LOVE IS IN THE ....u

For Rob

From Jeff

True of

First published in 2008 by

WOODFIELD PUBLISHING LTD
Bognor Regis ~ West Sussex ~ England ~ PO21 5EL
www.woodfieldpublishing.com

ISBN 1-84683-046-X

Love is in the Air

The Wartime Letters and Memories
of **Joe Pack** and **Margaret Dillon**

EDITED BY
JEFF PACK

Woodfield

Woodfield Publishing Ltd

Woodfield House ~ Babsham Lane ~ Bognor Regis ~ West Sussex ~ PO21 5EL
telephone 01243 821234 ~ **e-mail** enquiries@woodfieldpublishing.com

Interesting and informative books on a variety of subjects

For full details of all our published titles, visit our website at
www.woodfieldpublishing.com

~ CONTENTS ~

To the memories of
Joe and Margaret Pack

Introduction

Joe Pack was born in 1918 in rural Kent, the third of four children, three sisters. In 1940 he enlisted with the RAF and after about 12 months training was assigned to No.35 Squadron as a Halifax bomber pilot. On his 18th operational flight he was shot down on the German/Dutch border. His evasion and return to the UK involved the now famous *Comète* line ~ plus the efforts of a Dutch Inspector of ditches, a Basque smuggler and many other extraordinary people who put their own lives at risk to help stranded allied airmen evade capture.

On his return he was reassigned to flying boats ~ first Sunderlands and then Catalinas, involving some further training. In this process he came across Margaret Dillon, a WAAF Officer serving at RAF Oban. His advances were rejected and she was posted to RAF Davidstow Moor in Cornwall and he was posted to 265 Squadron in the Indian Ocean. At some point ~ and it is not clear exactly when or why ~ they had a rethink and started corresponding. The 180 airmail letters which survive (and there were clearly more) chart their courtship.

Joe returned to the UK in April 1945 and on 2nd June that same year they were married. They had known each other for about 2 years but almost entirely via airmail letters. Thus the reason for the title of this book will be obvious. I did, however, think about calling it *In The Company Of Remarkable Women*, because that is also the story of Joe Pack. The Comète line which saved him was predominantly run by remarkable women and Margaret Dillon surely also qualifies for that title.

The words in this book are almost entirely those of Joe and Margaret. The editor's contribution has been some light editing, filling in a few gaps to assist understanding, researching some official papers ... and lots of typing! *All words from other sources are shown in italics and, unless otherwise attributed, are those of the editor.*

Joe served in three different squadrons, flew three different aircraft types, crashed in one of each type and survived to tell the tale.

Joe very rarely talked about the war to his family. "Oh you wouldn't be interested in that," was his usual answer to questions. The amount he wrote, however, shows that it clearly meant a lot to him.

Jeff Pack, May 2008.

"The last of the many"

Cartoon by Leslie Sherlock, a commercial artist who worked for Joe for about 30 years.

1. Early days in Egerton

Written by Joe for the Egerton Local History Group

My mother was Delia Hopkins, a farmer's daughter at Newland Green Farm, born in 1888. My father was Jeffrey Pack, son of Robert Pack, a builder, of Victor Villa near Little Houses. They married on March 26th 1913 and travelled to and from the church in High Halden by a pony and trap, apparently to avoid the attention of being married in the local Egerton church. I was the third of four children Gladys, Margaret (always Meg), me and Audrey.

Robert was something of a tyrant to his family of five. Every night he would climb Egerton Hill to go to the George Inn, which he would leave only at closing time and return home, walking in the middle of the road. The local youths knew about this and would swerve to avoid him. The children were frightened of him when he returned each night. One dark night the inevitable happened and a cyclist knocked him into the ditch. He was helped home but still managed to make his usual visit to the George the following night. He was a tough old bird.

My other grandfather (Hopkins) of Newland Green farm, lived to be 102, I believe. He would walk out to the barn every morning and go to sleep in the straw, and then return at midday for his lunch. One day, however, he did not return; they found that he had died.

The Hopkins' employed one man who lived in the loft above the two horses in the stable. The rest of the work was done by his wife, son and three daughters.

We lived in Victor Villa, near Little Houses, with a workshop behind the house and a stable for the horse and cart. *[Whether this "horse and cart" was the "pony and trap" Jeffrey and Delia were married in is unknown.]*

My mother would light the kitchen fire every morning to boil the kettle. When the fire was hot enough she could use the oven at the side using the barest minimum of coal. Water was drawn from a well in the yard and sewage emptied into the cesspit which had an overflow into the road! Milk was delivered by Alan Murray, who carried a milk churn and ladled out measures with a jug. Later we would walk to Malt House Farm and collect our milk from there from Mr Waddington *(a connection that may have led to the interest in bell ringing described later)*.

There were only 2 or 3 vans in Egerton in 1914 belonging to local tradesmen. Possibly a couple of cars, and a Rolls Royce driven by the chauffeur for Major Stisted at the big house. He was a wealthy man and handed out money to many of the poor in the village – until his "empire" crashed, when life changed for many of the villagers and his employees.

Dr Littledale was available in the village about once a fortnight, his surgery was in Charing. He would send his bill for services sometimes months after – we rarely needed him. The village nurse attended to all births, it was well known that any baby born with a serious defect would have a pillow placed over its head at birth to extinguish its life.

There was a herbalist in the village. He would make up his concoctions from herbs he found in the countryside. He set up a little table in a Maidstone shelter for the clients who believed in him.

Most of the children attending the village school had to walk, some from a distance of two miles. The headmaster, Mr Sanderson, ruled with a rod of iron for many years. Egerton did not have a good reputation scholastically. The first ever in the school to pass the examination to go to a secondary school was my sister who got a scholarship to go to Ashford County School for girls (now Highworth). She cycled to Pluckley to catch the train, leaving her cycle at the pub near the station.

On one occasion at Egerton school a new teacher was selected to replace a retiring teacher. Her name was Miss Knight and she came from the north of England somewhere. Miss Knight fell in love with Hubert Pack (no relation – there were a cricket team of Packs in the village). I was not the easiest of boys and frequently received a blow around the head. Any slight movement by a teacher and I would put my arm up to ward off any blow I might receive.

When dancing around the Maypole one day to the music of the school gramophone, I found myself opposite the teacher, Miss Knight, and arm in arm I had to twirl around with her – which I did, but swept her off her feet! When the music stopped, she gave me such a clout on my head that I saw sparks! It was shortly after this that I found myself in favour with her, as my name was the same as her boyfriend, Hubert; she thought we must be related! It didn't last for long.

The highlights of village life were the annual flower show complete with swings and roundabouts. Also the Old Folk's Tea, a trip to Dymchurch with the church organist (we saw the sea for the first time), carol singing on Christmas Eve, pushing a hand cart with a harmonium around our hilly village and stopping at any wealthy house likely to give us a few shillings.

All children walked to the school. School was always interesting at lambing time. One of the classroom windows looked down over the field of sheep. At the right time a ram would be delivered to the field and the boys near the window would be watching carefully. When the ram mounted the sheep an audible whisper would go around the class "he's on" and the whole class would turn to the window to watch the spectacle – much to the embarrassment of the lady teacher who endeavoured to maintain order.

Homewood the butcher had two sons. I would often go to The Street to play with one of them. When bullocks were brought in to be slaughtered in the slaughterhouse, the smell of blood made them frantic. A noose at the end of a long rope would be placed from above one of the heads of the animal, passed through a hole to the outside where as many volunteers as could mustered would pull hard to get the animal's head onto the block where it had its throat cut and blood would gush out.

When pigs were slaughtered the slaughterer would remove the pigs bladder and give it to the boys who would blow it up and use it as a football!

One of the highlights of village life was the Stag hunt. The Stag would be released from a covered van when it would jump majestically over a hedge or gate and set off. A few minutes afterwards the hounds arrived controlled by a red coat. When they picked up the scent of the stag the rest of the pack would gather together and follow the scent with the huntsman following behind... [rest of story lost]

To arrange a boys football match or cricket match with a local side – Ulcombe, Pluckley or Smarden, it would be necessary to cycle to the village, find out where the Captain lived, and arrange to meet for a match. It has always annoyed me that Mr Rushton, Headmaster of Smarden school, always turned up to watch the Smarden boys matches – we would have no such encouragement. For some years Smarden were not beaten by any other sides, junior or senior.

Pluckley, mentioned above, is where the television series "Darling buds of May" was based and shot. Pluckley is just a few miles from Egerton and the series gives a perfect description of the bucolic way of life in both villages. Joe's story about a bicycle (written in about 2002) also captures this mood.

The Bicycle – 73 years ago

Breaking up from school for the long summer holiday should have been a happy time for we school children but it was not for me; the following day there was nothing to do, nowhere to go for an eleven year old boy (*this would have been in 1929*).

But there was something of interest happening in the village – we were going to have electricity "laid on". We did not quite know what that meant but we were told that the houses in which it was installed could have light from a bulb at the flick of a switch. It was difficult to comprehend. Many of the villagers around where we lived thought this electricity quite unnecessary – what was wrong with the oil lamps we had always used in the living room and the candlesticks we lit when we went upstairs to bed. Yes, what was wrong with that? And how about the cost?

In spite of this feeling work went ahead. About half a mile below our house a trench was being dug at the side of the road along the grass verge by about 10 navvies. The huge foreman in charge of the labourers would space the men equally apart and when he blew his whistle they would start to dig and not stop until he blew his whistle again, when that length of trench had been dug. In no time at all, it seemed, they had dug the trench and passed our house on their way to the village street. After a few days an electrical cable had been laid in the trench and the trench filled in, it was months before our house was eventually wired for light, but what magic!

It was during the summer holiday that our local garage displayed a brand new bicycle in their window. It was a boy's bicycle, the first I had ever seen, and the price was £12. When I hopefully told my dad about it he said "forget it, get the thought right out of your mind" and I knew what that meant. Apart from my 2d a week pocket money, I was getting a little money from delivering bread for the local baker. Perhaps if I saved this money, together with my pocket money, it would help to buy the bike. I delivered the bread three times a week after school for Mr Botting, the baker, to local houses. Mr Botting's name had always intrigued me a little. I would collect the bread in a large basket with instructions on where to deliver it. On these days Mr Botting would come out to the front of his shop to watch me climb the hill with the bread, probably to see if I was playing about with any of the other kids. When I thought I was a safe distance away I would turn around and shout "goodbye Mr Bottom" and he would quickly go back into his shop. One day after I had shouted my usual taunt he ran up the hill after me, picked me up, turned me over and bit my bottom! When I arrived to do my bread round the following week he told me he had found a less cheeky boy to deliver his bread. When I told Mum what had happened she told me "it serves you right for being so cheeky" My source of income had stopped, my 2d a week pocket money was hardly worth saving.

But there was another possibility; hop picking was about to start. Mum always took a half bin to pick hops for a local farmer each year. She needed the extra money to help buy winter clothes for me and my sisters and this was the only way to get the money. We would walk from home through the dewy fields to the hop field, carrying our wicker lunch basket and arriving at 7am or thereabouts at our bin to start the day's work. It was never easy to get started, the farmer would have to cut the hop bines at the base of the poles near the ground, the bine twined around the pole, he would pull up the poles and lay them near to a bin for picking. We children would have bines to pick into our peck baskets and when we filled them we would empty them into Mum's ½ bin. At midday the highlight of the day was having lunch sitting on a pile of hop poles now bare of their hops and bines. Our favourite sandwiches were marmite or cucumber with Mum's home made cake as a follow up – we were always very hungry. We had bottles of ginger beer to drink with a glass ball in the neck which exploded when pushed in. This was a great treat which we only had at hop picking time. Picking hops in the afternoon became somewhat boring and I would slip away to return at four in the afternoon when the farmer came to empty our bin to measure how many bushels we had picked. He filled his bushel basket, skimmed it off at the top to a level bushel and would empty the hops into a poke counting in a loud voice – One, Two, Three, Four – until the bin was empty. His wife would record the number of bushels picked into our Tally book for that day. On the first day I had earned 8/6d (6 peck baskets) but my interest in hop picking was slipping.

From that first day in the hop garden I spent a lot of my days playing around the farm, climbing the haystacks and inside the barn, helping to stoke the fires which dried the hops in the Oast and generally making myself a nuisance I expect.

My favourite time was to help bring in the cows from the fields into the milking shed. The farmer and his son, Alan (*Palmer, later to become a good friend*) would milk the cows, each sitting on a three legged stool with his head pushed against the side of the cow's belly. Pulling the teats of the cow produced a very poor squirt to begin with but it slowly increased to fill the bright shining pail held between the knees of the person milking the cow. I had strict instructions from the farmer not to go into the cowshed.

One day the farmer had not returned from the market at milking time and I crept into the cowshed and hid on the opposite side of the cow Alan was milking. He must have had a surprise when my head suddenly appeared from under the cow's udder with my mouth wide open. He duly obliged me by aiming some of the milk from the teats into my mouth, it was lovely, both warm and sweet. On another day I tried to repeat the exercise but he doused my face with milk, missing my open mouth completely. I think he did this on purpose, I didn't try it again.

Many families from the East End of London would come down to the farm each year to pick hops or fruit for the farmers. They would live in a long row of "hopper" huts with clean new straw on the ground to sleep on. The farmer heaped piles of spare wood nearby to use for fires to cook and boil water each day. I found the London children a diversion from picking hops and brought my cricket bat, ball and wickets along to the farm. We would pick sides and play in the nearby field. These cockney boys were good sports. I could not understand what they were talking about, cockney slang seemed a different language, but they would always let me bat first, because it was my bat and ball they said.

Hop picking over, I had earned less than £3 towards my bike, but there were other options. I had made a trolley from a plank of wood with a wooden box at the back supported by an axle and two pram wheels I had found. The two small wheels at the front swivelled to steer it by. It had to be pulled up the road to the top of the hill, our village was very hilly, then I would sit on it and have a ride to the bottom. At that time there were two tradesmen's vans and one car in the village and the occasional horse and cart and they did not worry me unduly. My trolley proved to be very useful.

It was a good year for acorns. They covered the ground under the oak trees like a carpet and I asked a farmer if he would like some acorns for his pigs and he said he would. Collecting acorns is a tedious business and I asked Meg, my middle sister, if she would help me. Meg was a tomboy. We were pals most of the time. She could climb trees, didn't mind worms, snakes or frogs although she didn't like horses or cows, I don't know why. She agreed to help me collect acorns into my trolley and the box was soon filled. The farmer was delighted and paid us well. We repeated this money-making exercise for two or three days until the farmer realised we were collecting the acorns from under his own trees. He refused any further payments and moved his pigs to the wood to feed themselves and save him money and that was the end of that.

My trolley had many uses. If I saw a horse and cart passing the house I would follow it with my trolley. If the horse obliged, as it did frequently with it's exertions on the hill, I would scoop up the droppings from the road with my shovel and bring it home for Mum's vegetable garden, which would always make her smile. I always kept the box fairly clean, but Meg wouldn't always ride in it, she was always rather particular, being a girl.

Conditions were now right for mushrooms. The best field for them in the village was quite some distance from our house and belonged to a gentleman farmer. I knew I could get a good price for early pickings if I sent them to Ashford market. Other boys knew of this field too. To be sure of a good basketful meant getting up early, long before the farmer was up. Meg agreed to help me, after a bit of haggling, and we decided to go the following morning. I was awake very early and woke Meg. We crept down and out the back door, which was never locked. We started off across the fields and were soon held up by a herd of bullocks which would not let us pass. We eventually chased them by running at them and waving our arms, they would turn and run away kicking up their hind legs in fun. Continuing our walk we eventually arrived at the field, just as it was getting light, and what a sight, mushrooms everywhere. We soon had our basket full to overflowing and were on our way home without seeing another person.

Mum was surprised to see us when we got home; she thought we were still asleep upstairs. She already had the kitchen fire alight and the kettle was singing for Dad's tea. She didn't question us too closely as to where we had picked the mushrooms. I think she knew and she put up the Carrier card in the window for him to call, a big "P". The carriers name was Percy. He arrived at 9 o'clock and agreed to take the mushrooms to a stallholder at Ashford market whom he knew. He called back later that evening and gave Mum the money for the mushrooms, my bicycle money was building up. Meg and I decided to repeat the early trip the following Friday. This was the next market day at Ashford. Unfortunately mushrooms were very plentiful by then and Percy had difficulty in finding a buyer and the price was very poor.

However there were other possibilities. My uncle Joe (*Hopkins*) had a mixed farm a mile or so from our house part of which was woodland. My Mum was born at this farm and over the years we children had often been down with Mum to fish the ponds, chase the poultry, pick strawberries, apples and cherries in season and prod the bad tempered sow (but we kept clear of the ram). Yes, there was always a lot to do on the farm. Uncle Joe was not always pleased with us but Mum was his favourite sister and he "put up with us". He had allowed me to put up my tent in one of his fields but the inquisitive bullocks soon had it down, it was lucky not to be damaged. I then asked them if I could erect it in the wood and he said yes and helped me clear an area of undergrowth for the tent. My next request was to set rabbit wires in the wood and around the edges, which he agreed to, providing I did not put them in the fields, because of the danger to his sheep. I had about a dozen wires which I put up in runs likely to be used by rabbits. When I got back to the tent it had begun to get dark. I managed to get my primus stove going to make a cup of cocoa before going to bed. Then I made a hollow for my hip, put my groundsheet over it, folded up a large old blanket I had brought with me and tried to go to sleep.

It was a bit scary in the middle of the wood, now dark under the trees, the noises of scampering animals and things dropping from the trees onto the tent. I began to wish that I was home in bed. Sleep eventually took over and I awoke when the dawn began to filter through the trees. I lay listening to the dawn chorus of the birds, unknown animals scampering around and once I thought I heard the squeal of a rabbit. When it was properly light I started off to check my wires and discovered my first rabbit. My Uncle Joe had told me what to do if I caught one. When I discovered the rabbit with the wire around it's neck running around in circles, frantic to escape, I think I was more frightened than the rabbit. I grabbed it by its hind legs, still attached to the wire, lifting it up I then chopped behind the neck with my free hand, breaking it's neck instantly. I had caught and killed my first rabbit. I was not so sure at the time that I liked the experience but I needed the money. Hanging the rabbit to a suitable tree by its hind legs, paunching the stomach with my knife, to remove the hot, steaming intestines was something I had seen my Uncle do with rabbits he had shot. The wires had to be checked twice a day and I caught quite a number of rabbits. I would take them home, Mum would help me skin them and send them off by Percy the carrier on Tuesdays and Fridays.

My Aunt Mary at the farm would give me something to eat each day before I made my way back to my tent for the night. I kept this up for a week or two but the end of the holidays was looming and I had to take up my wires, take down my tent and wheel it all home on my trolley.

There was not much to look forward to now, I was a long way from saving the £12 I needed for my bike, there was only school once again. The week before going back Mum took we children to Ashford to buy our winter clothes with the hop picking money and what did she buy me – my very first pair of long trousers, school would not be so bad after all. And that wasn't all. The following day Dad asked me how much money Mum had saved for me. I told him and wondered why he asked. Dad was no great talker and I wouldn't dare ask him. But the following day, surprise, surprise! An almost new second hand bike appeared in the shed. Dad had used my savings and added to it to buy the bike from someone he knew. When the bike was wheeled out of the shed it had no bar at the top – it was a girl's bike! At first I was very disappointed. Meg, my sister was highly delighted, she pointed out that the bike partly belonged to her, as I suppose it did.

Neither of us had ridden a bike before, we quarrelled a bit as to who should ride it first, but in the main Meg was a good sport, for a girl!

Bell ringing

Malt House was owned by Mr Waddington (known as "Boss"). He was an artist and a left arm spin bowler in the village cricket team. His son, Sandy (Alex) also played cricket and was the leading light of bell ringing. He taught many of us to ring. In our family my father, mother, three sisters and myself all rang. He would transport us on his motorbike to various ringing meetings.

[On Saturday 5ᵗʰ December 1992 the Kent Association organised a 60ᵗʰ anniversary of Joe's first peal, he would have been 14. The peal was of 5040 Plain Bob Major tenor 23 cwt in D. He was 74 when he rang it.

The earliest recorded peal he rang was at St Paulinus Church, Crayford in Kent on Saturday 21ˢᵗ April 1934. The "band" was Percy Stone from Nuneaton, Arthur Jones from Croydon, Phyllis Tillett from Ipswich, Walter Dobbie from Sittingbourne, Margaret Pack (Joe's sister), aged 17 from Egerton, John Gilbert from Sheffield, Joe Pack, aged 15 and a half from Egerton and Edwin Barnett from Crayford. This was the youngest band ever to accomplish a true and complete peal on Church bells. It may have been put together by Sandy Waddington.

RINGING MEMORIES in Crayford Parish Church on Saturday were members of a band who created a record 25 years ago. It was in April, 1934, that eight young people rang a peal of bob major in the same church. They created a record which stands to this day because their ages averaged just over 15 years. In this photograph are (left to right): Mr. roy Stone, Mrs. P. Marriott, Mr. Walter Dobbie, Mr. E. A. Barnett, Mr. John Gilbert and Mr. J. Pack. Mrs. Marriott the sister of one of the original record-breaking team who is now in America.—(K.T. Photo No. JM/2495.)

The previous average age for an eight-bell peal was lowered by an average of three years and the record is believed to stand to this day. It was a Peal of Bob Major consisting of 5024 changes and achieved in 2 hours and 50 minutes. The average age was 15 years 2 weeks; the youngest ringer being 13 years 3 months, the oldest 17 years 8 months and the conductor was 15 and a half! The Kentish Times featured a reunion of the band on April 24ᵗʰ 1959 when they rang the peal again. *Joe's sister Margaret could not be present having emigrated to California (see photo).*

From notes Joe kept he rang at Shipbourne on April 16 1932 with Glad and Meg, Charing on Sept 27 1932 with Glad and Meg, Dec 26 1932 at Linton with Glad, Dec 27 1932 at Charing with Glad and Meg, April 17 1933 at Charing with Meg and Glad, Aug 2nd at Charing with Glad, Aug 7th 1933 at Ulcombe with Glad, May 23 1934 at Charing with Glad, June 10 1934 at Hothfield with Glad and Meg, Sept 13 at Little Chart, Sept 26 1934 at St James' Egerton with Glad and Delia, Oct 12 1957 at St Albans with Glad and on 18th April on the 25th anniversary of the youngest peal at Crayford with Glad.

In the 1990's he also rang regularly in Kentish churches and Ealing churches including a quarter peal of 1260 doubles rung at the Church of Christ the Saviour in Ealing on 4th June 1995 to celebrate his and Margaret's Golden Wedding Anniversary and the same peal rung on 6th May 1998 to celebrate Joe's 80th birthday. Naturally he participated in all of these.

No church bells could be rung during the Second World War. When we returned to live in Smarden (*in the 1980's*) I found the local band, and on enquiring about Sandy Waddington, found they knew him, in fact they said that he collapsed while ringing at Smarden Church. I am wondering if Sandy's widow still lives at Malt House. At one time we collected our milk from Malt House Farm, in spite of a very savage dog they had named Tilly. Old man Waddington was an artist, he played cricket for the village and was a left arm spin bowler. His son Alec (Sandy) was also a fine cricketer.

Early career

Joe left home for his first job in 1934 probably without any educational qualifications. He describes his early years in some detail in his 1st December 1944 letter to Margaret:

I was so keen on bell ringing I got my first job at 15 and a half with Taylor's Bell Foundry, Loughborough, Leicestershire, as an apprentice.

In a letter dated Dec 1st 1938 from a Mr Tyler, of 22 Herbert Street Loughborough, presumably Taylor's bell foundry, he says' "This is to state that Mr J.T. Pack came under my supervision from June 1934 to June 1935 when he was serving part of his apprenticeship course as a drawing office apprentice. During that time I found him an energetic and industrious worker as well as a good timekeeper. I believe him to be honest and trustworthy and would recommend him to anyone securing his services."

This letter was presumably requested to apply for jobs after he had decided to branch out from his father's business, see below. It was while at Taylor's bell foundry that he was called to ring in the 1934 band, with his sister Margaret, that was the youngest ever and is described above. Joe later describes the Taylor's bell foundry as a "dead end job".

Joe then returned to Egerton to work with his father in his building business. During this time he attended evening classes to make up for his lack of education.

I managed to get a three-year course at Maidstone Technical School. I managed to get a lift occasionally in the bakers van delivering bread to houses in the valley but usually I cycled to Lenham station 6 miles away.

(He didn't do so badly – in the college of Preceptors certificate examination in June 1938 he scored 106 for scripture (minimum pass mark 67), 148 for English (100), 84 for history (67), 105 for arithmetic (67), 116 for trigonometry (67), 140 for mensuration (67) but struggled with algebra 40 (67)).

He also struggled to work with his father and eventually after 3 years decided to again leave Egerton and became an articled pupil with a local surveyor, passing some exams in the process, which led to an appointment with Watson's.

On 28th April 1939, J.D. & D.M. Watson, Chartered Civil Engineers of 3 Central Buildings, Westminster SW1 sent the following letter:

We confirm that we are prepared to offer you an appointment in this office with salary at the rate of £120 per year monthly. The appointment must be regarded as "temporary" but we have no reason to suppose that it would be of short duration. We understand that you would be able to start work on 15th May and shall therefore be glad to hear that you accept our offer. We return herewith the drawings which we think you left by mistake.

On 29th September the same firm wrote:

Mr J.T. Pack has been employed by us for the past five months as a junior civil engineering assistant and during this time he has assisted in the preparation of schemes of sewerage and sewage purification the chief of which were for East Middlesex, Luton, Plymouth, Bournemouth, and Blandford and Norton Manor Militia Camps. This work has involved the preparation of drawings, quantities and some estimating. Mr Pack is a willing and conscientious worker and his work has always been to our satisfaction. Owing to the war Mr Pack is leaving but he has our best wishes for success.

[In fact, as he explains in his letters to Margaret, "owing to the war" did not mean Joe was enlisting; in fact it meant Watson's had to release a quarter of their staff. He then spent 9 months in the Borough Surveyors office in Dagenham and must have continued studies started at Watson's since he received a medal from the Institution of Sanitary Engineers "for obtaining the highest percentage of possible marks in the Associate Membership examinations held in 1940". Shortly after this, in August 1940, he signed up with the RAF.]

2. September 1939

Written for the Egerton Local History Group

Life went on as usual in our small village of Egerton in the Weald of Kent; it was anything but a lively village. It had no railway, there were two Weald of Kent buses each day one to Ashford 8 miles away and the other to Maidstone but our main means of transport was walking. We were very dependent for fruit and vegetables on our front garden, we had a butcher, Homewood's, a baker, Buckle, and a village shop, Len Hopkins, which was doing its usual brisk trade. There were four pubs in the village. The monthly Saturday night dance continued to take place, although the windows of the village hall were now "blacked out", in a half hearted way. There were three shops and four pubs. The whole village was spread over a wide area at the top of the downs, spreading out into the Weald of Kent below the hill.

But in 1939 things were beginning to happen. There was unusual activity in the air. For several weeks we had been aware of new fighter planes, the Hurricanes and Spitfires flying in formation or having dogfights with one another high above us, over the Weald. They were operating from Detling, I believe. Later we were to see the dogfights taking place in life and death struggles with German fighters and bombers and occasionally several parachutes descending at the same time. Formations of German fighters could be seen high above us en route to London. At night, when we heard the drone of planes above, we would slip out of our blacked out homes or pubs and from the engine sounds would decide if they were "ours" or "theirs".

Not long after the declaration of war our armies were forced to evacuate from Dunkirk and thousands of weary soldiers arrived at Dover and coaches from all over the south of England were commandeered to bring the men back to London and beyond. I cycled over to the Ashford Maidstone main road on the Sunday morning to watch this nose to tail endless stream of coaches carrying their pitiful looking, dispirited soldiers, some only partly clothed, from the hell they had left in France. There was no joy on their faces having escaped from Dunkirk, they were dazed and dejected, still living the terror they had experienced during the past few days.

On 1ˢᵗ September 1939 Germany invaded Poland. Britain and France gave Germany an ultimatum to withdraw and, when this was ignored, declared war 2 days later. On September 27ᵗʰ Poland surrendered. The British Expeditionary Force then joined French troops to defend the borders of France, Belgium and Holland against the Germans. There then followed the "phoney war" when nothing much happened (except the subjugation of Poland by

Germany) from September 1939 to April 1940. Then on April 9th Germany invaded Norway and Denmark in order to gain control of the North Sea and access to the Atlantic and on May 10th attacked Holland, Belgium and France defeating them within 6 weeks. The British Expeditionary force was cut off by the rapid German advance and was rescued from Dunkirk by a hastily assembled fleet of about 900 ships of all kinds on May 26th.

Shortly after this in July 1940 the Battle of Britain began. In preparation for an invasion of Britain the Luftwaffe began intensive bombing raids on convoys, coastal defences, airfields and London and the major cities. The Luftwaffe had 2600 bombers and fighters, the RAF had 640 fighters but had radar and positioning systems that were more sophisticated than the Germans. Both sides sustained heavy losses and by October the Germans, who were preparing to invade Russia, decided they would not be able to defeat the RAF and this phase of the war was over. Joe would enlist just as the Battle of Britain was starting.

Enlisting

Yes, war had arrived – proper. It was in 1940, aged 22, that I thought I should join up to "do my bit". One or two of the lads from the village had been called up and several others had volunteered although conscription was not yet compulsory for my age group. I had a guilt feeling at still being out of uniform. There was an advertisement in the Maidstone paper asking for volunteers to join the RAF to apply at an address in Chatham and unbeknown to my parents I drove the 20 miles or so on my motorcycle to volunteer.

[The RAF never conscripted personnel, only ever seeking volunteers. Joe's father had been in the Navy in World War One and this plus the horror stories of the trenches and the glamorous image the RAF had as the Battle of Britain started may have helped his decision. Also of relevance was that it often took up to 2 years to train a pilot, Joe in fact took just one year, whereas Army gunners were on the front line within 13 weeks].

I was interviewed giving particulars of my age, education and so on. When asked what branch of the RAF I wanted to apply for I said I wanted to be a pilot. I felt a bit of a fool at the time because the previous night it was reported on the radio that 18 of our aircraft had been shot down the previous night. When I returned home my mother took the news of my joining very calmly

[RAF records show that Joe joined the RAF on 9 July 1940 at Euston for pilot training. He was given RAF Service number 1375376 and the lowest RAF rank of Aircraftsman Second class, which was the standard rank for new recruits. On 10 July he was placed on the RAF Volunteer Reserve and was probably sent off on leave until the RAF was ready for him. On 23 September 1940 he was called up at No 2 Recruit Centre, Cardington, Bedfordshire.]

Ten weeks after signing on I received the travel permit for me to report to RAF Cardington. Getting to the railway station – Charing, about 6 miles from Egerton, taking the train to Victoria and by bus to Euston station was quite an adventure in itself, it was my first trip to London. Arriving at Cardington station there was no transport to take me and others to RAF Cardington. The huge hangers there, where we did our drill training, had originally been built to house the ill-fated R100 airship which had crashed in France some time previously. I was issued with my RAF uniform; this was my last day in civilian clothes for several years. But we were not allowed out of camp until the end of the drill course when we were told we were smart enough not to disgrace the uniform. And so to Blackpool to continue drilling at the end of the pier to the amusement of the civilians from Lancashire, the usual Blackpool attractions were long since closed down. Our drill instructor was a huge army guardsman with a huge voice. The RAF had not yet been able to supply enough drill instructors to fill the vacancies.

And next to Torquay for another course (*probably on 25 October 1940 per RAF records*), theoretical this time, the successful ones then going to Cambridge (*No 2 Initial Training Wing on 12 November 1940*). I was billeted at Emmanuel College to live in undergraduate quarters and eat with them, many of the students were still in residence, in their dining hall. We stayed in the comfortable quarters of the college and ate in the dining hall, served by the College retainers, we felt quite important. Here we did our initial training as aircrew, having been raised to the elevated ranks of Leading aircraftsmen (LAC), (*on 6th Jan 1941 as under-training pilot*), and those of us who passed were issued with white flashes to put on our forage caps to show we were potential airmen. This paid us sufficient money – 3/6 a day – to buy several pints for 3 or 4 nights a week.

After experiencing the joys of Cambridgeshire we were sent for a few weeks further training at Babbacombe, Devon as pilots. So far being in the RAF had been most enjoyable and I looked forward to flying an aeroplane for the first time!

Our course was then sent to Elementary Flying Training Service (EFTS), either to the Empire Training School (Rhodesia or Canada) which had just started, or, just two of us, to Luton. *This was on 22 March 1941 at 50 Group (pool).* There I was taught to fly a single engine bi plane – Miles Magister Training aircraft, a single engined solo plane. We found ourselves joined to a course of New Zealand Fleet Airmen volunteers – not being sailors my RAF friend and I were excused all kinds of drills and unpleasant duties. And so one day I took to the air for the first time in my life, March 1941, (*6 months after enlisting*) sitting behind a dual controlled instructor. After a week or so of shouting and bullying from my instructor in April I went solo – flying on my own after 8 and half hours instruction. During the two months I was here I was taught looping the loop, spinning, stalling, emergency landings, steep turns, cross country flying and a host of other flying skills.

On one of these occasions, flying solo, I was lost, there was a strong wind and I was aware of Barrage Balloons around me (I was on the outskirts of

London). To my relief I saw a windsock, showing me the direction of the wind, and a small airdrome below. I landed safely and found myself at a civilian airdrome. The Duty Officer phoned Luton airdrome, who were beginning to worry for my safety, to tell them where I was. My instructor flew in and I followed him in my aircraft back to Luton – he was not amused.

On another occasion I was sent up to do some practice loops on my own. It was rather a bumpy day, several times I was aware of leaving my seat in the bumpy conditions, but it did not occur to me that anything was wrong. I was feeling sick so I flew away from the airdrome out of sight and did a few steep turns to waste a little time, but did not practice any loops. On landing, I taxied to the dispersal, stopped the engine and attempted to release my parachute which with this aircraft one sat on. The straps from the chute were brought over the shoulders and fixed to the straps from the chute that the pilot sat on. On attempting to release myself from the chute I realised that I had not been strapped in! My loops were never very good but had I attempted to loop the loop at about 3000 feet, as I should have done, I would have fallen out because I invariably hung onto my straps at the top when I was doing a loop. I nearly became a corpse on that day!

From Luton to Brize Norton Oxfordshire, (*on 31 May 1941 in 2 Service Flying Training School*), as a sergeant pilot to be trained to fly twin engine Oxford aircraft by day and night for the first time. After a few hours dual flying I had not too much difficulty taking off and landing day and night solo. It was during a night flying exercise that one of our course, George Washington, was lost but became aware of his aircraft touching down. He knew he was near the aerodrome. He was in a field at a higher level. Looking out of the side he realised he was on the ground; he throttled back and came to a stop safely. He had come to rest on a flat piece of ground several hundred feet above the aerodrome and several miles away. Later he took off and landed safely at base. George was the oldest fellow on the course, he was 31, most of us were around 20 years old. His home was in South America but he had pulled strings to come to England to fly with the RAF. Unhappily George's luck did not hold. A few days later, after his lucky escape, he was night flying doing circuits and bumps around the airdrome i.e. take-offs and landings, when, unbeknown to us, a German night fighter had joined in the circuit around the airdrome with the rest of us. Aircraft with navigation lights blazing were an easy target to shoot down, it was George Washington's aircraft that was hit (*10% of Bomber Commands losses occurred in training*).

I was flying solo on that night, when the lights of the airdrome were suddenly extinguished, much to my surprise. In such an event we had been told to fly around a certain beacon until the lights reappeared, which I did and landed safely. The following day I learned of the fate of poor old George, he had travelled a long way from South America to die in this way and so soon. We were not allowed to go to his funeral.

[On 9 August 1941 Joe was promoted to Temporary Sergeant and awarded his flying badge. On 16 August 1941 from Brize Norton to Kinloss, Morayshire, Scotland to join 19 Operational Training Unit.]

Here we flew night and day – mostly cross-country flying on old antiquated bombers, Whitleys, a twin engined aircraft with a huge wing span area. They were easy to fly but flying at night between the mountains of Scotland navigated by "sprog" navigators still under training was sometimes a little worrying. On 27th October 1941 I was finally posted to an operational squadron *[No.35 (Madras Presidency) Squadron, Linton-on-Ouse, Yorkshire, RAF Bomber Command]* for operational flying, less than 12 months after starting training and just over a year since enlisting (*this was remarkably quick, some pilots took up to 2 years to train*).

3.   35 Squadron

Written by Joe partly for the Egerton Local History and partly for friends and his own notes. Some of the records are from 35 Squadron diaries

35 Squadron were being converted from Whitleys to the new four-engined Halifax bomber. Learning to fly a four- engined bomber was very different from the previous plane I had flown, but I was soon taking off and landing the Halifax without too many problems. Flying at night was rather more difficult, the instructor who sat in the 2ⁿᵈ pilots seat was on "rest" after completing a tour of operations – 30 trips at that time – some rest! I was eventually teamed up as 2ⁿᵈ pilot with Sergeant George Steinhauer, a Canadian – although most of the Canadian aircrew were commissioned, George was quite sure he would not get a commissioning because of his German surname – and it seems he was right.

The Halifax Bomber

35 Squadron were the first Halifax unit in the RAF. The Handley Page Halifax entered service with the RAF in November 1940 but it was not until July 1941 that it's existence became publicly known, following the successful attack on the German battleship Scharnhorst on 10/11 March 1941 by 35 Squadron. It soon became apparent that the defensive armament of the Halifax was inadequate for daytime flying and by the end of 1941 they were only used for night time flying, which was what Joe mostly did, as will be seen shortly. The Halifax (6200 were built), the Lancaster and the Short Stirling were the backbone of Bomber Command. Halifaxs needed seven crew, three gunners to man nose, beam and tail positions, navigator, bomb aimer, captain and second captain.]

My first introduction to operations was on the night of **January 6/7ᵗʰ 1942.** We left at 0404 hrs and returned at 0700 hrs. The crew was Sgt Steinhauer (captain), Sgt Pack (second captain) and Sgts Goodrum, Meade, Campbell, Cowan and Mitchell. The aircraft was L.9606(R). We flew to Brest to attack the German battleship *Scharnhorst*, a potential menace to shipping in the Atlantic. We flew down from Linton on Ouse, Yorkshire over a DARKENED England, climbing slowly with a full petrol and bomb load, crossing our coast at a "safe" point, clear of our coastal defences. Crossing the French coast at about 12000 feet, all was quiet as we set course for Brest. We had no radio assistance at that time, but our (*illegible word*) and map reading navigation was good and within 10 minutes of our ETA to arrive at Brest, the skies ahead suddenly lit up with searchlights and enemy shells, the first of our aircraft had arrived ahead of us. Still some miles from the target area, we slowly nosed our way into the medley of bursting shells and searchlights, trying to home in on us with the enemy radars. There was a large concentration of ack ack guns in the target area and the coloured shells joined together. It was weird, they would come up in an almost leisurely fashion, yet they were obviously lethal – we called them "Flaming Onions". It was a relief to hear over the intercom "bomb doors open" as the bomb aimer guided us onto the target and later "bombs gone"(at 0610 hrs at 18000 feet) when the aircraft lifted vertically having shed its load. Turning slowly onto a course for our return, peace eventually reigned again as we scanned the skies for enemy night fighters".

Two days later, on the 8/9th Jan leaving at 0402 and returning at 0917, (with the same crew) we were back again. This time our plane was to be hit with shrapnel. With one engine out of action we landed at Abingdon, returning to Linton on Ouse the following day.

On 10/11th Jan leaving at 1759 and returning at 0002, again the same crew we attacked Wilhemshaven. There was slight damage to the starboard flap and the lower half of the rudder was missing owing to hitting a light on landing. The whole hydraulic system was U/S after bombing and both turrets froze up. The rear gunner's oxygen failed and he passed out for 10 minutes. Landed at Mildenhall.

On 15/16th Jan Kiel was attacked leaving at 1811 and returning 0040 by Sgts Steinhauer, Pack, Goodrun, Parry, Campbell, Russell and Dunlop.

On 12th Feb Steinhauer, Pack, Hawkes, Meade, Campbell, Cowan and Dunlop attacked the battle cruisers Scharnhorst, Gneisenau and Prince Eugen which were sailing up the Channel but without success due to poor weather, 10/10 cloud, severe icing and snow. This was my last trip with George Steinhauer as Captain, he was a Canadian. I was sent on a captain's course but he flew up to Kinloss, with a new second "dicky", to attack the Scharnhorst, which had by then gone into Trondheim. More than half the squadron was lost that night. George and his crew (several of whom had been regular crew members with Joe – Goodrun, Meade, Campbell, Cowan and Dunlop) did not return.

On 3rd March 10 aircraft attacked the Renault works at Billancourt. Joe's crew were MacIntyre, Pack, Chadwick, Perry, Jones, Wilson and Kaye leaving at 1737 and returning 2252.

On 8th/9th March 10 aircraft, including Joe, attacked Essen.

On 9th/10th March MacIntyre, Pack, Grierson-Jackson, Perry, Jones, Wilson and Kaye flew a mission.

13/14th March 11 aircraft to Cologne, including Joe. The trip to Cologne on March 13 was less than comfortable. We were shot up badly over the target area, lost an engine, iced up on the return journey and crossed over Dunkirk at 1500 feet (miraculously without being shot at). We landed at Manston without an air speed indicator. Although we lost an engine on several occasions, it was sometimes due to overheating i.e. glycol leaks.

Reconstructed Halifax at RAF Elvington [photos Jeff Pack].

Painting of a Halifax by Anthony [surname unknown].

On 16/17th April *Pack, in his first flight as captain, flew with Hill, Chadwick, Wing, Rome, Hopkins and Stevens. He notes his first trip was not without its moments:*

I had been given a new mark of Halifax to fly, it was the first of its kind to be fitted with a mid-upper gun turret. Half way across the North Sea the aircraft suddenly began to shudder and vibrate in an alarming way. My immediate thoughts were that the aircraft canopy was breaking up and what a bloody shame to go down like this on my first trip as Captain. Then the shuddering stopped. Only after enquiries over the intercom did I discover that the mid-upper gunner had been rotating his turret, with his new gun, with careless abandon, causing the vibrations. He was told what he could do in no uncertain terms!

The remarks entered in the squadron diary for this sortie were: "Took off at 21.27 from Linton on Ouse Lorient being the target. Weather clear, no cloud, slight haze. Target identified by Groix Island and later Gevre Point after searching for 25 minutes, using flares. Bombs believed to drop in the Dock area, but no bursts seen. One large red fire seen after leaving target".

On 19/20th May *Pack, Chadwick, Catley, McKenzie, Hopkins and Storey attacked St Nazaire, leaving at 2345 returning 0623.*

On 30/31st May *Pack, Pilborough, Chadwick, Catley, McKinstry, Hopkins and Storey were back over Cologne.*

On 1st/2nd **June** *the above crew were over Essen, one of 22 aircraft, all returned safely (this was apparently part of a 1000 bomber raid).*

On 3rd/4th **June** *the above crew were over Bremen, one of seven aircraft.*

On 6th/7th **June** *Pack, Chadwick, Gateley, McKinstry, Hopkins and Storey were again in action over Emden, one of eleven aircraft, one failed to return.*

On 7th/8th **June** *Halifax II W7701 TL-U, captained by Sgt Pack, was shot down. Ten aircraft had taken off to attack Essen, four failed to return.*

Bomber Command had started the war under the command of Sir Richard Pierce but had been ineffective. The strategy had been to attack a number of very specific targets. Unfortunately because of an ageing and under armed aircraft fleet casualties were high, to the point where daytime flying had to be abandoned in favour of night time flying only, and accuracy was low, and made worse by night time flying. On 8th January 1942 Churchill replaced Pierce by Arthur "Bomber" Harris. Harris changed the strategy to one of attacking one large target in very large numbers and trying to achieve collateral, morale-sapping, damage to German cities.

Joe's first flight on January 6th was probably one of the last daytime attacks. In the attack on March 3rd 1942 on the Renault factory he was one of 223 aircraft (10 from 35 Squadron) and the attack on Cologne on 30th May was the first 1000 bomber attack and the attacks on Essen and Bremen were only slightly smaller. This period of late May and early June 1942 was critical for the Allied war effort. Bomber Command had been losing their battle under Pierce, had Harris' tactics failed the result would have been catastrophic. After Dunkirk and for much of the rest of the war Bomber Command was the only direct way Britain had of taking the fight to Germany in offensive operations. The other services were essentially defensive until much later in the war. In so doing Bomber Command took large losses. 125000 men and women served in Bomber Command during the war and 56000 were killed. The odds for male airmen were even worse. Bomber Harris raised the stakes significantly by betting heavily on big results whilst accepting there would be aircraft losses. He succeeded although one aircraft loss, amongst many, was that of Joe Pack.

35 Squadron Operations record book 8th June 1942…

Ten aircraft took off from Linton on Ouse to attack Essen. Visibility and the weather were good but there was slight ground haze over the target area. Six aircraft returned safely to base after attacking the primary target and encountering intense heavy flak and considerable searchlight activity; four aircraft failed to return including Halifax II W.7701 (Captain 1375376 Sgt PACK J.T)

We regarded ourselves, as a crew, as reasonably lucky. I had flown on 18 sorties and we were still around, there seemed a fair chance of our completing a tour of operations (30 trips – then 6 months away from the front *line, then a further 20 trips*) but our luck changed on the night of June 8/9th – destination Essen.

We had got ourselves boxed in with searchlights and A/A. Diving, climbing, turning steeply, would not free us. I could smell the cordite, hear the sound of exploding shells... it was all very unpleasant. We eventually cleared the Ruhr at 21000 feet. Unfortunately in our efforts to get out of our difficulties we had flown out of the protection of the 400 bombers we had flown in with. None of the gunners reported seeing the night-fighter, which shot us down. Within seconds, it seemed, there was a large burning hole where my instrument panel had been. The plane was on fire and four of the crew were killed. 3 inches of steel behind my back probably saved me from instant death.

A little later, I was swinging across the skies on my parachute, like a huge pendulum and, 20/30 minutes later I hit the ground, which I had not seen. I expected to be immediately arrested, but there was complete silence. I discovered, later, that I had landed to the west of Aachen (*cannot explain this reference, as we will see later he landed 40 miles or so north of Aachen*).

19 aircraft were shot down that night on the raid on Essen, crewed by 125 airmen. 97 of the airmen were killed, 19 became prisoners of war, 7 were recovered after their plane crashed in the North Sea and 2 survived their crashes and subsequently evaded. Both the survivor/evaders were from 35 Squadron – one was a Canadian, F/Lt McLean, who would become Minister of Fisheries in the Canadian government after the war. The other is the subject of this book.

4.   Northern Europe in June 1942[1]

At the outbreak of the Second World War in 1939 the British Expeditionary Force took up defensive positions along the Franco Belgian border. By May 1940 there were more than 390,000 men. There were also nearly 2 million French troops manning the defensive Maginot line along their German border from Switzerland to Belgium. On 10 May 1940 the German Western Offensive started but they struck through Holland and Northern Belgium avoiding the Maginot line. By the 14th May Holland had capitulated and the Germans swept through Belgium driving the British forces back to the coast. By 19th May the Germans had reached Abbeville on the channel coast and the retreating British Expeditionary Force was trapped and surrounded. On the 3rd and 4th of June 340000 men (including 112000 French and Belgian troops) were rescued by 900 ships at Dunkirk (Joe refers to seeing the stream of dispirited returning soldiers from Egerton in Chapter 2). Thousands of troops however could not be evacuated and remained stranded in France and Belgium. Many were caught and but many also were left stranded.

Later in the war Joe would meet a Private MacFarlane. MacFarlane's M.I.9. report is interesting (M.I.9. was a department of the War Office whose specific remit was to assist and support evaders and escapers and to debrief them on return to see what could be learnt. They also supported escape lines in Northern Europe).

"The whole of our Company was captured in the town of Abbeville on 6th June 1940, when the whole battalion had been surrounded and the order given to surrender. We were marched through Northern France into Germany and, after passing somewhere near Brussels; we arrived at the Rhine, and about the end of June were put on barges. After a journey of three days, during which we had no food, we were disembarked and sent to a holding camp at Sagenheim. From there we were sent five days later to Stalag IX/C (Bad Sulza). I was only two days there before being sent on a working party to the cement works at Steudnitz, near Dorndorf about 7 miles S.E. of Bad Sulza. There were 70 men in this work camp and we all lived together in two rooms near the factory. I was among those who worked in the quarry filling wagons with chalk.In Sept 1941 I was transferred to the salt mines at Unter-breizbach, about 10 miles S.E. of Hersfeld where I was employed in the

---

[1] *Publishers note:* because this chapter was written entirely by the editor, in the interests of clarity and aesthetics we have abandoned the convention used elsewhere in this book of italicising the editor's words.

turning shop. Again there were about 70 men in the camp, which was about 10 minutes walk from the mines. About the beginning of 1942 I was planning to escape..."(more of this later – Ed)

There were also large numbers of individual stranded soldiers. These men were of little concern to the Germans, if they had rounded them up they would have had to feed and accommodate them so many soldiers remained living rough, perhaps eventually escaping, sometimes living with local families and occasionally marrying. Many individual Belgians and Frenchmen and women helped the soldiers, providing food, shelter and other help and occasionally creating loose organisations to do this and this was the genesis of the Comet line (La Ligne Comète in French). The Germans were fairly relaxed about this at first but this was to change.

In the meantime the Germans entered Paris on the 14th June and by the 25th June1940 they occupied the whole of France down to a line from Bordeaux in the west to Lyons in the east. Below this line the country was governed by a French administration which had signed an armistice with the Germans and was based in Vichy and run by the 85 year old Marshal Petain. The Germans already occupied Holland and Belgium.

As the RAF became more active there were increasing numbers of aircraft being shot down with aircrew often escaping. This increased dramatically in early 1942 with Bomber Harris' change of tactics. The Germans were much less relaxed about the safeguarding and escaping of trained airmen, who, if recovered, could be bombing again within days. The British too were understandably more anxious to recover pilots who had taken up to 2 years to train than squaddies who had taken just a few weeks.

To repatriate Allied personnel the local patriots had to look South and West for routes as the whole of Northern Europe was occupied and the Channel impassable. Many patriots helped the Allied servicemen, either individually or in the organisations that formed. Thousands of Belgians and Dutch would be looking out for airmen shot down overnight. The question then was what to do with them once found. One organisation that formed, and there were many, was the Comet Line (La Ligne Comète*)*.

There were many thousands of people involved in the Comet line but three families were central to it and Joe's escape – the De Jongh family, the Dumon family and the De Greef family, all the members of these families were involved with the Comet line. Other prominent families were the d'Oultremonts, the Marechals and the Itterbecks.

The De Jongh family

The Comet Line was started by the De Jongh family in Brussels. Frédéric De Jongh was a schoolteacher and his daughters were Andrée ("Dédée" – the French diminutive of Andrée) and Suzanne. They started by helping allied servicemen with food, and Dédée had worked in a hospital for wounded Allied soldiers but then sought ways of repatriating them.

In August 1941 Dédée escorted two Belgians who wanted to go on fighting and a Cameron Highlander, Colin Cromar of the 1st Gordons to the British Consulate in Bilbao and persuaded the Vice Consul to finance such evasions. She explained that her family had been helping British evaders since Dunkirk and simply needed help and especially funding to be able to continue. Remarkably the Vice Consul agreed almost immediately, she was given the codename of "postman" (and she often referred to her airmen as her "parcels") and he offered 6000 Belgian francs per serviceman to cover the expenses from Brussels to St Jean de Luz and 1400 Spanish pesetas for the mountain crossing, although he asked that she preferably bring British servicemen only and eventually only airmen. She did this and she founded one of the most successful of the escape routes across Europe – the Comet line.

Most of the other escape routes had political affiliations or were organised from London. Hers was severely independent and autonomous. She specialised in the release of aircrews shot down over occupied Europe; individually they were regarded as the most valuable. More than 2000 airmen escaped or evaded the Germans during the war and got back to England. The Comet line was responsible for 800 of these – British, Polish, Americans, Canadians and Australians. The Comet line also brought to safety many of the helpers who were in danger of discovery. Dédée herself made more than 17 crossings of the Pyrenees on foot escorting escapers. Once the escapers had been delivered she would return the next day back over the Pyrenees.

There were in essence three parts to the Comet Line - Brussels, Paris and the Pyrenees. There were also a number of smaller groups who fed airmen into the Comet line in Brussels. One small group were called Broken Wings who covered the Limburg area and another line was known as JAM which was based at Liege. Once they had retrieved the airmen their job was to get them to Brussels to be taken on by Comet.

In 1942 the RAF were making their big raids on Germany and numbers of pilots were brought down in occupied territory. Bombers, using the shortest route in and out of Germany, were mostly brought down in one strip of country, and this became known as Death Valley. Many thousands of men and women were brought into the Comet organisation. They were organised into groups of beaters and each night they went out into Death Valley to find the British pilots. It was a race to get to them before the Gestapo.

At the outset of the Comet Line Frédéric De Jongh, Dédée's father was entirely responsible for the Brussels end of the line, organising the collection of evaders, their lodging, security clearance and eventual despatch. In Feb 1942 the Gestapo were on his tracks and in April he went to Paris.

The Dumon family

Others took over (they had actually been working with him from the start) including 2 teenage sisters "Nadine" (Andrée Dumon, later Antoine, also Dédée, but Nadine to avoid confusion with Dédée De Jongh) and her sister "Michou" (Michèline Lily Dumon, later Ugeux – the famous "Lily" to many airmen). Their work was to collect airmen and pass them on to colleagues for despatch to Paris. They also helped forge ID documents. One major contribution made by Michou was to discover the identity of a traitor in their midst, Jean Masson. For a while the Brussels organisation had been completely disrupted by Masson and if Tante Go's organisation in the South (see below) had been penetrated then the whole line could have been lost. Michou's determination to find the traitor will have been increased by the fact that her sister, Nadine, was to be betrayed by him.

Nadine was arrested by the Gestapo in August 1942. The Germans had been looking for Dédée and may have mistaken Nadine for her, perhaps both of them being Dédée added to their confusion. Many other Comet helpers were betrayed by Jean Masson at the time. The Gestapo were also closing in on Michou and in January 1944 she finally agreed to use the Comet line herself to escape to England. She had helped more than 250 evaders through the Comet Line.

Evaders who had been given safe houses in and around Brussels and Belgian ID were then escorted to Paris, usually by train and tram and passed over to the organisation there.

In Paris the same process took place of housing the evaders, arranging French ID and preparing them for the journey to the South. It very soon became clear that Dédée could not go back to Belgium, the Gestapo were looking for her and she initially and then her father moved to Paris and conducted operations there until they were both eventually caught.

Quote from Dédée: "At long last my good luck failed me. On Jan 13th 1943 when near the frontier a Spanish smuggler denounced me to the Gestapo. I was taken back to Bayonne and afterwards spent four months in solitary confinement in various French and Belgian prisons. Later I was to know the horrors of the concentration camp at Ravensbruck. Here two out of every three women captives died from their experiences" (Ravensbruck was a women's prison). When arrested by the Germans all Dédée would admit, under torture, was that she was the leader of the Comet line. This probably saved her life as the Gestapo could not believe that a "mere girl" could be that.

Following Dédée's arrest her father, Frédéric, took leave of absence from the school in Brussels and on April 30th he moved to Paris to continue the operation. But the Gestapo were getting very close to him, the price on his head was 1 million BF. He was arrested in June 1943, betrayed by Masson, and executed on March 28th 1944. Others continued the work started by the De Jonghs.

The De Greef family

In the South of France the evaders were taken over by Mme Elvire De Greef ("Tante Go" – the name came from a pet dog called Gogo). Her husband, Fernand, was the interpreter for the local German Kommandantur. In this position he was able to help with information, passes and stamps and took incredible risks including personally helping to spring Florentino from jail (see later). In this he was helped by the permission he had from the Kommandatur to pass freely in the streets at night as part of his job. In 1942 Tante Go was 43 years old and her children Jeanine and Freddy also helped. They were a Belgian family who had tried to escape to England at the start of the war but had been trapped and settled at Anglet in South West France. Tante Go and her family operated in Bayonne throughout the war procuring food and safe houses and arranging the guides and acting as a base for the Pyrenean crossings and was as an inspiration to all. Tante Go was the Comet Line chief in the South.

Route over the Pyrenees

The route for each crossing was broadly the same. Florentino (the guide across the Pyrenees) and Dédée would pick up the evaders at St Jean de Luz or Ciboure, walk to the farmhouse "Bidegain-Berri" in Urrugne (the home of Francia Usandizanga), rest, continue for 4 hours to the river Bidassoa, then on to Oyarzun, then there was 2 hours to go. The landmarks.were the lighthouse at Fuenterrabia, the lights of Irun, the Bidassoa and the peaks of the Trois Couronnes. Border crossings ended in July 1944, the Germans had now occupied the whole of France which was now a war zone and it was impossible to get to St Jean de Luz.

The Comet Line

There were a number of remarkable things about the Comet line. Firstly it was female dominated and many of these brave ladies were very young mostly in their twenties but some in their teens. Despite being so young the spirit created was unique, no matter how many of the line were arrested others would come forward to keep it going, it continually reinvented itself despite being virtually destroyed several times.155 members of the Comet line died in the Allied cause and many more were imprisoned It was also a very Belgian group, it resisted any attempts by M.I.9 to help, it did not want to be run from London. It was also a classless group with about 12000 helpers working for it most of the time and a wider group which has been quoted as up to 400,000 men and women involved in various ways including priests, teachers, doctors, peasants and a Baron, a Count and a Countess.

The Comet line repatriated 288 airmen from the British, American, Australian, Canadian and New Zealand air forces. They also repatriated 73 Belgian, French and Dutch helpers who were coming into danger.

Meanwhile back to Joe who we have left dangling on his parachute somewhere over Northern Europe. Joe will have known little about the potential support on the ground (he will have known nothing of the Comet Line) and little about the other servicemen he would encounter but he will have known that there would be lots of Germans on the ground. He just had to be lucky with who he met first.

5.   Escape and Evasion

The following is a mixture of what Joe wrote for his own purposes and for friends and the official M.I.9 debrief which he submitted when he returned and one or two other sources.

9th June to 12th June

M.I.9 Debrief report dated 27 August 1942

I was pilot of a bomber aircraft which left Linton on Ouse at 2300 hrs on 8th June 42. The other members of the crew were F/Lt (Roy Blackwell) Chadwick, navigator, Sgt (William Edgar) Pilborough, (a Canadian), bomb aimer, Sgt (John Ralph) Storey, engineer, Sgt (John Andrew) Catley, wireless operator, Sgt (John) McInstry, second gunner and Sgt (William John) Hopkins, rear gunner. I do not know what happened to the others.

(Sgt Catley, 1006939, from Nelson in Lancashire was the only other survivor, having baled out at 500 feet and survived, although I don't think Joe ever knew this. Catley was captured on 9th June, the same day as they were shot down and was a POW for the duration of the war, although he made several escape attempts. The others are buried at Heverlee war cemetery 3km south of Leuven.)

For the rest of his life Joe would would think quietly about his crew each June 8th. Now, his grandchildren meet every June 8th to think of Joe.

Joe's notes

After leaving our target at Essen we were shot down and baled out about 0150 hrs on 9 June. I came down in the region of Kirchhoven, near Heinsberg, still in Germany. *(Kirchhoven is about 100 km south west of Essen and Joe's route back to Linton on Ouse would have been north west from Essen after the attack. The probable reason for being so apparently off course is that the Essen raid was one of the huge attacks with hundreds of bombers from squadrons all over England and they would have had to come into formation before the attack and well away from Essen and then again done the same after the attack before returning home to their various airfields. This would have been necessary to avoid collisions with aircraft arriving from all directions. The assembly area was presumably south west of Essen).*

I landed in marshy country and hid my parachute and the rest of my equipment in a deep filled drain. I tried to get a bearing on a small compass with which I had been issued, but it was not much use, because I held it in my hand and it kept swinging. I started off west but I had considerable difficulty, as all the paths seemed to run N.W. I did the only thing that occurred to me; I hid my chute, took a bead on the North Star AND RAN AND RAN AND RAN in a south-westerly direction. For the first hour I walked across marshland, in which there were occasional crops and woods, and skirted the few buildings I saw. I got onto a road and came to a hamlet about 0300 hrs. I walked through this hamlet and was not challenged. I continued along the road west, passing through more small villages. Just after dawn I began to meet workmen on bicycles. I hid from the first few but as any who saw me did not show any interest in me, I walked along the road. I had torn off my stripes and kept my head well down when passing anyone.

I walked on till about 0530 hrs by which time I had arrived at a fairly large village on the canal to the East of the Meuse (*Maas in Flemish*), which at that point forms the frontier, and not far from Ophoven, across the river in Belgium *(the village would have been Stevensweert which is actually in Holland)*. By this time there were crowds of people about, so I walked along the canal for a short distance in search of a hiding place *(from the crash site at Kirchhoven to Stevensweert is a distance of 25 kms by a windy road today, somewhat less by a more direct route across the fields. In heavy boots and uniform to cover this distance in 4 hours or so is remarkable)* There was very little cover, but I eventually hid in a small patch of fern and firs. Come the dawn I hid in a wood, sleeping most of the day. The following night I continued my progress. By dawn I was near a village *(this would have been Neeroeteren, 18km from Stevensweert)* and very wet; it had been raining. I tried to sleep and about 0830 hrs I heard workmen very near and occasionally got a glimpse of them.

Two Dutch workers discovered me. I could not avoid them. I was on the border between Germany and Holland *(actually some distance now from the border between Belgium and Holland)*.

M.I.9 report

They appeared to be surveyors and occasionally they had to get their chains through my shrubbery. About 1030 hrs they chopped a path about 2 feet from me and saw me. I pretended to be asleep and they continued working. They were talking Flemish which I thought was Dutch. About 1100 hrs I decided to try to talk to them. I went up to the youngest, a man of about 24. There were 3 men working. I spoke to him in English. He made a rush towards me, pointed to the sky, and asked if I was an aviator. When I said I was, he shook hands with me and called the 2 others, one of whom was his father and the other probably the local surveyor. After they had told me I was near Maaseik they hid me in a deeper shrubbery. I had told them I wanted to get to Switzerland and they promised me clothes and help.

The young men went to see various people on my behalf. About midday he offered me his lunch. The bread smelt fusty, the butter, which had been made from fish, had bones in it, and the cake tasted like cattle cake. I found it difficult to swallow and the ersatz coffee did not help much.

The Bidelot letter

In 1980 Joe received a letter from Albert Bidelot. It is shown in full in Chapter 20. Edited extracts are shown here." I will now describe in detail how I came to find you back in 1942. Being an inspector of bridges and gutters as well as "Géomètre expert" (a surveyor) I was, that day (this would have been the 10th June), out to measure the area in which I found you, because the canal was to be made larger. I had 3 helpers with me that day, and one of them was next to me when I discovered you and mistook you for a German soldier, that is why I first spoke to you in German. You addressed me in English and offered me the money the RAF had given you in case of such a situation and I refused it. I gave you a little of what I had on me to eat and told you to wait for me while I went off to find some civilian clothes for you. I sent my boys home and cycled 8 km home where I rang one of my neighbours (a Doctor) and asked him for some civilian clothes ... and asked him if he would accompany me back to Neeroeteren... but he said it was too dangerous but he would put me in touch with somebody who could help. He brought me a suitcase with a shirt, tie, shoes etc and I set off on my bike and when I reached the place where I left you – no Joe Pack. I called for you, but received no reply. I had tears in my eyes. I thought the Germans must have found you, or that you had given up waiting. I was told later that G. Grosermans of Ophoven had returned to the forest accompanied by Hilven of Ophoven, and that the latter had taken you on his bike, having given you an old pair of trousers, took you home with him, accompanied by the "helper" Grosermans. I was furious, I knew Hilven, but Grosermans was a good for nothing, he might have betrayed us all. But I was assured that you were in good hands and would be taken to Gertrude Moors at the Mill at Dilsen.*

M.I.9 report

During the afternoon the young man *(Grosermans)* brought a friend, a man of about 50, who claimed to be in the Belgian Secret Service *(from correspondence after the war this was Mathieu Tras-Nijs from Lanaken who Joe was to meet after the war)* and said he would take me to Switzerland on the back of his bicycle.

About 1600 hrs the young man brought me some clothes and took away my RAF clothes. About 1830 hrs I left my hiding place and travelled on the back of the "Secret Service" man's bicycle across the canal and river and round Ophoven. About 2200 hrs we reached a large house, from which a man came out with dogs. My helper whistled like a bird and was answered from the house, from which a man came out with dogs. He proved to be the gardener and took me into the house, where there were two oldish ladies. I was given a good meal and champagne and shelter for the night. All the people who were helping me kept asking when the invasion was coming and said they could not hold out much longer. I left the house on the afternoon of 10 June *(this was probably the 11th)*. *(The M.I.9.report finishes*

---

here and there is then a second supplementary report of the same date. It sounds as if they broke for lunch and then carried on – Ed)

A second supplementary M.I.9 report also dated 27th August 1942

On the night of 9 June *(this would have been the 10th)* I was taken (as described in my report) to a house some distance to the N.W. of Ophoven *(Hilven's house)*. During the afternoon of 10 June *(the 11th)* a woman of about 25 brought me some better clothes and a light mackintosh, and about 1930 hrs she and her fiancé came on bicycles with a third bicycle for me. I took with me a parcel which contained the top of my battledress, I had been told in England to carry with me some proof of my identity and I thought this would meet the case. I cycled with the man, the girl keeping about half a mile behind, mostly on tracks to a mill at Ophoven, where I was told we were waiting for our doctor. (There had previously been some talk of a doctor who would take me to Switzerland by car).

Ed – This is almost certainly the mill at Dilsen not Ophoven, home of Gertrude Moors and her family. Albert Bidelot refers to it in his letter and enclosed a photo of the Mill, shown below.

Dilsen (Limburg)
De Molen en Molenaars huis

The doctor arrived at about 2230 hrs. He had an English wife and spoke English. He asked me various questions about the RAF in order to test my identity. The doctor left about 0100 hrs *(11 June - probably the 12th - Ed)* after telling me to put complete faith in my helpers. His impression was that I would be got to Portugal. At 0430 hrs the lady of the house whose husband is with the Belgian army in Scotland took me by tram to Liege, which we reached about 1030 hrs.

The Doctor is probably Dr Groenen who "is in touch with an organisation working for British Intelligence" (details from Leslie Baveystock who had passed the same way just days earlier) and would have screened Joe (Joe tried to contact the doctor after the war but without success, he would not have known the doctor's name at the time, indeed he will have known none of the names of his helpers at the time for obvious security reasons). The Germans were very aware of the success of the escape lines and made strenuous efforts to break them often by infiltration. There were several attempts by Germans posing as airmen to do this and it would have been essential for someone to screen airmen as early as possible and before they got to know too much about the escape line and it's personnel. Dr Groenen will have asked questions such as what is the official form number of an RAF leave pass and what colour is it. The Mill at Dilsen was quite secluded. Airmen not able to answer the questions and suspected of being infiltrators could, if necessary, be shot. Joe clearly passed the tests.

12th June to 20th June

The M.I.9. report above says he reached Liege at 10.30 hours the next morning (12th June). It is likely that Joe forgot quite a lot of intervening detail. In the letter sent by Albert Bidelot he refers to the map he enclosed and says it "shows the places you stopped at after Asch and before Lanaken where our

friend Mathieu Erab lives". He has ringed Ophoven, Neeroeteren, Lanklaer, Dilsen and Neerharen. He also enclosed pictures of 2 trams, (shown left), presumably indicating that Joe had used them.

The trams were a) from Weert to Molen-Beersel to Maaseik and b) from Maaseik to Lanaken. From Weert to Lanaken was an often used evasion route. It seems unlikely Joe would have been taken north to Weert, see map below. Perhaps he was told to meet someone arriving on Weert tram at Maaseik whereupon they then travelled to Lanaken on that tram. Then Joe writes:

After several days I arrived at the now famous Maastricht (probably written at the time of the EU Maastricht treaty). It was a bit of a shock to find the Town Hall full of the German military. It sounds as if he was being moved around while plans were being made for his eventual journey.

HOLLAND

BELGIUM

• Weert

• Molenbeersel

Geistingen •
Ophoven • • Stevensweert

• Maaseik

Neeroeteren •

• Kirchhoven

• Heinsberg

Dilsen •

Lanklaar •

GERMANY

Neerharen •

Lanaken •

• Maastricht

1 INCH TO 5 MILES

This map shows all the towns and villages referred to in Joe's evasion thus far
and was drawn by Joe's granddaughter Arabella.

Joe's notes

On the way *(to Liege)* we met two men who shielded me from other travellers. A young man took me by tram to the Cathedral at Liege *(this was l'église St-Barthelémy)*; he handed me a rosary and left me kneeling down, to be joined by a man who interrogated me in broken English for a while. When we left I noticed he was saluted by all the policemen we passed *(this was one of the Commissaires of Police for Liege, Louis Rademeckers)*. Later, he met me outside in the street and took me to visit his friends; the butcher, the baker and others. On being introduced, they would produce a bottle of Cognac and we would toast one another. In my tipsy state we boarded a tram, together with a bunch of German soldiers; I pushed them to make room for me, without a care in the world. He took me to the house of two elderly ladies *(Jeannine Marie Rosalie Ritschendorff and Mathilde Virgile*

Théodore Ritschendorff, they were 48 and 53 at the time and lived at 30 rue de Waroux in Liege, they hid about 40 airmen during the war, Rademeckers' assistants were close neighbours), who kept me for 10 days. During that time I was provided with another suit of clothes and (by a British lady) with English books *(probably Mme Docteur Lindemann, actually an American married to a Belgian).*

After hiding in a room about 10 feet by 7 feet for about 14 days *(actually just a week or so),* my friend collected me and I travelled by tram to Louvain *(Leuven in Flemish).* There my next helper, I was told, was the Chief of Police at Louvain Maurice Collignon. He was caught and shot on 4th August 1943. Maurice Collignon was a formidable patriot who helped many allied personnel.

20th June to 4th July

On 20th June I was taken by the chief of the organisation *(Paul Schoenmeckers),* a retired Belgian officer, to Louvain, whence a young Belgian took me to his flat at the Ministry of Justice in Brussels. Brussels was full of armed troops. Occasionally I would see a man or woman with the yellow Star of David stitched to their backs. I know now that this was to distinguish Jews for transporting to the extermination camps of Poland. After the young man had taken my photograph his father took me to stay with friends about 20 miles out of the capital.

Joe would have required Belgian ID with a photograph to get from Brussels to Paris and French ID and photograph to get from Paris to the Pyrenees. It is not known which of these photographs is which. He is without a moustache in both which otherwise he had for his whole life. It was probably felt that an RAF moustache was a bit of giveaway.

The friends 20 miles out of the capital were Roger and Stephanie Leblois who became family friends. She was a secretary at the Ministry of Justice in

Brussels and (as we will see later, the Resistance was very active at the Ministry of Justice) she would smuggle out copies of her typing to the Resistance – how she hated her employers! Her husband was a racehorse trainer; he had 6 or 8 looseboxes and was very frightened (who can blame him). I spent 2 or 3 days and nights hiding with his horses; later he moved me into his house. The Leblois' lived at Hoeylaert which is outside of Brussels. *(It is possible the Leblois' had a flat in Brussels as well as their stables at Hoeylaert since Joe referred often to spending time in Brussels.)*

Although Joe does not mention this church most airmen were taken at some point to the Eglise St Joseph in Brussels for transfer from one helper to the next. They would be left sitting in a pew and told that when someone approached them and asked the time the correct answer was "always the same".

That night (*not sure which night - Ed*) I was taken to the gatehouse serving the entrance to the Palace of Justice in Brussels. The family living there were employed to open and close the large metal gates when the German limousines, with Swastika pennants, drove in and out of the Palace (*the Palais de Justice was used by the Germans as a headquarters*). That night the family invited friends to a party at the gatehouse, in my honour. I seemed to be the only one present that was worried for their safety. They photographed me and, days afterwards, produced a passport and work-pass. Before the year was out the couple and their three teenaged children had "disappeared". Only the mother appeared again, after the war.

This is the Palais de Justice in 1930 but it had not changed by 1942.

The gatehouse Joe refers to is the grand entrance on the right side of the building which faces the Rue aux Laines. The main entrance to the Palais is on the far side facing the Place Poelaert. On the far side of the Place is the Rue de la Régence. The buildings to the left of this road (under a barely discernable Martini sign) were demolished sometime after the 1930 photograph above and the Ministry of Justice building was put up. The Ministry today is shown below but has been heavily renovated since the war. There were ground floor apartments on the right hand side and the left hand side of the Ministry building occupied by service staff. There were also two concierge lodges and one apartment in the Palais de Justice building on its Rue aux Laines side. The apartment may have been occupied by the Chauffagiste, the heating engineer who managed the heating for both the Palais and the Ministry; both buildings being connected by tunnels under the Place Poelaert and under each building

Baveystock, in his book, refers to be taken to an apartment opposite the Palais, i.e. in the Ministry of Justice. He also says that the Evrard family lived there and hid him and that the other apartment, on the other side of the Ministry, was occupied by the Van Steenbecks. It seems likely that Joe was hidden by the Van Steenbecks and that they were the gatehouse keepers who therefore had access to the gatehouse where they held the party in his honour. Mr Van Steenbeck was also a photographer and Joe refers to being photographed for his documents. Mr Van Steenbeck was shot by the Nazis in the basement tunnels in May 1943.

The Ministry of Justice today. The apartments were at the left and right ground floor extremities.

The month of July 1942

On the 1ˢᵗ of July F/Sgt B. Evans, in his M.I.9 report refers to meeting "a young RAF pilot, whose name I do not know, at the station at Namur, whereupon they then caught the tram to Louvain with Pilot Officer Watson RCAF.

On 4 July I went to Brussels at night and was given an identity card and German pass for the frontier. On 5 July I was taken to Louvain with F/Sgt Evans (S/P.G(-)809) and a pilot officer *(Watson)* who is now a prisoner in Spain. *It was normal practise to travel to Paris starting outside Brussels, which was very heavily policed; through trains attracted less attention than trains starting from Brussels.* Our guide was a young girl *(Nadine).* In Louvain we boarded the Paris train and travelled via Brussels. *It is possible Joe may have confused his dates. Evans' M.I.9 report states that they caught the 2130 hours train to Paris, arriving 0630 hours on 2 July and were taken to the Hotel Luxembourg in the Latin Quarter. Watson and Evans went to one house, Joe to another.*

We had some difficulty at the frontier *(between Belgium and France),* when the pilot officer *(Watson)* kept on doing the wrong thing in reply to the official's questions, but the girl *(Nadine – she was arrested in August and this will have been one of her last evasions)* passed us all off as mutes. The passengers were now thinning out and German officers searched everything and everyone. Our girl was in tears, passing us off to the officers as deaf mutes Fifteen hours after boarding the train, standing in crowded corridors, we arrived at the Gare du Nord, Paris. On leaving the train we split up; there were watching military personnel everywhere. At the barriers, German soldiers going on leave would show their credentials and salute with the words "Heil". I crept through on the other side. As I crossed the road outside the station I was confronted by a German officer with yellow lapels. He didn't say a word. I put up my hands – he searched me and my bundle of clothes, razor etc., dumped them on the road and left me. I **had been searched by the Gestapo** *(this was probably not the Gestapo since they did not have a uniform but it was still a dangerous situation).*

Map of Belgium showing the towns and cities Joe visited after Liege. [drawn by Arabella]

In Paris I stayed for 14 days with M. and Mme Coache and for another 14 days with Monsieur André (Frédéric De Jongh), the father of Dédée.

The Coache's were a wonderful French couple. The wife would take the three of us (there were two Scottish soldiers hiding with me) on the Metro to Paris (they lived at 71 Rue de Nanterre, 92 Asnières, about 11 km northwest of the centre of Paris). On Bastille Day, 14th July, although strictly forbidden by the Germans, we displayed Blue, White and Red ribbons in our buttonholes and Madame wore her national scarf. On another occasion, she took us to see the German A/A gun, positioned over one of the Seine bridges; a few weeks previously the same gun had been firing at us when we bombed the Renault works. *Madame Raymonde Coache was taken by the Gestapo early in 1943 (another victim of Masson). Her husband René, escaped to England but then returned on a secret mission for M.I.9.and was arrested in April 1944 but freed 6 months later. Raymonde survived two concentration camps and the Coache's became family friends after the war. Raymonde's exploits were acknowledged by both Governments with medals that she refers to as her "souvenirs".*

Joe's second 2 weeks in Paris were spent with the De Jonghs. When in Paris Frédéric De Jongh lived at Saint-Maur in the Val de Marne and Dédée stayed at 10 Rue Oudinot, near the Rue de Babylone with Elvire Morelle and

Jeanine De Greef when she was in Paris. It is likely Joe stayed with Frédéric De Jongh until Dédée was ready for the next stage of the trip.

I left Paris from the Gare d'Austerlitz on 30 July with Sgt Norfolk (S/P.G(-) 815), Sgt Wright (S/P.G(-)816) and Pte MacFarlane (S/P.(G)821). Our guide was Dédée.

31st July to 27th August

Joe's notes

The events leading to our eventual train journey south are too detailed to record. The masterminding of our eventual escape was all due to our leader, a young Belgium girl, the now famous Andrée De Jongh. She and her father (who was later caught and shot), together with her sister (*Suzanne De Jongh, married name Wittek*), laid the foundation for many British airmen to escape via the "Comète Line". *Andrée De Jongh was awarded the George medal after the War by the British. Her own Government made her a Countess. She survived the War and lived in Brussels (she passed away on 13th October 2007).*

We travelled from the Gare d'Austerlitz, after previously bribing the railway officials. We occupied a compartment of a carriage reserved for German officers and German collaborators. There were eight of us; Andrée De Jongh, a lady (*Tante Go, Elvire De Greef, née Berlément,*), her two daughters (*she only had one daughter, Jeanine De Greef, who was 17 at the time, the second young lady was probably Elvire Morelle*), and four of us Brits. (*Joe refers elsewhere to another traveller with them being "B" Johnson – Albert Edward Johnson, always known as "B", an Englishman who had been working for Count Baillet-Latour, President of the IOC, in Brussels before the war and then worked with Dédée until he was forced to escape to England in March 1943. He escorted 122 Allied evaders over the Pyrenees in 14 trips). In recent years Jeanine De Greef has written that the train compartments had 6 seats not 8, and that Dédée and Jeanine travelled with the 4 evaders and B Johnson and Tante Go were in a different compartment. Dédée and Tante Go never travelled together.* Whenever our compartment door was opened for one reason or another, the girls would talk across us; we would say OUI or NON to a slight nod or shake of the head by either of the girls. There was always a German in the corridor.

Private William MacFarlane

One of the party was a Private William MacFarlane who had been captured on 6th June 1940 as described in the previous chapter. His M.I.9. report then continues:

"About the beginning of 1942 I began planning to escape with Pte. James Goldie of my unit, with whom I had been since capture. We saved chocolate biscuits and tea from Red Cross parcels and discussed ways of getting out of the camp. The mines were worked in two shifts. I worked from 0600 to 1800 and Goldie from 1400 to 2200. We decided to escape on the night of 21st March. This was a Saturday and we reckoned there would be a chance of our not being missed on the Sunday. I made a jemmy in the turning shop (which we would use to burst open the gate on the East side of the camp which was only used by the guards and the women working in the kitchen. We were locked up at 2100 in our huts and the doors were not opened again until 2245 hours when the second shift came in from work. There were two sentries and four women who worked in the cookhouse. After the women finished at 1900 hours the two guards became responsible for the feeding of the second shift when it came off work. One of them ought to have remained on guard outside but we knew that they both generally went into the dining room. I broke the lock of the gate about 2030 hrs and the gate remained open till 2245 hrs when Goldie and I left. Two other men of our regiment were to have come with us but they did not turn up though we waited ten minutes for them.

The following is a summary of our equipment and plans. **Clothes** – we wore ordinary battle dress on top of which we had blue overalls with "KG" in red on the back. We were able to conceal these letters with rucksacks which we made out of sacks. **Food** – we had collected sufficient chocolate and biscuits for ten days, six tins of sardines and about six lbs of tea. Our idea was to use the tea as bribes. **Maps** – we had two maps of Germany and adjacent countries, one of which Goldie had got from an anti-Nazi German working underground with him in the mine and the other of which he got from a Pole who worked at the head of the shaft. I told the Pole I was going to escape but did not tell him how or when. **Plan** – there had been a number of other attempts from the camp but none of the men had tried to escape other than on foot and they had all been recaptured. We decided to try to jump on railway wagons at Gerstungen about 12 miles N.E. of Unterbreizbach.

We took six days to get to Gerstungen walking in a circle to avoid detection. We walked at night, avoiding villages, and slept in the woods by day. There was snow on the ground up to our knees, and quite frequently we had to use melted snow instead of water. On our second night we left our hiding place rather early and were crossing a main road near a village when we were stopped by a German (civilian presumably). We told him we were Frenchmen going to Gerstungen and when he asked us why we did not speak French we admitted we were English (this must have been difficult for Scotsmen! – Ed). By giving him cigarettes we persuaded him to let us go, but we suspect that he reported our presence to other villagers, because we were chased very shortly afterwards. We managed to hide in a wood and our pursuers did not come in after us.

We reached the goods station at Gerstungen on the night of 26th March. We broke the lead seal of a closed salt wagon and entered by the door. We then opened a window, came out by the door – which we re-sealed – and got back in by the window. There were quite a few railwaymen about, but no one saw us. We had plenty of room on top of the sacks of salt inside the wagon. Unfortunately the train only moved for a few hours at a time and then laid up for half a day or a day, so that the journey to Belgium, which would have taken about two days normal travelling, lasted eight days. We had neglected to take water with us and did not leave the wagon during the numerous stops for fear of being seen. We suffered terribly from thirst, and during the last few days were unable to eat the food we had brought with us. We knew the wagon was bound for Belgium as we saw the destination (Hasselt) written in German on the notice on the side of the truck. IN Belgium a French notice was substituted for the German one.

We were able to check our position on one of our maps by watching the names of the stations we passed through. On Good Friday (3rd April) we arrived in Hasselt. We remained in the wagon all day and most of the night and then dropped out at about 0400 (4th April). We walked to a stream on the outskirts of Hasselt where we washed and made tea in tin cans picked up on the road. We then walked to Tirlemont, the jour-ney occupying two days. We had to walk by day because we could find no cover for hiding. We were still in our blue overalls over battle dress but, though we walked on the main road, no one challenged us. On 5th April we stopped at a house in Kessel Loo and asked for water to make tea, speaking in broken German, which the people understood. An old woman took us in and kept us for the night. Early next morning we were taken by bicycle to Louvaine where we were sheltered for six weeks before an organisation arranged the rest of our journey.

Joe wrote after the war: The Scot you mention as being in our party (MacFarlane) to cross in July '42 – he and his friend stayed with me in hiding in Paris. They had a real escape to tell. They were taken as POW's, ex-Black Watch (actually the Argyll and Sutherland Highlanders), at Dunkirk and eventually to a POW camp in Poland (actually Germany). The two of them escaped from the camp and made their way on foot through the Black Forest in terrible conditions sleeping in snow. Boarding a goods train without food or drink. They eventually ended up in Paris where I met them. Their story is now only vague in my memory but I do recall that they had been told they would have to see out the war with nuns in Paris. Having successfully escaped, so far, from Poland, they decided they would make their own way to Spain from Paris. This presented a great danger to the escape lines and it was decided to take them over the Pyrenees, but only one at a time. They agreed to this and that is how they came to be hidden with the Coaches. The Scot who travelled with us on the train to St Jean de Luz had blond hair which represented danger as there were no blond men virtually anywhere at that time. When we arrived at St Jean de Luz Germans were everywhere and we avoided eye contact. Our Scottish friend had been instructed to leave the station by a different exit. *This was an often used route for conspicuous evaders. The station gentlemen's toilet had a locked door that led straight to the street. A duplicate key had been obtained and the door would be unlocked so that when necessary the normal ticket barrier could be avoided.* All went well and the four of us were able to meet again outside the station. Here we hid in a café; the following night the Basque guide who was to take us over the Pyrenees *(Florentino)* was blind drunk. He was paid £100 for each of us "delivered safely".

William MacFarlane and James Goldie were awarded the Distinguished Conduct Medal by the King on 10th November 1942 as pictured below.

SCOTS DECORATED.—Private Mac-farlane and Private Goldie, both of the Argyll and Sutherland Highlanders, photo-graphed with a young friend outside Buckingham Palace after receiving the D.C.M. at a recent Investiture.

The above pictures are courtesy of Moira Bradley, William McFarlane's daughter.

Crossing the Pyrenees

The crossing had been planned for the 18th July. According to Jeanine (Tante Go's daughter) there had been some trouble that night and Dédée had to start again on the night of 20/21st July 1942. [In fact it is likely that it was not 20/21st July but the 31st July. Airmen crossing were asked to write a short message before the crossing. Joe wrote the following words taken from the actual book.]

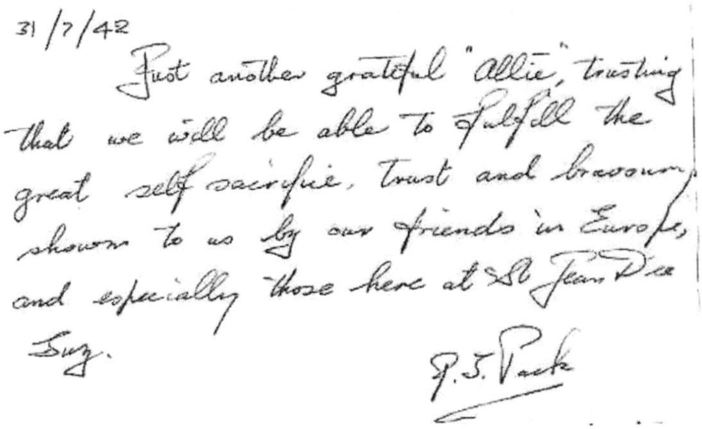

31/7/42

Just another grateful "allie", trusting that we will be able to fulfill the great self sacrifice, trust and bravoury, shown to us by our friends in Europe, and especially those here at St Jean De Luz.

Suz.

P. J. Pack

Intriguingly the very next entry in the book is by Angus MacLean, the only other survivor/evader from the Essen raid. He wrote:

"Dear Friends, it is impossible for me to put into words the gratitude I feel for the way I have been treated by my friends on the continent and especially by those here in St Jean de Luz. I hope that our friendship will go on for many years" Fl Lt Angus Maclean RCAF.

A further extract from another book kept by Elvire De Greef is shown below. It shows the scrupulous accounting that had to be done. The numbering on the left (51 to 54) probably refers to the total of Allied servicemen taken across by Comet and the numbering on the right (33 to 35) to total airmen taken over. The book is still in the possession of Jeanine De Greef, Tante Go's daughter, who originally maintained it.

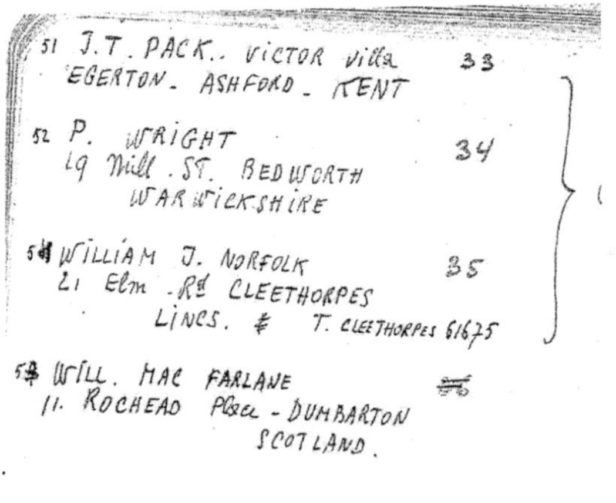

```
51  J.T. PACK.  VICTOR VILLA       33
     EGERTON.  ASHFORD. KENT

52  P.  WRIGHT                     34
     19 Mill. ST. BEDWORTH
          WARWICKSHIRE

54  WILLIAM J. NORFOLK             35
     21 Elm. Rd CLEETHORPES
          LINCS. $ T. CLEETHORPES 61675

53  WILL. MAC FARLANE
     11. ROCHEAD Place - DUMBARTON
                    SCOTLAND.
```

Joe crossed with P. Wright an RAF Sergeant of 76 Squadron from Warwickshire, William Norfolk, an RAF Sergeant, also 76 Squadron from Cleethorpes (Wright and Norfolk were members of the same crew and had been shot down on the 1st June 1000 bomber raid on Essen which Joe had also participated in only to be shot down himself a week after them also in a raid on Essen) and William MacFarlane, an Army private in the Argyll and Sutherland Highlanders from Dumbarton, Scotland. This group were the 33rd to 36th to make the crossing. The first crossing was made on 20/8/1941 and the last was made on 04/06/1944. In between 288 allied personnel were helped across the Pyrenees to safety. For most of this period the guide who took the airmen across was Florentino.

Florentino Goikoetxea

Florentino was a Basque from Hernani in the Pyrenees. He was born in March 1898 and so was in his mid forties when he guided hundreds of airmen over the Pyrenees. He is described as a free and anarchic personality who loved living in the open, enjoyed a drink or two and was involved with the extensive smuggling that took place over the Pyrenees. He was recruited by Dédée for this role. The crossing would begin in St Jean de Luz or Ciboure on the Basque coast. Dédée would take the airmen to the farmhouse at Urrugne to meet Florentino (this was the home of Francia Usandizanga, who would later be captured and die at Ravensbruck in April 1945) and it then took about 8 hours to reach the river Bidassoa, the border between France and Spain. Crossing the swiftly flowing Bidassoa could be hazardous and occasionally impossible. When crossed there was then a 1000 foot ridge to climb, then on to Renteria. Climbing those mountains in rope-soled espadrilles represented an exhausting, gruelling 15 hours or so.

Dédée accompanied Florentino on these crossings. Florentino had hidden brandy bottles at numerous points in the crossing which helped keep him and the airmen going. He also, apparently, had a habit of stumbling every so often which led to Dédée falling on top of him which he seemed to like. He was caught and shot in the leg in July 1944 but managed to escape (in fact his escape was organised by the De Greef family taking extraordinary risks). Florentino was awarded the "Kings Medal for Courage in the cause of Justice" by the King himself, he was introduced as a man who had worked in the field of "import/export" i.e. smuggling! He was also awarded the French Legion of Honour. He died in 1980.

In 1966 we had a family holiday in San Sebastian. One day Joe announced that we were not going to the beach that day but instead would meet someone for lunch. There was no forewarning or explanation. The lunch, I only now realise, was with Florentino. He spoke nothing except Basque of which we spoke none. We spent a lot of time smiling at each other. After the lunch Florentino went out saying he would be back soon. He came back dressed in the Basque uniform of which he was obviously very proud. Joe never explained who this person was and why he was so important.

The reason I am certain it was 1966 is because of the World Cup. We had seen the early matches at home before setting off to Spain and then saw most of the England matches at our hotel. Then the unplanned happened and England were in the final. We could just make it home for the match if all went well. Unfortunately things didn't go well. There were storms in the Channel and England was cut off! We watched the match in a French café in Calais and were surprised that all the French were supporting Germany, there was complete silence at the end.

A further ten-mile walk took us to the outskirts of San Sebastian; there were plenty of Germans there – on leave, I suppose *(they were not on leave, German officials were allowed to operate freely in Spain and Gestapo and Abwehr officers were stationed at all Spanish police stations).* From St Jean de Luz to San Sebastian is a distance of 33 km all of which had to completed at night.

A couple of nights at San Sebastian, then a rendezvous with a British Embassy car (with furled pennant), in which we drove to Madrid.

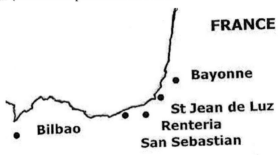

Map by Arabella showing the route taken

From his M.I.9 report a Captain Collie RASC was at the British Embassy in Madrid on 9th August 1942. In his report he wrote:

> *"When I was there the other British escapers and evaders consisted of four RAF sergeants and a boy from 51 (H) Div (Seaforth Hrs) who had escaped from Germany. The four RAF sergeants must have been Pack, Norfolk, Wright and Evans and the "boy" Private W. MacFarlane, 7th Argyll and Sutherland Highlanders.*

We stayed in wooden huts in the Embassy grounds with about sixty others of various nationalities. When the decision was taken whether we would take the train to Gibraltar or to a Spanish prison, I was fortunate and took the train to Gibraltar. *The Embassy staff could not send all escaping men to Gibraltar and will have had to prioritise those likely to be of most value.*

By the 13th August he was certainly in Gibraltar as he sent a telegram to his parents which is shown below.

ELT Pack Victor Villa Egerton Ashford quite well Probably home soon havin grand holiday how is everyone Reply RAF Camp Gibraltar
Joe

By devious means *(this may refer to many airmen having being given false papers showing they were French Canadians)* I was lucky to be walking across the causeway at Gibraltar on August 24th 1942 *(probably August 14th in view of other dates)*, seeing British soldiers and hearing British voices was an experience I never really expected to happen, reporting to the RAF. In less than 24 hours I had exchanged my tatty civilian escape clothes for an RAF uniform.

In Gibraltar Joe would have been interviewed by Donald Darling, M.I.9.'s representative. He would have been given strict instructions not to talk to anyone about his evasion except M.I.9. and he could expect a further interview on his return to London. Breach of this instruction would lead to a court martial.

It is not known exactly what this photo is for. It may have been taken in Madrid or Gibraltar. He is not yet back in uniform and has re-grown his moustache.

After a couple of days I was able to scrounge a flight in a Sunderland doing circuits and splashes in the swell in the outer harbour– I was not impressed, it was a very hairy experience. The heavy swell (I was told) was throwing the flying boat into the air, it seemed to stall from 40 feet up, before sticking on the water, quite frightening to a mere land airman. The Gibraltar authorities, in their wisdom, got me a passage in a destroyer, detailed with two others to guard a large, slow convoy – travelling at 5 knots. *[Joe's M.I.9. report states that they left Gibraltar on the 20th August but it was probably the 19th August since this is the date his fellow travellers have stated.]* We had to sail way out into the Atlantic before going north (to hopefully avoid subs). We had only one scare, dashing around the convoy at 30 knots, throwing off depth charges – but nothing was sighted – who would be a sailor?

It was many days before we arrived at Londonderry (**25th August 1942**) – just 3 months after leaving Yorkshire. Then from Larne to Stranraer by ferry, train to London, with strict orders to report immediately to the Air Ministry *(occasionally returning evaders were escorted by military police to ensure they reported back as quickly as possible and spoke to no-one)*. But it was Sunday morning when I arrived at Euston; the Air Ministry was closed, so I took a train to Charing in Kent and got a lift to Egerton, my home Village. My knock at the front door was answered by my mother. She had received the second telegram from the Air Ministry the previous day – "Missing, believed killed on active service". After all these years I can still shed a tear to think of that meeting *(this telegram must have been a bad shock after the telegram he sent on the 13th August just a week or so earlier. His parents must have assumed his boat home had been sunk)*.

Joe's memory is probably playing tricks. He arrived back in Londonderry on Tuesday 25th August. His M.I.9. debrief took place on Thursday 27th August in London which is about as quick as you can get from Londonderry to London by ferry and train. Norfolk's debrief took place the day before and Wright's took place also on the 25th immediately before Joe's. He may then have been sent back to 35 Squadron in Yorkshire to report back to them, returning to London on Sunday 30th August. The Air Ministry that was closed was probably the clerical/administrative office, the operational side of the RAF did not stop for Sundays. It is also interesting that the telegram received by Joe's mother was sent. The RAF will have known he was safe since arriving at Madrid and certainly after arrival at Gibraltar some 2 weeks earlier. This presumably shows the secrecy of MI9's operations. They may not have wanted to accept that it was him until the debrief was conducted and perhaps then it was too late to stop the telegram.

6.   119 Squadron ~ from Bombers to Flying Boats

Having returned in late August 1942 I was given 2 weeks leave before being recalled to Lytham to "pass out" American ferry pilots onto Halifaxs. *This would have been with 44 (Transport) Group and No 3 School of General Reconnaissance, RAF Squires Gate, Blackpool.*

The Air Ministry then allowed me to choose my RAF future and I asked for a flying boat squadron.

On 16 December 1942 he was posted to 119 Sunderland squadron at Pembroke docks operating in the Bay of Biscay and the Western approaches for anti submarine operations. Pembroke docks were, at the time, the world's largest flying boat station with more than 100 aircraft. Some wartime pictures are shown below, courtesy of John Evans of the Pembroke dock Sunderland Trust.

On 31st October 1942 he had been commissioned and promoted to the rank of pilot officer (equivalent to a Second Lieutenant in the Army) with a new number of 136697 (because he had now left the RAF volunteer reserve and was part of the main RAF).

On 1st January 1943 he was mentioned in despatches (announced in the London Gazette of the same date) which was the standard award for a successful evasion.

119 Squadron had been formed in March 1941, disbanded in Dec 1941, reformed in April 1942 and would be disbanded in May 1943. 119 Squadron patrolled the North Atlantic either on escort duties or reconnaissance.

The Sunderland was manufactured by Short Brothers and was nicknamed "the Pig" by its crews. It entered RAF service in 1938 and by 1941 had developed into the Mark III of which nearly 500 were manufactured for the RAF. It was fitted with 18 machine guns, the greatest number of guns carried by an RAF aircraft. With all the gun turrets sticking out, the Germans gave it the nickname of the flying porcupine.

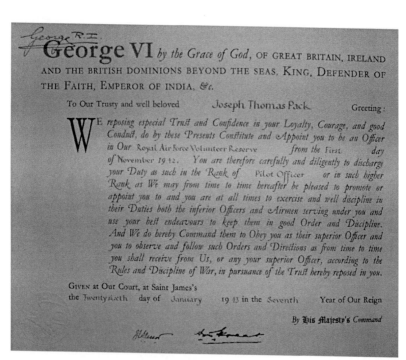

Joe's promotion to Pilot Officer.

His first flight was on Feb 8th 1943 from Pembroke dock up at 0645 down at 1737, nearly 12 hours flying. He was flying as "second dickie" being new to the aircraft and the squadron. He flew 9 sorties in February and March with the squadron diary noting only the sighting of Spanish fishing vessels. His 10th and last flight was on March 29th 1943, up at 0833, then 1920 "A/C went aground on landing, no casualties, Scillies".

Short Sunderland flying boat.

In later years Joe talked about "writing off" 3 airplanes during his RAF career. The first was of course the Halifax on June 9th 1942. This is presumably the second although the report does not refer to a write off, merely going aground; the third comes later in the story in November 1944.

Nearly 50 years later Joe wrote a letter to John Evans, then of Paterchurch Publications, more recently project manager of the Pembroke Dock Sunderland Trust. The letter is shown in full in chapter 20. Excerpts from it are:

".. 29th March 1943 .. we had been flying an anti-sub patrol in the Bay of Biscay.. Pembroke Dock had closed in weatherwise and we were diverted to Mountbatten (Plymouth). Here they had close hauled the defence balloons for us and the cloud base was down to 500 feet. There are some high hills near to Mountbatten and, flying in cloud with only a rough idea of where we were, caused a certain amount of panic. When we saw through the clouds, the sea together with a few boats and the odd balloon, we gathered we had arrived and got down to the water ASAP. Unfortunately we landed down wind, we certainly had no intention of going back into the clouds. Landing down wind (which was quite strong) is a dangerous manoeuvre, the Sunderland with the wind behind would not come to a stop and that is why we hit the opposite shore. We tried to get out of the aircraft thinking it might catch fire and several of the crew climbed onto the wing. Although the engines had been switched off, the propellers were still windmilling slowly and one of the crew jumped through the props without being hit, onto soft ground below, about 15 feet, he was very lucky.

Pictures of the damaged Sunderland are shown below.

The reference in the Squadron diaries to the Scillies is puzzling. The crash was certainly at Mountbatten near Plymouth. The aircraft was not a write off, Bill Stark of the RAAF was one of the crew involved in its recovery and took the photos below. Shorts then restored the aircraft which was back in

service with 10 Squadron by August but then disappeared with its new crew in the Bay of Biscay in October 1943.

Note the bombed out buildings in the background.

119 Squadron diary

On 14th April 1943 (just 2 weeks after the above crash) the Station Commander informed the squadron that it was to be disbanded, the squadron aircraft were to be transferred to other units and aircrew, officers and airmen were to be sent on leave.

In late April 1943 Joe started a conversion course to Catalina's at 131 O.T.U Killadeas, Northern Ireland. Over the next 6 weeks he was flying almost daily, sometimes twice a day, to become accustomed to the new aircraft. His first flight in sole charge of the aircraft was on the 4th May.

Whilst at Killadeas (Enniskillen) Joe wrote to the Caterpillar Club and received the following letter in reply dated June 23rd 1943:

"*Dear P/O Pack, many thanks for your letter of June 5th and I regret the delay in replying, but this has been due to pressure of work. I am very glad that one of our chutes was the means of saving your life, and send sincere congratulations on your escape and return to this country. I have pleasure in welcoming you as a member of the Caterpillar Club and have ordered your membership card and Caterpillar pin. These I will send on to you as soon as they are received. You state that at the time of your jump you were an N.C.O but do not say what your rank was. I have therefore ordered your pin and card to give your rank as P/O, but if you care to let me know your rank at the time of baling out, I will be pleased to have these altered. Yours, Leslie Irvin, Irving Air Chute of Great Britain Limited.*"

We still have the Caterpillar pin.

On 14th July 1943 Joe was posted to 302 Ferry Training unit, Stranraer, and then back to Oban to be crewed up for his eventual trip to the Indian Ocean. The picture below is believed to be the crew.

"Crewing up" was an interesting process. After airmen had undergone their technical training as pilots, navigators and so on they then had to be formed into crews. This took place in O.T.U's (Operational Training Units). Up to a hundred trainees of each position, ten pilots, ten navigators and so on, were assembled in a hanger and instructed to form crews. Instinctively one might imagine the pilots looking round for the best navigator, bomb aimer and so on. Apparently it was quite the reverse, it was the navigators and gunners all looking for the best pilot, in whose hands they would entrust their lives. Once the crews had formed they stayed together subject only to illness or injury. This process generated great camaraderie and many crews, including Joe's, stayed in contact after the war. This must count as an early forerunner of modern speed dating. Joe would have undergone this process for each of the squadrons he was in.

For the pilot there was then a final stage of preparation when he flew as second pilot or "second dickie" with an established crew. This was to learn how to apply the lessons learned in practice – don't fly in a straight line and level, positioning within a formation, banking searches, side slipping, night fighters, weather – all these were rather different when you were surrounded *by flak and fighters. Having proved himself as a second "dickie" the pilot then returned to his own crew and started operations.*

A last point of interest is that the pilot was not necessarily the most senior airman in rank of the crew. Because crews were allowed to form naturally there could be any mix of ranks. When Joe started flying with 35 Squadron his navigator was a Ft/Lt and a commissioned officer and Joe was a Sergeant Pilot and non-commissioned. This would give the odd situation that he might have had to salute his navigator before getting into the plane but once inside the pilot, whatever his rank, was in charge and gave the orders. It also could mean that some crew used the non-commissioned Mess and others the commissioned one. It was not like this in the Luftwaffe where the most senior airman was in charge whatever his position. Since it would have been completely unworkable for a rear gunner, who might be an officer, to be in charge this must mean that crews were allocated, perhaps changing from mission to mission, denying them the camaraderie that characterised the RAF crews.

Joe was with 302 F.T.U until 3rd November 1943 practising circuits and loops, compass swinging and night flying, until eventually being assigned to his next operational unit.

7.   Margaret Dillon

Whilst in Oban crewing up for the Indian Ocean Joe met Margaret Dillon. Their acquaintance at Oban, of which much more later, can only have been about 10 days at most.

Margaret was born on 12th Feb 1921; she was about 3 years younger than Joe. She was brought up with her three brothers in Poplar in the East End of London. She got a scholarship to George Green's grammar school in 1932 but had to leave in 1935 to start earning money to support the family, she was 14 years old. Although her education had been cut short she always spoke fondly of the 3 years she had enjoyed. During this time she had elocution lessons and eradicated all traces of her cockney background and developed quite remarkable powers of expression and communication as will be seen later in her correspondence with Joe.

Margaret in WAAF uniform - the story behind this picture
will emerge during the course of the book

She enrolled on 27th March 1941, aged 20 (service number 442556) with the Womens Auxiliary Air Force (WAAF) as an Aircraftswoman Second Class (the lowest rank) under training as an Accounts clerk. She was posted to Gloucester. On 10th April 1941 she was posted to the School of CA and then on 13th May 1941 to RAF Abbotsinch, Renfrewshire. On 1st November 1941 she was promoted to Aircraftswoman First Class. On 23 November 1941 she was granted a commission as Acting Section Officer on probation and attended a training course at Loughborough until 13 December 1941. On 9th December 1941 notice of her commission appeared in the London Gazette.

On 27 May 1942 she was posted to 2 Initial Training Wing and on 19 August 1942 attended a course at Loughborough until 22 September 1942. On 25th September 1942 she was posted to RAF Duxford and on 6th November 1942 promoted Section Officer (War Substantive) with effect from 1 October 1942. On 24 November 1942 she was confirmed as Section Officer. A Section Officer in the WAAF was equivalent to a Flying Officer in the RAF or a Lieutenant in the Army. "War Substantive" means that the promotion is annulled when the war is over.

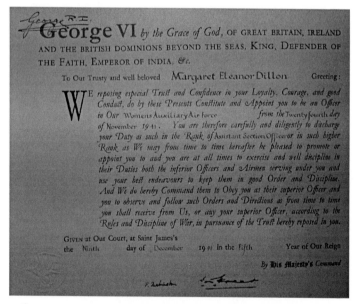

On 4th January 1943 she was posted to RAF Oban, Argyllshire, and then on 30 April to RAF Davidstow Moor, Cornwall. On 7th December 1943 she attended a course at Roborough, Plymouth, Devon until 21 December 1943. On 7th March 1944 she was posted to HQ Coastal Command Northwood in the Operations room (senior WAAF's were Group Officer S.V. Williamson and Squadron Officer M.B.Ker). On 7th August 1945 she transferred to 105 Personnel Despatch Centre for release from the WAAF. Her WAAF records show that *her civilian occupation was a bought ledger bookkeeper. For much of the war until the very end Margaret was senior in rank to Joe.*

The WAAF played a major part in the RAF and the war effort generally. In 1939 there were only 2000 women in the WAAF, by 1943 this had grown to 182000. The WAAF undertook almost every job except operational flying, including operations rooms, signals, intelligence, radar, maintenance and many other tasks. The influence of women in the RAF was probably greater than in any of the other services.

8.   265 Squadron

On 7th December 1941 Japan attacked Pearl Harbour which brought the USA into the war within days and then on February 15th Singapore fell to the Japanese. The threat to Australia and the Pacific was suddenly very real. Additionally by 1943 supplies of all kinds were becoming a key issue for both sides in the war. Germany, by opening an eastern front against Russia, was surrounded by war areas and came to rely on Japan for much of its provisions. England also received no food or other essentials from Europe and relied extensively on Commonwealth countries. In both cases the goods had to be shipped and the Indian Ocean was becoming of strategic importance. Sea routes through the Mediterranean were closed for most of the war and shipping lanes around the Cape of Good Hope were vital. 265 Squadron, and others, were expected to hunt for enemy submarines, warships and supply ships and escort allied convoy ships.

Madagascar before the war was a French colony. With the fall of France it fell into German hands. Diego Suarez, at the north of the island had a fine harbour and the island held a vital strategic position in the Indian Ocean. In May 1942 30,000 troops of the Royal Welsh Fusiliers took Diego Suarez. The whole island was taken by September 1942.

The source of this photo is unknown but may be showing the taking of the island.

On 11th March 1943 the troopship Lancashire arrived in Mombasa, Kenya, with personnel for the reformation of 265 squadron (disbanded in Jan 1919) but as no aircraft were available at the time, detachments of the squadron were sent to help other units. The first Catalina for the squadron left Stranraer on 26th March1943 arriving at Madagascar on 25th April. Others followed and the squadron was built up at Diego Suarez. The area to be patrolled was vast and to cover it required detachments to be spread at distant places. Kipevu in Kenya was found to be more suitable as a maintenance base than Diego Suarez so a large section of the squadron was based there from May 1943, while training and patrols were flown from Mombasa. Other patrols started out from Tulear in Southern Madagascar, Mauritius and Pamanzi (now known as Dzaoudzi) and many ended in different places from where they had started. On 21st April 1945 the first aircraft left Diego Suarez for Mombasa with stores and personnel, the last patrol having been flown on 12 April and on 30 April 1945 265 Squadron was disbanded. (from RAF History section on Internet)

265 Squadron had a song sheet; most of the songs are unprintable. One of them is the Squadron's theme song and all Squadron dinners were to be concluded by the theme song:

[Signal to begin – C/O rising from seat]
"Have you ever caught your b****cks in a rat trap?
In a rat trap, hairs an' all?"
[To be repeated until the bar is reached; to the pounding of feet]

It is not clear what tune this is to be sung to!

Catalinas were 2-engined seaplanes, they could only take off and land on water (later versions were made amphibious but the RAF never adopted them), thus every flight was started and ended with a boat trip! Without a smooth runway to rely on, night time landings were hazardous. Catalinas were made by Consolidated Vultee of Buffalo, New York and the RAF bought hundreds of them. They had limited offensive capability (up to 4 stores of 1000lb bombs or depth charges) and limited defensive capability (4 blisters or turrets with machine guns). What they did have was an incredible range of up to 3000 miles. Max speed was 190 mph and cruising speed was 115 mph thus the flying range was up to 24 hours. Catalinas were amongst the slowest combat aircraft of World War 2. Max ceiling was 18000 feet; they were thus used for reconnaissance, especially antisubmarine and shipping operations, for escorting and for searching. The RAF nicknamed the plane the "Catalina" and it stuck and the name was used by the USAF also. The original designation for the aircraft had been PBY. Years later Joe owned a car with the registration letters PBY. Although he never mentioned it, it must have given him pleasure, 50 years or more after the war, to be driving a "Cat" again.

On 6th November 1943 Joe was posted to Diego Suarez in the north of Madagascar. He wrote an account of his journey from Oban to the Indian Ocean which reads like a geography lesson.

Catalina off Mombasa by Arthur Banks above and a wartime photograph below

Like many CAT crews (I imagine) we partially crewed up at 131 O.T.U Killadeas, N.Ireland, and completed the crewing at Oban, Scotland, 302 F.T.U

It was on the 6th November 1943 that we left Oban for Mountbatten on the South coast of England (*a distance of about 600 miles*), en route for

Madagascar. We were fortunate in flying with another CAT bound for a squadron in East Africa – we were all pals together.

The following evening *(1745)* we took off for Gibraltar *(about 1400 miles, 15 hours)*, across the Bay of Biscay in the gathering gloom. Then, well clear of the French coast (and its German night fighter squadrons) into the tops of clouds to avoid possible detection and, come the dawn, Gibraltar, with happily only a small swell running and a safe landing after 15 hours flying.

Our white knees and tropical clothes seemed a little out of place with the old diehards there. We met up with the other crewmembers and celebrated the start of our great adventure to Africa and beyond..

After two or three days *(on 10th Nov)* at Gib we took off for Port Etienne *(now called Nouakchott, in Mauritania, a distance of about 1400 miles)*, flying close to the West Coast of Africa, landing after 11 hours in the air flying at 1 to 2 thousand feet above the sea. The landing area was a few hundred yards inland from the Atlantic with the desert stretching away inland.

The local Africans were dressed in rags or sacking, reputedly existing on a handful of rice and a pint of water issued by the RAF camp, they were the poorest of the poor.

The mess was very primitive with a bar constructed of beer crates and a very limited selection of liquor. The other Cat Captain, P.O. Moore (I think), and myself were briefed around midnight by the Station Commander; there seemed to be a large landing area at Bathurst *(now called Banjul in The Gambia)*, our next port of call, with no swell and no problems.

We took off well ahead of the other aircraft for the short trip to Bathurst (4 and a half hours *and 400 miles*). The landing was difficult, I could not see the surface of the water, there was no wind, not a ripple. I did a careful landing, lots of engine, the aircraft nose well up until we hit the water safely. A control boat led us in to the moorings, we tied up and were taken by dinghy and on to the operations de-briefing room. After a while there was obviously something wrong, the place was in an uproar.

We followed the general rush out to the water's edge and half a mile or so across the water was a great column of black smoke – which had been the other Cat with its crew of our chums. Most of the missing bodies were retrieved during the next 24 hours, savaged by Barracudas, we were told.

We became pallbearers at the RAF cemetery on the edge of the camp, with brightly coloured birds, red, blue and green, flying around. It was very peaceful there, with a silent group of jet black Africans standing respectfully at the edge of the cemetery watching the burials.

Landing a Catalina, indeed any flying boat, was the most hazardous part of the operation. If the water was rough it would be like trying to land a conventional aircraft on a heavily ploughed field with the furrows moving. There will have been occasions when the water will have been too rough to land which would have been a problem if fuel was low. Equally landing when the water surface was smooth, as happened to P/O Moore at Bathurst, *will have been difficult in terms of correctly judging the descent. Night-time landings initially were impossible although later in the war they found ways of doing them and we will see that Joe performed the first night landing in 265 Squadron on 10th June 1944.*

Many years later Joe told a story of landing in a heavy sea and bouncing severely and later being told by his crew in the mess that they had bounced right over an unseen vessel. He was grateful to his crew who should have reported the incident but didn't.

After 3 days at Bathurst, on 14th November, we took off again for Freetown (*Sierra Leone, about 350 miles*), about 4 and a half flying hours down the coast, where our plane underwent a minor inspection. Some of the officers and NCOs had already spent about 2 years in the sweltering heat of Freetown with no sign of a home posting and were slightly "round the bend". Some of them were trying to work their passage by bringing non-existent dogs into the mess on the ends of non-existent leads, keeping them under control with realistic commands, and it was impossible to detach the dog owners from their fantasies. I imagine the MO witnessed this charade nightly. The speciality of the mess was the bread, baked on the Station and containing an assortment of weevils – well baked of course.

And so to Lagos, *on 26th November,* (across the bit of Africa which juts out, *and about 1000 miles*), a very bumpy ride, the poor old Cat was certainly thrown about and so were we. Lagos proved to be quite a modern town compared with other places we had landed at. After two days rest on to Leopoldville (*now Kinshasa, about 1200 miles*) in the Belgian Congo where the Mistral (I think it is called) which blew at this time of year, with continuous rain, and the odd cu. nimbus, trying to pull us from the 500 feet we were flying up into it's raging interior. Then land and later Leopoldville took us 11 hours flying time after take off.

We landed in a backwater of the Congo, which flowed at about 10 knots, bringing tree trunks and whole lumps of land and trees broken from it's banks floating down on its surface. Occasionally one might see an animal trapped on a floating island. A mile or so from where we moored, with buoys fore and aft, a waterfall kept up a continuous roar. I pitied the guards who were "supposed" to sleep on the Cat each night.

Leopoldville was an interesting place to stop at and we managed to go U.S. with the connivance of our engineer. Each morning lines of prisoners were led out to work past our hotel, chained to one another by their Belgian captors, an unusual sight for we Brits.

From Leopoldville to Stanleyville, *on 6th December,* (*now Kisangani, and 750 miles*) took 6 and a half hours, flying over forests and scrubland, map reading was not so easy without roads, villages or towns to pin point and with little radio contact. At 500 feet we witnessed herds of giraffe, zebra, gazelle below and sometimes lions, elephants and other African wildlife. It was quite a trip!

It is not certain that this Catalina is Joe's but this is Stanleyville

Stanleyville, situated somewhere near the centre of Africa *(from the map below it would appear to be the precise centre of Africa)*, was a small town; we landed in the river. We took a walk along the main street where numbers of native workers were stitching clothing, sitting outside their huts, all using, would you believe, SINGER sowing machines!

Onward to Kisumu, *the next day, (about 500 miles)* on Lake Victoria, the terrain as for the previous day and the mighty Victoria Falls could be seen way to port an hour or so before we landed

After a short stay at Kisumu, *actually quite a long stay until 20th December, nearly 2 weeks*, we took off for Mombasa *(400 miles)* to complete our trip from the west to the east of Africa. We flew most of the trip in cloud at a high altitude (for the Cat) to clear the highlands and well away from Mount Kilimanjaro, which has a height of 30000 feet.

Mombasa, an RAF permanent base, was humming with activity and the powers that be subjected us to a certain amount of red tape after delivering the aircraft, the checking of the inventory was most thorough. I wonder what happened to the Navigators OMEGA ASTRO watch?

265 Squadron diary 16/11/43 Captain F/O J Pack to join squadron shortly.

We took off for Diego Suarez, Madagascar, in Cat FP311 from Mombasa, arriving about 7 hours later *(900 miles)*. The native type huts that we were to sleep in (Bandas) left a lot to be desired. There were great celebrations in the mess that night, not because of our arrival I suspect but we found it was Christmas Eve (1943) much to our surprise.

It had taken nearly 7 weeks for them to fly from Oban, which they left on 7th November 1943, to Diego Suarez, where they arrived on 24th December. It is likely that the Catalina will have been modified somewhere en route for tropical conditions. The total journey was nearly 9000 miles, quite a commute to get to work.

In the early hours of the following morning I staggered over to my bed (a straw palliass on the ground and a blanket). I used one of my kit bags as a pillow (it contained spare clothes) – weeks afterwards I was aware of faint squeaks coming from my "pillow" and discovered that a family of mice had adopted me. I hadn't the heart to disturb them; they eventually left of their own accord.

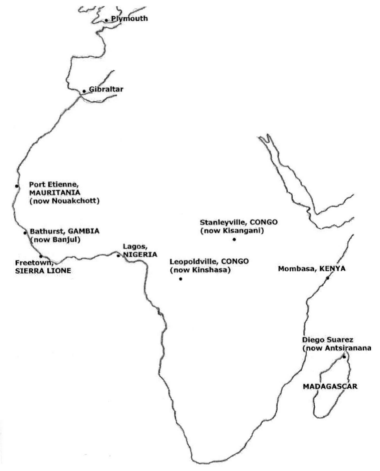

Joe's route to Diego Suarez as mapped by his grandson, Joe.

Diego Suarez was a grim place to be stationed at. A wind blowing at 40 mph blew red dust onto our food and into our clothes for several months of the year, and the rainy season! The homemade showers helped to wash off the grime and the mosquitoes waited for us to strip off! Our squadron engineer had the brilliant idea of throwing oily waste into the holes which had been dug for loos and setting the waste alight to kill the large bluebottles which had taken up residence there. The waste did not kill the hardy bluebottles and the smell of the oily waste wafting up from below was not conducive to pleasant relaxation.

However there were many occasions for light ribaldry and morale was high; any boredom was broken up by trips to Mauritius, Pamanzi, Seychelles, Durban and Ceylon. The Pyrotechnic lads on the station had a novel way of fishing. They would make up explosive charges; we would go out into the harbour in a motorised dinghy and at full throttle throw the explosives over the stern. After the explosion the stunned fish, including Barracudas, would come to the surface and were collected up as required. It was later in the year that one of our Cats was missing from patrol 300-400 miles to the east, I believe they sent out a signal to say that they were attacking a Jap sub and presumably were shot down by the sub. We searched (with other aircraft) but with no luck, we missed our friends in the Mess, but life has to go on.

We were fortunate in having as our Flight Commander the late Peter Seymour and W/Cdr Louw as our C/O both of whom were great characters. S/Ldr Seymour had a bubbly sense of humour which was with him all the time.

Having arrived at Diego Suarez on 24th December 1943 we had to wait 3 weeks before being given our own Catalina FP260, flown from Mombasa, and on the 17th January we flew to Tombeau Bay, Grand Port, Mauritius, our first experience of "operations" in the Indian Ocean.

We were away on the 19th January for an anti-sub/anti shipping patrol, to the east of Mauritius, of 18 hours duration. I don't think we realised, at the time, that these were probably the most important trips of our Indian Ocean tour. During the next 9 days we flew four further patrols, approx 18 to over 20 hours duration, 1000 nautical miles into the Indian Ocean and returning. I notice in my logbook that I describe them as "Blockade Runner Patrols". No doubt at the time we knew we were searching for the German tanker used for refuelling U-boats, now known to be the Charlotte Schliemann. We did not find her but we did find some horrible weather, in fact there was a cyclone in the area. I notice from the description of the "Charlotte Schliemann is hunted down" that it was found and sunk on 12.1.44. If this is correct, we must have been on anti-sub patrols or was there a communications problem? *The Charlotte Schlieman was in fact sunk on the 12th Feb 1944.*

The German submarines operating in the Indian Ocean were refuelled by two tanker ships, the Charlotte Schlieman, the largest, and the Brake. This was to avoid the long journey back to Penang. The Schlieman carried 300 tons of diesel and munitions. Much RAF and Navy effort was devoted to sinking these vessels which would have made it very difficult for the submarines to operate. Joe flew a number of patrols from 19th January 1944 looking for the Charlotte Schlieman but further patrols were stopped by a cyclone "we had been flying at 500 feet when the complete horizon disappeared in blackness". The Schlieman was positioned roughly halfway between Madagascar and Australia, a vast area to search. The Charlotte Schlieman was eventually sunk by HMS Relentless on 12th Feb 1944, and the Brake soon after, both having been located by Catalinas from 259 Squadron and with their sinkings the menace from German submarines in the Indian Ocean finished although Japanese submarines remained a threat for another 6 months or so but mainly further east. 45 German submarines had originally been sent to the Indian Ocean, only 3 returned. After the sinking of the Schlieman by a combined RAF and Naval effort Admiral Jimmy Somerville visited 209, 259 and 265 Squadrons to address all personnel. He gave lavish praise "Thanks to you a lot of German submarines will never find their way back to base". The operation was so secret that most of the listeners hadn't a clue what he was talking about!

Of great importance to the above operation will have been "Ultra". The Germans used the Enigma encryption machine to code their messages and they believed it to be impenetrable. In fact in early 1940 Bletchley Park (Ultra) had cracked the code and were intercepting and understanding messages. Polish mathematicians played a major role in this. To prevent the Germans suspecting their codes had been broken, and changing them, the Allies disguised their knowledge by not always taking action or acting as if they did not have the information. The location of the Charlotte Schlieman was known for some time but many sorties were flown to disguise this knowledge. It is said that Ultra shortened the war by 2 years.

After our last trip on January 30th searching for "armed raiders", we returned to base, to find the cyclone, and the resultant swell in the landing area, was nearing Mauritius.

After 19 hours in the air and four or five hours ashore we were off again, together with our maintenance ground crew for Tulear (southern Madagascar), another 9 hours flying, taking off at about 2am – yes we were a little tired but it was a relief to get away from the cyclone. It was here at Tulear that the swell caused the refuelling bowser to hit and bend the spar of our Catalina (refuelling is always done afloat). A replacement spar was ordered from Durban and four weeks later it arrived by ship. During that time everyone got a bit fed up with waiting. Bill Graham, our Australian navigator, got himself in trouble by shooting stray dogs with his revolver. The dogs would run along the sands at the waters edge, about 100 yards away, with the Cats moored beyond. It was after bullet holes had been found in the hulls of the Cats that questions were asked – they were certainly not caused by enemy action. The Aussies could get away with anything. Bill seemed most of the time to be half cut, he took his alcohol aboard when on a trip (unknown to me of course) but he was a damned good navigator – at all times.

The spar arrived eventually, the station-engineering officer arranged for about 50 locals to help beach the Cat. At full tide, early morning, I taxied FP260 to a previously chosen spot until we ran aground on the sand; it was then that we needed the local lads to assist us to prevent the aircraft slipping back with the tide, then to sit on the floats, opposite to the damaged spar. These nude natives were useless, splashing around in the water and laughing their heads off, to them it was one big joke, they were quite uncontrollable. Our crew, led by Blondie Ashworth, our engineer, did a great job, and the spar was changed with half an hour to spare before the next tide came in.

Working on the Catalina.

Local labour was brought in to keep the port wing down while work progressed on the other side

We flew back to Diego Suarez on the 5th March and from there we flew anti-sub patrols every two or three nights, sometimes from the island of Pamanzi or from Mombasa. We grew accustomed to taking off at last light – the night coming on, watching the moon or part moon appearing (sometimes), the galaxy of stars, the prominent Southern Cross and, after a long time, the first dawn appearing. I don't know how it comes about, but the first dawn seemed to disappear into darkness, then the second dawn and the new day slowly emerged.

The weather was usually reasonably good; there was usually a period of 5 or 6 hours when we might be in the "search" area on a trip. We had no radar and after 2 or 3 hours flying at 1000 feet the eyes could not be guaranteed to see anything.

During most of May 1944 we ferried our W/Cdr Louw, from one detachment to another, I don't remember why. Then in June various operations, nothing too strenuous, and on the 29th a trip to Durban with W/Cdr Louw who enjoyed shooting up the beaches at 0 feet around Durban, to show the locals there was an RAF.

We spent a week in Durban and were entertained royally by the local people who seemed most anxious to get us attached to their daughters – mainly, I think, because we were true Brits, i.e. pure white, this was most important to them in those days. W/Cdr Louw was a South African who constantly made fun of the "English" but he was a great officer, sometimes in a good mood and sometimes a bad mood. I can recall some very happy times, one driving across a football field, with the game in progress, with six well inebriated aircrew in a jeep – we were nearly lynched.

On another occasion in the officer's mess at Diego Suarez I got myself into trouble with him. We aircrew enjoyed throwing beer mats into the large slowly circulating fan in the ceiling, whence the mats were dispatched, sometimes with interesting results. Normally we stopped this little game when the C.O. came into the mess. On this occasion I threw one last mat into the fan. W/Cdr Louw had his glass in his hand, about to drink when the mat hit his glass and it shattered on the floor. It was not one of his best days. "Who did that?" "I did sir," I said coming to attention. "Report to my office in the morning"

At 8.30 sharp I knocked at his office door – "Come in". He kept me standing at attention for a few seconds, then – "Hello Joe why are you here?" "You asked me to report to you sir" " I don't remember that, you had better cut along and get your breakfast". That was W/Cdr Louw. He got his DSO (or was it a DFC?) for landing a Catalina in the Med and rendezvousing with a submarine to pick up the French President M. Petain, probably in 1941 – I may have the wrong President.

On another occasion at Diego Suarez news came through that he had been awarded the British Empire Medal. Knowing his apparent dislike for the "English" I wondered if this gong was awarded to him because of his South African connections. On the strength of the award he stayed at the bar for 24 hours. At about 3 am I was awakened by a "boy", to be told to report to the C.O. in the mess. We drank and chatted together for a couple of hours. The M.O. was his next drinking partner and he eventually ordered W/C Louw to bed. W/C Louw was not normally a hard drinking officer.

From July 1944 to February 1945 we flew hundreds of hours searching for subs and occasionally as a convoy escort, and we didn't see a single sub

– except on one occasion the magic words came over my earphones PERISCOPE ON THE PORT BOW. Sure enough there it was, showing the white wash of the periscope. We were at about 1500 feet. I turned the CAT inside out to get down to the attacking height (200 feet I seem to remember) and as we approached, what did we see – three large whales, one of them spouting water, that was the wash we had seen. I was tempted to depth charge the whales but hadn't the heart (*Although others apparently did, whales took a bit of a hammering from bored pilots*)

In September we flew to the then Ceylon via Addu Atoll which is about 1000 miles from the Seychelles. Addu Atoll had a radio beacon at that time, to "home" on. There was always the possibility of the beacon being unserviceable and if we had bypassed the coral islands we would have flown into thousands of miles of empty ocean.

We arrived by dead reckoning navigation – spot on. This was done by plotting the aircraft track on a chart, finding the wind strength and direction by dropping a flare onto the sea below and measuring the drift of the aircraft. By applying the drift required the aircraft course could be worked out until the wind direction changed. A flare could be seen at night as well as by day. At night if the conditions were unsuitable we were able to "fix" on the stars or the moon with an astro fix. These astro fixes had a varying degree of accuracy but, like the occasional W/T fix, were better than nothing.

Landing at Addu Atoll was quite an experience. Clear blue waters, a horse shoe coral lagoon and the seashore not more than 6 feet above sea level and less than 100 yards in width. The ocean on one side of the sand and the lagoon on the other. Ashore all the population had the secret of eternal youth. There seemed to be no middle aged or elderly people living there, everyone looked youthful.

This account does not have any particular sequence but it was when we were at Mauritius that a cyclone hit the island. Our aircraft was reasonably safely anchored on the leeward side of the island and we were sheltering in the basement of a large single storey house with the wind roaring above. I don't know how long we sheltered there but we had a couple of bottles of gin with us which helped to pass the time. I remember the "core" of the cyclone passing over us and then the roar of the wind again. When we eventually emerged the carnage was impossible to describe. I particularly remember the trees, those that were not flattened were lying at the same angle of about 30 degrees.

It is difficult to pick out events in the Indian ocean which might be of interest to you but this is an event which I must tell you about, if only to clear myself. We had flown direct from Mombasa to the Seychelles with four sailors aboard who were to rejoin their ship, a Corvette I believe, which was in the Seychelles mooring area.

I landed in the correct channel (the landing area in the Seychelles has reefs everywhere with deep channels marked by buoys) leading to the mooring area.

As I was taxiing up the channel the naval boat began to flash with it's Aldis lamp. The Navy could always send morse by Aldis faster than the RAF. I tried to help the crew read the message when – crash – I had hit a reef. The crew quickly told me that water was coming in and later that we were sinking. Now back in the deep-water channel I made for the slipway. As the flying boat filled with water I had both engines fully open to make any "way" at all and as we approached the causeway Blondie Ashworth, our engineer, reported that the temperature of the engines was so high that they would either melt or explode.

The Catalina was a complete write off I believe.

My C.O. W/Cdr Louw flew into the Seychelles the following day and I had a message to report to him in the mess that evening. I was in quite a state when the time came, I was quite sure I would be court-marshalled. If my records had caught up with me W/Cdr Louw would know that I had escaped from a Halifax bomber at 20000 feet in July 1942, been involved as 2nd pilot with a badly damaged Sunderland on returning from an A/S patrol in the Bay of Biscay and now a Catalina in an unnecessary accident.

W/Cdr Louw was not in a good mood when he arrived at the Seychelles and I feared the worst.

What happened, he demanded. I told him how I was distracted by the Navy's signalling and wandered from the deep channel. When I had finished – there was a little silence, then he said – consider yourself admonished – another little silence, a smile and then – what are you having to drink Joe – and that was that.

Another incident from the Seychelles which might interest you. There was no operational flying for a while, so I decided we would do some air firing practice – the CAT had a .50 gun at each "blister" to the rear of the hull.

I flew well away from the main islands and spotted a tiny island with half a dozen coconut trees and a single native hut built nearby. Obviously the hut was used "during the season" when the coconuts were being collected. I flew low over the hut a couple of times but there was no movement – the hut was obviously uninhabited. Every sixth round of ammunition to our guns was an incendiary and it seemed good practice for the gunmen to ignite the hut with their guns.

The crew opening up the blisters put on the safety harness and when the aircraft was in a suitable position took aim and fired – first from one side and then the other. It was rumoured that it was possible to shoot oneself down with one's own guns.

Although I circled the hut several times the tracer bullets were not within many yards of hitting the hut – were the gunners scared about hitting our boat?

As I turned to give the gunners a final burst, out of the hut came a black man followed by his wife and family, waving their arms.

I did not hang around, safe in the knowledge that we could barely hit the island much less the hut, but I hoped the man or his wife could not read the aircraft letters.

We left Diego Suarez on March 15th 1945, via Dar-Es-Salaam and Mombasa to Nairobi in a Dakota, then Juba, Khartoum, Wadi-Halfa, Cairo and the UK.

Within a couple of months I was flying Sunderlands for BOAC via Cairo, the Persian Gulf, Karachi, Calcutta and Rangoon.

I now find that some of the crew stayed on in the RAF. John Bishop, my 2nd pilot, was one of them and later flew Sunderlands. He achieved the impossible, to my mind, do you remember the airlift into Berlin when the Russians refused entry by road. John Bishop flew on 200 occasions into Berlin with supplies, flying – guess what- a Sunderland flying boat – the mind boggles.

Bill (Paddy) Macklin and Roy Marshall stayed with the RAF for some time, I believe. Ken Ashworth became I/C postings and Johnny Elms became a captain of industry with Marley Tiles. Yes – they were a grand crew, its nice to be in touch with most of them again. It's a pity we cannot locate Bill Graham, our Australian Navigator, particularly as I owe him a fiver.

9. Letters between Margaret and Joe

Margaret and Joe exchanged more than 180 letters. From the first letter, dated 23.1.44, it is clear that there had already been correspondence and then the next letter is not until June 1944 so it is likely that as many letters again have been lost. Many letters went missing generally during the war. The surviving letters are shown chronologically but it is clear that they often took weeks and sometimes months to arrive so it should not be assumed that any letter replies to the previous one. Interspersed with the letters are extracts from the 265 Squadron diary to show what Joe was doing while he wrote his letters, all his operational flights are recorded. All of the letters are stamped as censored and there were strict rules about what could be written and what could not.

265 Squadron: Joe is on the front row at the extreme left. Bill Graham, who flew with Joe and is referred to in his letters, is on the back row fourth from the left. Jack Barber also flew with Joe and is in the middle row on the extreme right. Wing Commander "Fats" Louw is the centre of the front row.

265 Squadron diary 17th Jan 44 ~ M265 (S/Ldr Seymour, F/O Pack) arrived at Grand Port, Diego Suarez to start the detachment, having flown from Mauritius on the previous day, but had been diverted to Tombeau bay whilst in the air, despite the strictest instructions for the maintenance of W/T silence…Grand Port was not ready to receive the detachment…It was found that the caretaker who holds the keys to the buildings was still hung over from his Sunday binge and had taken the week off!

Catalina M265 flying to Mauritius from Diego Suarez on 16th January 1944, taken by Joe Pack from Catalina FP260. All Catalinas carried photographic equipment to record sightings. This photograph is courtesy of Peter Seymour, Squadron leader.

We were away on the 19th January and in the next few days flew four further patrols from approximately 18 hours to over 20 hours, 1000 miles into the Indian Ocean and back (*this was the search for the Charlotte Schlieman*).

An emergency signal from 246 wing ordered the immediate evacuation of Mauritius pending the arrival of a cyclone. M265 took off for Tulear.

265 Squadron, East Africa Command Joe to Margaret 23rd January 1944

> F/LT J.T.PACK,
> 23.1.44   265, SQUADRON,
>   EAST AFRICA COMMAND.
>
> My darling,
>   Just a quick letter to let
> you know that I am getting your
> mail o.k. again. Sorry about
> this panic dear, but perhaps you
> understand. Big letters

I received you stopped loving me between the 8th December and the 21st with the consequent lack of mail about a fortnight afterwards at this end. You just must not do it sweetheart, I imagine all manner of things have happened to you.

Right at the moment my mood is so black I am unable to write a decent letter but promise to write tomorrow.

I believe I have told you that many of the chaps in this part of the world appear a little strange, and are said to be " around the bend". The new name for them is now "Harpic" (clean round the bend) – should I apologise?

A little rhythm I heard the other day seemed rather clever and thought you might like to hear it – it is called The Turtle.

The turtle lives twixt plated decks
Which practically conceal its sex
I think it clever of the turtle
In such a fix to be so fertile.

You don't like it? You know sweetheart I should not have tried to write now but the mail will close in a few minutes and I thought you might like to know about your letters arriving.

Pleased to know you like the bag will try and get some skin to use for winter gloves and scarf.

I love you darling Joe

265 Squadron diary

5th March 44 M/265 (F/O Pack) arrived from Tulear

6th March 44 – F/O Pack could not get away until first light owing to bombing up and that the squadron had only one refueller. CAT M265 A/S Patrol from Diego Suarez. Suspicious object was a WHALE. Up at 0537 Down at 1135. Crew were F/O Pack, F/O Barber, F/O Graham, F/Sgt Marshall, F/Sgt Sharpe, Sgt Elms, Sgt Nicholls, Sgt Macklin and Sgt Ashworth

7th March – M/265 returns on the afternoon after uneventful search

8th March – M265 left for convoy duty at 14.30. A/S escort to HMS Recorder and HMS Mastiff. Up 1430(8th) Down 0325(9th) from Diego Suarez

11th March – M265 took off for Pamanzi

17th March – A/S patrol Up 1415(17th) Down 0820(18th) from Mombasa

21/22 March – pulling down of Bandas (2 a day) for wooden hutting – "Personnel employed on the demolition of the bandas became somewhat disorientated. The C.O. had all NCO's together and instructed them that being NCO's it was their job to lead the men and not to side with them..Work progressed smoothly once again"

1st May – G265 Up at 1947 (May 1st) Down 1220 (May 2nd) A/S escort to 3 E/V's & 2 A/C carriers

4th May – G265 arrived in the afternoon from Seychelles after completion of a major inspection at KISUMU

13th May – The Squadron beat 201 Battery (Army) 5-0 at football

13th May – W/Co Louw began his tour of inspection and was ferried by Joe to Mombasa(13th May), Pamanzi (16th), Diego Suarez (16th), Mauritius (18th), Pamanzi again (22nd), Mombasa again (23rd) returning on the 26th below.

25th May – drew 0-0 at Hockey

26th May – G265 returned from Mombasa on completion of the AOC's tour

Map prepared by Joe Jnr, showing the places his grandfather flew to.

Joe to Margaret 1st June 1944

My dear Margaret, its wizard hearing from you again if perhaps a little annoying. You see, little girl, at the age of 25 years (26 now) it is somewhat unbalancing when one finds oneself once again doing and thinking silly things, because of a girl. I thought I had finished with all that after my 21st birthday! But that was at Oban – it's a long time ago now. You must keep writing to me, it is most important, because if you do not I may not be able to find you when I get home again, and that is even more important. It's damned silly I know, but out here one thinks of wives and a family and so on, you envy the fellow with a picture of his girlfriend or wife and kid stuck on his dressing table. Probably lack of feminine company, or perhaps one is learning to appreciate a more settled existence? Or maybe the thought of someone really caring what happens to you, I don't know, perhaps it will wear off.

There is so much to tell you I do not know where to start. To begin with I will try and write once a week if you would like me to. At the moment I am miles from anywhere and this letter might not be taken to the mainland for weeks as there is no regular mail plane. Fortunately I expect to be leaving quite soon.

I hate to tell you but poor old Jack Moore with all his crew including Eric Lister all were killed at Bathhurst on the way out. I watched him come in about 20 minutes after I had landed and burst into flames about a mile away – it was horrible. Several of the fellows were got out the following day and we saw them to their resting places, a very quiet spot miles from anywhere, with palms and flowers. And the birds were singing the whole time. I shall never forget the birds – why do the best fellows have to go? Sorry if I have to finish on this note, Goodbye my love, Joe

265 Squadron diary

2nd June – G265 carried out a 4-hour local flight completing photography of gun emplacement for Army HQ, camouflage section and taking the opportunity of checking the D/F loop.

5 June G265 took off for local training but returned after 2 circuits when it was found that water was entering the "tunnel" compartment thru a broken flare chute

10 June – G265 and B265 (F/O Smith) carried out air to air homing on the IFF Mark III. B265 reported little success, whilst G265 reported contact established at 117 miles.

10th June – G265 (F/O Pack) "foxed" the critics by returning in fine style after dark, coming into a night landing (as noted in the previous chapter this was a difficult manoeuvre – Ed).

14th June – 4 aircraft, including G265, Diego Suarez to Tombeau Bay, Mauritius. Antisubmarine sweep. Up 0556, down 1656

15th June A/S sweep from Tombeau Bay to Diego Suarez, up 1410(15th) down 1350 (16th)

22nd June – G265 left for Tulear on their way to South Africa. All concerned were in high spirits (Durban on leave – see below –Ed)

On the 18th June Joe was promoted to Flying Officer with effect from 1st May 1944

Joe to Margaret 25th June 1944

My dear Margaret The weekly letter I promised you is not materialising so far I fear but the reason, excuse or whatever you care to call it is this. The

Gods have been good to me and decreed a week's leave in Durban and who could possibly write letters in such a place? And who should I meet there but one of your <u>special</u> (old) boyfriends Sopey (Jeeves). He really looked after me, although it is to be regretted that he is a changed man. For some amazing reason he has decided to get married (it is not you darling is it?) and will rarely now touch the "grog". But I must not be too hard on him; all good men fall sooner or later.

Durban is a grand spot, one is short of nothing but money, and that quickly becomes very acute. Imagine arriving in time for lunch and not being allowed to buy a drink at the Mess bar for 24 hours! And the fellows were decent enough to see that one was not short of a drink during those 24 hours.

The daily drill was to rise at 1100 hrs, the bar opened at 1215, liquid refreshment to 1345 then lunch. A taxi then took you off in a gloriously mellow condition. Once in Durban anything might happen, girls actually drop gloves, ask you for a match and so on. If you keep them off you arrive back with many slips of paper giving names and telephone numbers, if you don't you are taken smartly to a night club or dance and wake up the following morning less £5 – it's a grand place – for a week.

Many apologies for writing this drivel about my leave, little girl, but having just finished it, it is still fresh in my mind. Not having been back at base for several weeks I cannot answer any recent letters of yours which I am sure must be waiting for me? There are still a great number of things that I must tell you about, if you would like to hear about them. I saw so little of you at Oban, I feel that you must either think me a damned nuisance for writing or – well, I am not too sure what you do think. I am running short of paper so will have to stop once again. Bye bye for the present, Love, Joe

10. July 1944

12th July In the evening a game of rugger was played at Port Victoria football ground. Officers vs. NCO's and airmen. It is worthy of note that Americans, Canadians, Australians and Association Football amongst other types mingled to give the game a character of its own. It attracted a large gate of local inhabitants. The NCO's and airmen were the winners.

13 July A/S patrol and sweep – up 1430(13th) Tulear, down 0745(14th) Tombeau bay, Mauritius

15 July A/S Patrol up 1955 (15th) Tombeau bay, down 1435 (16th) Tombeau bay

16th July Up 2205 (16th) Tombeau bay down 1730 (17th) Tombeau bay

19th July A/S patrol 1835(19th) Diego Suarez down 1210(20th) Diego Suarez

Between the 13th July and 19th July Joe flew 74 hours.

Frithwood House, Watford Road, Northwood, Middlesex Margaret to Joe 19th July 1944

Joe, Dear, your letter is dated the 1st of June – and believe it or not I received it today! I can't begin to tell you how happy it made me to hear from you again – I felt sure that you must by this time be completely uncaring – whether you wrote or not.

The news of Jack and Eric is simply too dreadful – Joe darling – do take care won't you? – I don't mind admitting that I care a great deal about your safety – and just recently have wanted you to be here so terribly. Why didn't I admit it to myself before you went away? I was so afraid it would just be another of those things which are here one day and gone the next.

Joe darling – I believe I love you very much – do you believe me? – but I didn't fully realise it until you had gone away – and I knew I couldn't see your funny face anymore.

Dear Joe – if you love me – will you tell me so? – I shall be your girl – I think I am anyway – deep down inside – I shall write thousands of letters – and send you a picture – a glamorous one – completely unlike me to remind you that there is a face something like that somewhere in the world – and eyes which want to see you again rather badly. And Joe – can I have a picture of you too? – anything – just so that you are always with me – by my bed – and in my pocket when I'm working. I shall look at you many times all day – and think of all we shall have to say to each other when you come home – I wish it were soon.

Darling – did you think it was silly then – to say that you loved me in Oban? – I only wish I'd had the courage then to accept something which could have been so wonderful – but Joe – if you find me – when you come home – I shan't be changed – and if you are not either – then we shall make up for all that – can we?

Your letter was a very sad one – is it so lonely? I wish I could be posted to Nairobi – at least we should be on the same continent – we might even be able to get leave – my gosh! – what a leave that would be.

I seem to spend most of my time here visiting relatives – they'll soon be removing the welcome mat – I fear.

Joe dear – are you 26 now? I'm 23 – did you know? – sometimes I feel 17 – other times about 90 – especially after night watch.

I'll write again tomorrow and as many days as I can, when there is enough to write about – just to make certain some of them reach you anyway. Goodbye for now, all my love – darling, I do love you.

PS Joe – my darling Joe, its true – I love you – It sends a warm queer feeling through my whole body when I think of it. Thousands of kisses – and one very special one – the first one – when we meet again – please God make it soon.

Margaret to Joe 19ᵗʰ July 1944

Joe, darling, I felt I had to write at this psychological moment – and having no air letters and it being too late to go and buy any – here's another screed in an ordinary envelope – Lord knows if it will ever reach you. Your second air letter reached me the day after the first – most extraordinary – considering the second one was written three weeks later.

Joe – you said you were leaving your present abode – dare I hope it might mean you will be coming home? – Oh Gosh! If only I could believe that – what a celebration we'd have – would you want to?

Also dear, what on earth do you mean by asking if Jack Lever is marrying me? I told you ages ago that he was a very good friend of mine – and absolutely nothing more – I liked him – he'd a tough time – and he was a queer man – I simply felt sorry for him – but as for marrying old Jack – well, I can't think of a more impossible person.

In any case Joe – in spite of severe criticism on my part on several occasions – I'm terribly pro-English – and if and when I marry I have no doubt it will be to an Englishman. I'm not trying to sell you anything, honey, but just trying to tell you that I don't fall in love with every man I meet – and I certainly was not even remotely in love with Sopey.

I wish we'd met a year before we did – we should know so much more about each other – I should at least have had time to give you a picture – and you to give me one darling – can you send me one? It will be a very poor substitute – for you – but if I have your face to look at – at least – I can wait till you come back – shall I wait Joe? I shall anyway because I very badly want to. I shall also buy some air letters tomorrow – perhaps if I write often enough you will cease to be annoyed when you hear from me.

Write often – I must hear from you as often as humanly possible. All my love darling, Margaret

Margaret to Joe 21st July 1944

I have written two ordinary letters – just two or three days ago – it will be interesting to see which reach you first. Your leave in Durban sounds like heaven – no raids, no work – nothing but sheer pleasure – I wish I could have been there too – but Joe – isn't Durban in South Africa? It must be quite a journey from where you are – or did you fly? Have you heard yet the news of the trouble the Germans are having? Perhaps we shall meet sooner than we anticipated. I'm longing to meet you again – we shall have so much to tell each other. There is much I want to say to you – that I should have said a long time ago – if I hadn't been such a coward.

Darling – how often do you get leave? We have had none here since the start of the Second Front but in any case – it really isn't of much use to me because my family have been in London – until recently, when Mother went up to Manchester to stay with friends – but Daddy is still here. I see him every week. It would be so wonderful if you were here – at least not too far away to ring up sometimes. Sometimes I dream that you are having an ops rest and have been sent to HQCC for it and we meet every day, and when we have a whole day free we go to all sorts of places and do the most incredibly lovely things – even just walking seems lovely.

Joe, dear – although I don't imagine you will be frantically interested – I think Sopey Lever must be marrying the girl he told me about in Oban – she is a divorcee I think – and – I wish you'd known at the time – he was very fond of her. How many of my letters have you received? I have written quite a number. I can't remember exactly how many. By the way Joe – is Jack Barber still flying with you? In a way I think I'd rather he isn't because you were never really happy about Jack – were you dear? How long is the tour in your particular part Joe? It seems like years since you left. Padre Lake is in France – I'm very glad for him – he wanted to go very much. Did you know Daphne was out of the service? She's about to produce an offspring. I met Judy Read last week – do you remember her? A tall fair girl – very calm and collected always. Darling – don't think too much about Jack Moore – he was a sweet boy I know but these things just happen. Be happy and safe, all my love, Margaret

Margaret to Joe 25th July 1944

There is not much work to do at the moment and as I have been thinking of you all day anyway – I thought I might as well write – it makes you seem nearer. Do you remember you wrote about the divorces in Kenya? Strangely I happened to be reading a book on farming in Kenya yesterday – and it was only then that your remark meant anything – I had no idea that the divorce figures were so large out there – it's rather strange that in normal life – when the Kenya families in the majority of cases live so far apart that there is the opportunity for disloyalty or changes of affection – but perhaps that is the reason – that people are alone for so long – when they do meet others – their emotions are unstable. There is a strong rumour that leave will start soon – I believe I mentioned it before – I shall go down to Wales I think – and spend a week with Pauline – did you ever meet her Joe? She's a terribly attractive blonde – and one of the nicest people I have ever known – but awfully unhappy poor thing – she fell in love with a married man and now cannot find any interest in anybody else – and of course there is nothing that can be done about them – his wife is an invalid, and he can't bring himself to divorce her – Oh Lord! Why do people get so mixed up? I wish you were coming to Wales too.

In a way it's rather good to be near town – it means we can do a lot of satisfactory shopping. Did I tell you I'd given up smoking? My mess bill nowadays is almost invisible – and I feel so much better physically – I just hadn't realised how bad it was for me to smoke so much. I play more games too – especially squash which I simply adore. I shall have lost so much weight when you come home you just won't know me. How is your sister Joe? Has she volunteered for overseas? I think I must be getting old – or something – because the desire to go overseas has practically disappeared – its very strange because only a short time ago I would have given anything to go. I even asked if I could go to Nairobi – near you – but never had any real hope that it would be done.

My stock of air letters is running out – I must replenish it very quickly. I do hope you are getting all my letters dear, and after waiting all this time for yours – I hope when it comes it will be several and not just one. Joe – you can't imagine how much I long for your return – perhaps it sounds strange – coming from me – but I don't think I'm imagining things – it wasn't until you had gone that I realised how much you had grown on me – and not until I had met so many strange people – that I realised how much I wanted to stay with you. But perhaps some day I shall be able to explain to you – in words – and not on paper – just what had happened last year just before I met you – I have said before I only wish to God I'd met you before I did – things would have been very different. Write soon, all my love, Margaret

Joe to Margaret 25ᵗʰ July 1944

S.O. or Flt/O? When you get up tomorrow morning try and imagine a shining black boy in rags cleaning your shoes in the doorway of the hut. There will be a bucket of water in the corner and when you pour it into a large tin to wash yourself, you will have to skim dozens of ants from the top. You find a clear spot and dip your toothbrush into the murky water and refresh your mouth. During your toilet you will notice mice of various sizes darting about, but the mousetrap in the corner will probably be empty. The smell of bad alcohol from the corner indicates that your navigator has spent the previous night on South African Rum or Brandy and has not yet ventured to become conscious.

Breakfast at 0745 will be a pleasant meal even if there is no bread, but if there was a party in the mess the previous night, a wise person will, after breakfast, avoid the bar section of the hut.

As you gaze out at the hills devoid of all vegetation you will notice that the wind is strengthening to gale force and by 1900 will bring clouds of dust from the plain behind. The camp, being a collection of badly made huts allows the dust to cover most things and the flies too appear in their hundreds to torment people with hairy legs. An experienced person will return to his net at 10.30 to emerge in time for lunch at 12.30. It is a little dusty of course (the lunch I mean) and it is necessary to keep the flies off with one hand and eat with the other, but a full stomach gives one the inclination to get the head down for the afternoon nap.

But why is everyone showing a smile and why is that excellent spirit (that the RAF is alleged to foster) so prevalent? The answer is because it is Monday: everyone knows it is Monday because it is the day the Padre gives his weekly service. And why does everyone return almost reluctantly to his net and there fight off nature's desire to sleep?

The answer comes at 15.30 when instead of an empty crew room a crowd of fellows may be seen looking out anxiously to the West. A few words spoken by watchers with powerful glasses increases the excitement. The speck grows. Minutes later a sigh of relief goes up and experienced pilots watch a bumpy landing come to rest and murmur subconsciously "wizard landing".

A general adjournment to the mess and everyone is chattering together over a cup of tea, an observer would notice heads held higher and the fly swotting becomes more accurate. 17.30 sees the shadows lengthening and smelly bodies have the red dust washed away by tepid showers. Few miss the opening of the icebox at 1800 and who but a glutton could possibly want more than ½ pint of beer? A goodly variety of malts however in a galaxy of colours and labels and the hardiest types continue their fight against abstinence.

But why this hopeful expectancy, why the glances at the doorway? A mailbag thrust through explains everything and one finds oneself fighting in a mob to that bag of hopefulness.

And 10 minutes later! Here and there a man with a heap of mail, the Canadian with his parcels and mail, and some have gone to their huts to read alone. Then there is the few who have read their only letter and are trying to appear as if there is nothing wrong. And then there is always the odd person or two sitting up at the bar, hand clenching a glass, gazing at nothing with a fixed expression on his face – he has had NO mail. Little wonder he gets morbidly tight that night.

And the Mess does not liven up to a drunken party on Mondays, most of the chaps will be writing, others still reading and most of them will have a strangely contented look on their faces, which flies, fleas, dust, rats and mice cannot take away – that night! Sorry about all this darling, Bye for now, Joe

11. August 1944

265 Squadron diary 2nd August 1944 A/S Patrol Up 0325 Diego Suarez down 1210 Tulear

Margaret to Joe 5th August 1944

Joe darling, I wish there wasn't so much that we <u>can</u>'t put in letters - there is such a lot I want to talk to you about – really interesting things – but I can't – isn't it stupid? Darling I do so love having letters from you but there aren't enough of them – are you forgetting again? Please don't – it means a lot to me. Next week I'm going to have a new photograph taken – and shall send you one – I do hope it reaches you.

Today produced an unexpected and wholly delightful incident – I was coming up the hill – pushing my bicycle and feeling rather done in when an old man – a local yokel – to coin a phrase – offered assistance and walked all the way home with me. He talked all the way about farm life and crops and animals and flowers and was so charming and just when he left me I was conscious of peace and content and in that moment realised just how beautiful is the country – in England – and how much I love it. I realised too, dear, how much you belonged, in my mind, to all those lovely things which the mere thought of gave me so much pleasure.

Darling sweet Joe – when are you coming home – I want to see you so much. This beastly war – but perhaps if it hadn't happened – I should never have met you and whatever happens, darling, I shall always treasure that thought – do come home soon because all the places and pubs here are just waiting for us to go and drink their beer and see their beauty and make friends – and I'm just waiting to see you. All my love dearest, Margaret

Margaret to Joe 6th August 1944

Joe darling, I started writing this yesterday – but suddenly piles of signals came in and I didn't get a chance to resume until now. I'm going on leave – to Wales – tomorrow and will write from there – I do think the powers that be might let you come too – it would be such fun.

I went along to a little pub called "Minnie's" last night – it's such a quaint, tiny place that everybody has to hold their breath while they're inside – it's so silly really – there are dozens of pubs – half empty ones – dotted about all over the place – but everybody, especially the Coastal types, <u>must</u> go to Minnie's. I think you'd like it too.

Darling – I'm not sure whether I asked you before – but is there anything I can get for you over here – do please let me know – because I should love to do anything for you. I did ask before – but just in case you didn't receive my letter I shall ask again – please may I have a photograph? I really do want one – for a very good reason – this letter seems to be filled with a lot of junk about me – please write lots about you – I want to hear it all – even things like whether you had a cold or whether your socks need mending or if you remember to put on your bedsocks at night, if you can play games, you like games dear don't you? Do you like boating on the river? I simply adore it. If you would care to – when you come home – we could spend whole days on the river – it would be such fun.

Darling – do you like black? I'm going to buy a black suit with lots of bits and pieces and save it to wear when I meet you again – I wish it were soon – it seems such a waste of time – you there and me here – so far away when I at least would so much love to have you here. You have all my love darling – you must believe that, it would break my heart if you didn't. Indeed – now that I have at last admitted it to myself – the knowledge is with me at very moment and I really feel just a little frightened at the thought of meeting you again. I can't even write silly letters as I used to and I certainly cannot express all that I feel – on paper – it means so much – and I'm afraid to say it anyway – for fear that you might have changed. Dear Joe – please don't change, I love you so much. Goodbye my dearest, all my love, Margaret

265 Squadron diary 7th August 1944 A/S patrol and search for survivors up 1650 Tulear, down 1820 Pamanzi

Margaret to Joe 7th August 1944

Darling, I've just remembered two sweet little stories I'm sure you'll love.

The first is about Rosemary, one of the many little girls recently sent out of London – who was going to bed on her first evening in the country. Her hostess asked her if she said her prayers before going to bed. Rosemary said she did. "Well then kneel down and I'll listen as your mother does". Rosemary repeated the usual "now I lay me down to sleep" and then improvised a tailpiece of her own " and God, please protect Daddy and Mummy from those German bombs. And do, please God, take care of yourself because if anything happens to you – we're sunk" – isn't it rather lovely?

Then there's the story about the wren – high on a ladder in the British Admiralty's war room – stood a wren – sticking pins in a map which marked the progress of a North Atlantic convoy. A crusty old sea lord walked in, glanced upwards at the map, and said "Captain, that wren will either have to wear pants or we shall have to move the convoy to the South Atlantic"!! Joe – do you have a cinema?

Darling, I'm sitting at the station waiting for my train to Wales – I've been thinking of you all the morning – you never seem to be out of my mind now – although you are lovely to think about, you trouble me, take my mind away from what I'm doing all the time. Do you mind that I think about you so much? I feel so sorry for all those people who haven't you to love – is that silly, Joe? It isn't really you know – they don't know what it's like to remember what loving you was like, to want to love you again and they shan't.

Indeed if they did I should be wild with jealousy. It isn't easy to write all these feelings in a refreshment room on a railway station but they are there all the time and whatever I do they don't go away. There's a very old man sitting opposite and I think he would so much like to know what I'm writing – I wouldn't care if he saw what I was writing – in fact I should love to tell him about you – that I love you dearly and it grows more and more with every day that passes. I pray for you every night, that you may be safe and come home soon. All my love, dearest, Margaret

265 Squadron diary 9th August 1944 A/S patrol up 1010(9th) Pamanzi down 0205(10th) Pamanzi

Joe to Margaret 10th August 1944

My dear Margaret, It seems ages since I wrote to you last but in actual fact it is about 7 or 8 days. The expected leave in Kenya is not to be, the Gods decree otherwise. Instead of leave I have collected another "Moggie" (*Not sure what this is, if a Moggie today is slang for a cat and a Cat is what airmen called the Catalina, perhaps Joe was collecting a new aircraft – Ed*) and am all set for some more works. It is a bit of a disappointment as we all needed that leave, but if it means getting home a week earlier, its OK with me. Incidentally I had intended spending leave with Bob Butler and "Red" Finley from 209 Squadron whom I believe you know – decent types.

I am now in Kisumu, Lake Victoria, but expect to be back at base in a few days. I am running a sweepstake with myself as to how many of your letters will be awaiting me – Darling, I can't wait. There is a hotel here in which the BOAC harbour their wives. It is horrible to see the things that go on, as each woman has at least a dozen men after her and at least 50% of them are looking for divorces – they make me sick. I would much prefer the native women who smoke long pipes, spit with great precision, and shave their heads. They work hard for their lazy husbands and can balance amazing bundles on their heads and invariably have small bundles on their backs from the top of which a small head appears. They are inclined to be a little unfaithful I believe but a night spent with an Askari soldier will probably reward her with his greatcoat.

Please excuse this drivel, little girl, but if I write about what we can do together and when I shall see you and so on, I get very unhappy because even 3 or 4 months seems a hell of a while to wait.

You ask in a letter if mail to and from is regular. Yes darling it is, but I spend a lot of time away from base and it cannot often be sent on. Bye for now, sweetheart, Joe

265 Squadron diary 11th August 1944 A/S Up 0258 Pamanzi, Down 11.35 Pamanzi, Up 1725 Seychelles, Down 1200(12th) Seychelles... A long day, 27 flying hours in 2 days!

13th August A/S up 1331 (13th) Seychelles, down 1734(14th) Seychelles... Another long day, 28 flying hours

Margaret to Joe 16th August 1944

You can't possibly have had even half my letters. I wrote ages ago telling you of my promotion. I thought it might amuse you. They've made me a Flt/O Plotter at HQCC.

Joe – your description of mail day was just marvellous. They're playing "Blue Champagne" on the radio – you should be here sweet – to dance with me – or just to hold me – darling – will you? I love you. When you come home – you will be changed won't you? Will you still care for me I wonder? I have just had a weeks leave in Wales – it was absolutely lovely – and I did absolutely nothing but lie around with almost nothing on – all day in the sun – eat and sleep. It was so lazymaking – the sun. I really seriously intended to do lots of shopping in Chester – which I think is lovely city – but I didn't ever get as far as the bus.

Darling – did I tell you I saw a man on a bus one day, who had eyes exactly like yours? It made me feel as though you were really there – just for a moment – and I couldn't breath – it was a full two seconds before I realised that I was staring very rudely – and he had begun to look inquiringly at me, no doubt wondering if I had sunstroke. Joe my dearest – your letters are dated a whole month apart – could you not write more frequently my darling – please? Because a letter from you keeps me quite light-headed for days – and I like the feeling – of being quite stupid and exhilarated to the point of complete irresponsibility. And now my sweet brown eyed Joseph – when you wake up tomorrow morning will you imagine something for me? Imagine that you see through a window – a long rolling view of green meadows and lovely fresh flowers, and trees, hundreds of beautiful trees, and long purple-rich grass and in the distance – merging with the line of a sky so blue it's hard to believe – a sea – sparkling – silver – in the sun – and then go down the stairs – out into the scented air – and on towards the sea and then meet me – don't say anything – just walk to me quite slowly – and then darling take my hand – we shall go on towards the sea – the breakers will rush to meet us – dissolving into thousands of baby white drops at our feet – and as they rush on and on – they will shout for joy that life is so good – and the world so beautiful – and I shall answer – with a full overflowing measure of joy in a busting heart – not in words – but just by turning to you – and looking deep into your eyes – and then, gently darling, so gently, kissing you. I believe then – dear one – that you will know just what is in my heart – that of which I was so afraid – but which I can now acclaim with such joy – darling – just to see you – now – for a moment – and I should cry – with happiness. All my love dearest, Margaret

Joe to Margaret - Undated – Margaret numbered Joe's letters and this one fits in between the 10th August letter and the 20th August letter

Darling, I laughed when I read in one of your letters that you had bought a hat, buying a hat seems so feminine, and I have only known you as a servicewoman. How do you look in civvies, clothes can change a person. If you wear black and wear bits and pieces with it can I get you some Indian filigree work to go with it, black to my mind is the only colour for it.

Glad to hear you had a pleasant turn in Wales, I did not think it was possible! Wales and the Welsh – ugh! – anything but. It might be all right "Going around with nothing on" as you put it, but for anything else! – And even for that there are always prying Welshmen to contend with, no darling, we will go some other place, unless you nag me into it?

Did you have to give up smoking especially for the leave, economy, or are you shedding your vices, dear? And the lost weight? I can hardly remember how you were, you had a beery tummy then, all very lovely. Which leads me to the promised photograph, is it in transit, please? Sorry about the leering specimen I sent you the other week.

I have had one sea-mail letter in which you told me of "Soapy". I met him a few weeks back, a shadow of his former self. Margaret, he rarely drinks! Miserable! He is dying! Reason? He is saving to get married! Is it worth it? How would you like to give everything up and have babies and things? What does Daphne think of it anyway, is it a young Doug, or not? Darling aren't I horrible?

Excuse the light-hearted vein, but this news is so damned good, and I am so ridiculously happy immediately followed by being hopelessly miserable, and its all your fault darling, what are you going to do about it? You can't just let things go on you know, you will have to recall something or me.

If you should ever be near Norfolk you must look up my favourite sister, Audrey, She is a grand kid you would like her. I am writing to tell her, or warn her – a Flight Officer, whew! Why not write and say hello? Her address is Cpl. Audrey Pack, Flying Control, North Creake, Egmere, Wells-on-Sea, Norfolk. Bye for now, darling, write tonight (and tomorrow night) Lots of love, Joe

Margaret to Joe 17th August 1944

Darling Joe, An ordinary letter because there is not enough space by far in an air letter to tell you all that I have to say. I wrote yesterday mentioning my leave in Wales - it was so lovely - as an author would have it - just like wine - and to be with Pauline again was such great fun - I hated coming back to work.

Darling – can you tell me, the next time you write – how soon you receive these letters? Yours to me take almost a month – but they are air letters – so these probably take even longer. It's such a pity we are so restricted in letters – I'd so much like to tell you about places and things which would interest you – I'm sure.

I dreamed last night that you were here – and we went to Town. I wore a lovely long dancing frock – with flowers – and you wore your uniform – you are very charming in uniform, dear, and we really stepped out – we drank champagne – and went to every place in Town – there was a carriage – drawn by two beautiful white horses – every time I stepped out of our lovely carriage – you kissed my hand – I kept wishing you'd not stop at my hand, but to kiss me properly – and Joe – how we danced! We seemed to be floating in a mist of heady perfume – your face was against my hair, and I felt that I never wanted to wake up – all through the dream I could see your eyes – looking quite steadily one moment – then twinkling – and darling – sometimes sad – why sad Joe? I wish I could dream of you always – I should sleep every moment off duty – and if I could – all day and all night – especially at night – because when everything is still – and the night is soft and dark – that's when I like to be alone – outside – under the sky – thinking of you – and wishing all the time that you were here – that I could hear your voice – and to reach out a hand – to feel you were there – warm and close to me.

Oh Joe, you disrupt my whole life – if I see a dark head – my heart jumps – music, all kinds of music sets me off dreaming – dance music because I want to dance with you – and the purest compositions of masters – because I know how you love them – Oh Gosh – it will be absolute heaven to see you again – please God – make it soon – I think if it's too long I shall just die of wishing. Darling, you have all my love, I love you, Margaret

Margaret to Joe 17th August 1944

Joe Darling, Please don't mind, but I just feel so beastly fed up that I had to get away by myself and write again. I'm writing up in bed, with a mood so black I even frighten myself. I should like so much to be able to sit down and tell you all my troubles and woes – you are the only person who would really understand – but you are in beastly Africa – and anyway must have quite enough to make you unhappy – without a stupid female wasting precious air letters with moans. In any case – mine is a very small moan really – just one of the other Plotters has annoyed me – hurt my feelings in fact – and I could hit her – only a Lady (?) doesn't do that. You must think I'm a dreadful bore – writing such dull letters – but when I write it makes you seem near, and that's what I want most of all.

Darling – you mentioned in your lovely account of Mail Day – that the mail boat comes in every Monday – does that mean it also takes the mail out once a week – have you moved? Because before you said that it's so difficult because the mail is not regular. I do hope that is so – because the infrequency of your letters drives me nearly to despair. Do you know how much your letters mean to me?

Do you remember Judy Read – in Oban? She has been posted to the South too and came over to dinner the other night – it was great fun – especially as there was a dance in the mess – we talked about old times – she asked about you and told me, I hope I'm not repeating old news, that Padre Lake is in France – did I tell you that I wonder? She was terribly amused to find I was a Flt/O – especially as I never was promotion-minded anyway.

Joe – have you any monkeys near the camp? You said there was no vegetation but surely there is jungle – or am I being terribly ignorant? Oh Gosh – I know I drip all over the place – but darling – I dream all the time about when we meet again – where will it be I wonder? And when? And what shall we say? Probably nothing at all, or chatter, I at least, nineteen to the dozen. One of the navigators here is leaving this week, so a whole bunch of good types are going to Minnie's (you remember I told you about it) to give him a decent send off. It would be perfect if you were here.

Joe, dear, what news of your sister? Is she abroad – or anything exciting? Darling, do you remember that lovely Coty lipstick you gave me? Did I ever tell you what an adorable colour it was? I save it for only very special occasions – it is hardly used at all – I shall wear it when you come home. I have a white blouse with red things all over it – exactly the same colour – I think you will agree it's an awfully good colour match. Please write lots and lots of letters – the postman is getting awfully tired of saying – No Air Mail for you – it's unhappy-making. Bye, sweet, all my love, Margaret.

Margaret to Joe 17th August 1944

My dear Joe, It would seem that you <u>have</u> forgotten me – well and truly – or does the absence of letters from you indicate disinclination to write? Of these two terrible things – heaven forbid that either should happen – I am not at all sure which one I would choose – if I had to.

If you were in this country there would be a chance of seeing you but now that you are so far away I can't even be sure that my letters are reaching you. We had a small gathering in the WAAF mess last night, a thing we call "Wednesday At Homes" – It was quite fun. I heard a sweet little story about a dear old lady who had never seen an elephant in her whole life – when suddenly – one day she saw one which had escaped from a zoo, eating up all her cabbages, picking them up with his trunk and chewing away quite happily – horrified – she phoned the police and said "Please come straight away – there is a strange animal in my garden who's picking up the cabbages with his trunk – and I'd hate to tell you what he's doing with them!" 17/8/1944 Darling, this is an air mail letter which I wrote months ago – before I got your first airgraph – I thought it might amuse you – to receive it now – as a matter of fact I mislaid it – and just today, when I was turning out my sports shoes, found it sandwiched in between a whole bunch of dirty old rubber shoes. So I'm afraid it is not very elegant – do you mind? My photograph for you is done, but I cannot collect it for about 3 weeks – it should take no more that 3 or 4 weeks to reach you from here – I do hope you like it – and, my dear, please may I have one of you? Please send one, if you can, anything, or something which I can keep with me all the time – because I long to see you so much sometimes – if I could only see your picture it would help a lot. All my love, darling, Margaret.

265 Squadron diary 18th August 1944 A/S up 0650 Diego Suarez down 1253 Tulear

Margaret to Joe 18th August 1944

Joe, darling, August – the 18th day of the 8th month – and the 1,944'th year. How much longer I wonder before we can be ourselves again – and forget that we have known so much tragedy and unhappiness – and how much longer before all those lovely memories – which thank heaven balance the sordid side of war – become a deep glow of happy remembrance in the back of our minds?

Perhaps not so very long now – sooner than one even imagines maybe. Last night – just before I turned out the light – I saw through the window – a Spitfire – high up – caught in the light of a half a dozen searchlights – with it's navigation lights on – it was pitch black all around – but in that vast expanse of nothing – there was this tiny silver thing – seeming to be supported by enormous bars of light – reaching from the ground – it was quite incredible – it was flying so high that there appeared to be no movement at all. There is something fascinating about an aircraft at night – the deep roar of engines – ploughing through the air – in total blackness – it seems they cannot know where they are – but knowing all the time – that they must – of course. Please take care of yourself – I think it must be far more dangerous at night – especially flying your kites – than during daylight. I used not to think twice about flying, and certainly love to fly myself, but every time I think of you doing a trip – I wish not once, but many times, that you were not going – and yet it seems illogical I know, I have the utmost faith in your flying – I should so love to fly with you sometime – don't laugh darling – but I know I should be quite safe. I cannot say that for every pilot I have flown with. That sounds like the most blatant line-shoot doesn't it? But you know what I mean – just any flip I have been able by begging borrowing or stealing – to scrounge from anybody – sometimes from the most reluctant people – who have finally relented merely in order to prevent me crying or even throwing a fit – it's really amazing what people do to avoid tears – and yet more often than not – they're only assumed grief anyway.

I did once see a man cry – I have never before or since experienced such terror – it was awful – I felt as though my body would collapse – it just robbed me of the power to move or speak. It was during the Blitz on London – in 1941 – and this poor man had lost his family – they were buried in a shelter – he was lying flat on the ground – trying desperately to move great mounds of earth with his bare hands – all the time he said not a word – until suddenly his hands were still – his head dropped hopelessly onto them – and then came the sound of dry – tearing – sobs – oh God! It was awful – everybody became silent – only faintly understanding his grief and incapable of doing anything to help him – he had to be alone – in the tragic knowledge that his whole world was locked in that shelter and lost. But even worse – for an onlooker – than the presence of death – was the sound of his crying – I never – say I'm a coward if you will – in all my life – ever want to experience such horror again.

Darling, what is the tour in East Africa? You have done almost a year already haven't you? I wish they would post me to somewhere near – at least near enough to see you on leave in Durban or something – or even to talk to you on the telephone – I can imagine my whole months pay would be used for the phone. I'll write again tomorrow, bye for now, dear, all my love, Margaret

Margaret to Joe 19th August 1944

Margaret to Joe 19th August 1944

I'm on night watch, its 3 o clock – everybody else has gone down and it's with great relief I can now allow my mind to wander where it pleases – and, as usual, it's wandering quite certainly in your direction. I have not yet ceased to be amazed that one can think so often about one person – and never get tired of it.

I wish they had rockets which fired letterboxes – from 265 Sqdn to Northwood and back again. Think how marvellous it would be to exchange letters every few days – instead of sometimes weeks and months.

Today has been a dull but nevertheless very pleasant one. – I came off watch at 1.30, wandered around the house in slacks for a couple of hours, read "For whom the bell tolls" – then slept for a couple of more hours – and came back on watch again at 9 tonight – until 8.30 tomorrow – or, this morning. When I come off I shall be free for 2 days – two whole days – what could we do – if you were here – and had two days too? Pictures, swimming, sunbathing, walking, talking, having tea, dinner, boating, beer in an old old pub – dancing – Joe – imagine – two whole days of sheer delight – I wouldn't mind working these beastly watches if that could happen.

There's one pleasant thing about life here – I share a room with an awfully nice girl – a cipher officer – who is about 29 – great fun – likes me – I like her and we get on like a house on fire. Darling – do you mind – I told her what I feel about you – I had to get it off my chest – and now she thinks you're pretty marvellous – and – without doubt – accepting my word of course – quite the best pilot in the RAF. I really believe you're the nicest anyway. You know, my little prairie flower, I shall not be happy until you send me a picture of you – and shall certainly keep asking until you do – will you – please? The work is just piling up on my table – but I can't bring myself to leave you just yet.

There are times when I need you very badly, my darling, please believe me, when I feel very sore and tired and nobody is enough or has the power or understanding to cure the depression – which descends – like a great cloud to make unhappy my whole mind and spirit – when I could be tossed here and there – and lack the will to protest. It may seem strange – since I knew you such a short time – yet time has taught me that there are only very few people with whom we feel completely at rest and to whom we can go and find complete sympathy and understanding – with no need of explanation. I feel that about you Joe, truly.

Dear, please write often – I want your letters so badly – but not as much as I want you – perhaps when you come home – I shall be able to tell you all that there is in my mind and heart, even if by that time, your heart has changed.

I cannot know – since you don't say – if you have changed – but anyway – I must tell you that I love you – that my one dream is of your return – regardless of what happens then – and every day – this feeling of being lost and alone grows – it's illogical – when I look round and see the crowds of friends I have here – but its true – not any of them can replace you in my mind – and time – which is supposed to be a healing factor – serves only to increase my longing for you. Darling Joe, please love me, Margaret

265 Squadron diary 20th August 1944 A/S 10.50 Tulear 20.40 Pamanzi

Joe to Margaret 20th August 1944

My dear Margaret, I wonder what you thought of my description of "Mail Day", at 265 Squadron? At the time of writing I was feeling very low as I had not received a letter from you for several weeks and life was grim. Return to the Squadron after a short detachment I found three awaiting me, including a sea mail letter – I live again!

There is so much I want to tell you, I think of you in the air, it helps to pass the long hours pleasantly but letters are most inadequate. And there is so much I do not understand – Oban. Why, Why, Why? You were so difficult to understand and you made it so obvious that you only wanted friends? You and you alone realised just how much I wanted to be with you, to get to know the real you, but you would not allow it. It was the first time I had ever wanted so much from a woman since my teens. And you hurt all of me, when I found a letter I had written you, in the Mess. Daphne told me about it, she told me it had been around for a week and admitted quite openly that she had read it, and gave me some advice on the spot about putting so much in writing – nice person!

I thought that I would never tell you about that letter, but it is like getting something off my chest – am I crazy darling? It is one of those things that gets one's pride I suppose. It is nothing I suppose but my feelings were so personal and private between you and I – or perhaps only on my side at this time?

You must please know my dear that your letters about boating, your black costumes, in fact the thoughts of sharing anything with you, sends me energy and delight. Sorry about this letter, I promise I will only write about nice things in my next. Lots of love, Joe

265 Squadron diary 21st August search for survivors up 0300 Pamanzi down 1930 Pamanzi

The survivors they were looking for were from H-265 which was shot down by U-boat U/862. This submarine had a remarkable history. It sank countless Allied vessels as well as the Catalina and caused much havoc around the Pacific and Indian oceans as well around Australia and New Zealand. It was never caught and at the end of the European war went to Singapore where the Japanese took it over and renamed it I/502.

Margaret to Joe 22nd August 1944

> We
> Darling,
> Tuesday 22/8/44
> So much to say – + so little space to crowd it in. First + most important is that I miss you badly – + wish all the time that you were here – + parties don't help – because that is when I find that all my resistance to the awful sense of loss – breaks down –

– and I could easily cry – a thing I have never done in my life before – at least not in my grown up life.

There was a party here last night – a navigator has been posted and we were all sending him off cheerfully – if, in some cases, rather drunkenly. There were some very funny moments – such as a ballet dance done in a most inspired fashion by a tall – very ugly- navigator – with a dirty white handkerchief stuck in his collar – so tightly tied that it threatened to choke him at any moment. I seem to be always talking about navigators, darling, it's simply because most of the people we work with here are in the navigation section and are practically the only people we have anything to do with at all. What a queer bunch they are too – all shapes and sizes – with positively the most wonderful collection of accents I have ever heard.

Leave has started gain – I was extremely lucky in getting a week before the new leave period starts – so I still have 4 weeks to come for the new year. You will soon be due for some more leave won't you? I have written a lot of letters in the past few weeks, I don't know how many of them you will receive – I do wish the mail was more reliable – it would make life so much easier.

One extraordinary thing happened to me the other night. Whilst waiting outside Baker street station for a taxi I had my pocket picked – at least – the old lady – for such it was – was not quite successful because I caught her hand in my pocket and when she realised she'd been discovered – hurried off into the darkness as though the devil were after her. She was a funny old thing, with dirty straggly hair and her clothes were all in rags, her hands were the most alarming though – terribly thin with long dirty nails and bent, giving the appearance of claws or talons. For a moment I was quite shaken and then became amused – because in my pocket she would have found no more than the magnificent sum of twopence.

We are on three watches now – which means no days off – unless we run around on the day we should be sleeping – after night duty – which isn't very clever – because after a short time doing that – one becomes a positive mental and physical wreck. I don't intend to grow into that state – so it looks as though there is going to be nothing but work and sleep for some weeks. I'm not a bit sorry really – because just recently I have been getting far too little sleep, being stationed so near Town presents too many opportunities for amusement and that would seem to be a bad thing if one has also a job of work to do. So – I retire to the seclusion of my room and, maybe, read good books, or, finish all the knitting and sewing I have to do. Darling – more letters is the cry, please? All my love, Margaret.

265 Squadron diary 23rd August A/S up 0900 Pamanzi down 1130 Diego Suarez

24th August Search for survivors up 1125 Diego Suarez down 1710 Pamanzi

9 Catalinas at Pamanzi in the Comoro islands. Photograph courtesy of Jim Lawlor

Joe to Margaret 24th August 1944

My dear Margaret, it is probably impossible to give you an accurate description of life at the Squadron. More frequently than not we are away from base, at the many little islands in the Indian Ocean but on the occasions when we are "at home" we really go to town

The bar is well organised up to about 1800, or 20.00, when the officer behind the bar gets drunk too and serves out drinks without being asked. That starts a "session" of course. We all pay for it in the morning. A few months ago we had bamboo huts and then the S/L (a hell of a good chap) and the rest of us would have races (of up to 24 hours) over the roofs of the huts. I can say quite honestly that I was the only person to give old Peter (the S/L) a good run. Everything went well until he fractured his arm in the mess and about two days after Jack (Barber) broke his toe in a rugger game we had at the return of our and another squadron. Jack was there too (do you remember him at Oban?) and about 7 days afterwards we were out searching for him – in vain – he probably did a good job – how I hate the thought of dying – now!

Damn, I have filled a whole page of this Airmail without writing a thing of interest to you. Please blame it on 150 hours of flying that I have completed this month – its true! Darling, you are making me do silly things. I am always daring to think that we "cope" together – gosh, how much and how little I seem to know about you. But having you as a very dear friend makes life worth living, there is now something worthwhile to stay alive for – no kid! Believe you me it is not always too good out here. Write a lot my sweetheart, tell me you like me, I won't believe you but I shall want to. Love, darling, Joe

265 Squadron diary *26th August 1944 A/S up 0735 Pamanzi down 0955 Diego Suarez*

Joe to Margaret 28th August 1944

My sweetheart, I find that I now have ten of your letters and will try and answer the many questions you have asked, and if this epistle is more disjointed than usual you know why. Must skip through them as I am off at 05.30 in the morning and it is now almost midnight.

Many apologies if I have not congratulated you on your second ring – wizard show – I am sure you deserve it. When I went to your dance at Oban you were like a mother to your WAAF and frightfully official – horrible word. I guess you are getting quite snobbish now, or are you, not a hope. When I see you again if you are not exactly the same as I left you, look out, I prefer you that way, it's the only way I have known you. Have you a temper darling? Do you have moods – I know so little about you, when may I spend lots of hours with you?

Your early letters tell me that you are off the Alc. I wonder if you are now? Being selfish I hope you are, I do not like the idea of you drinking with anyone but me. Does a semi - pub crawl on the Norfolk Broads appeal to you? And can you really dream of a caravan in Dorset or Devon – or perhaps only a tent? (two tents). Darling is it silly to hope that you like these things too, and perhaps - this bloody light!

Darling, it is now Tuesday, the light refused to stay on last night and I am now in Mauritius. Mauritius is a dream island in the Indian Ocean about 35 miles by 25 and the inhabitants are of French descent. – but I will not bore you with this. Your letter of yesterday telling me of your leave in Wales urges me to write, write, write but I find I cannot. You write of lovely things, it is wonderful to know that you love them too. It is those little things that can make me so happy but I am a very humble being and find it easy to appreciate them – do I talk in riddles?

I am getting sentimental, it is your letter, could I feel otherwise, but how inadequate, I want to shout, sing, in fact go completely crazy and the reason? I think it is the thought of sharing part of you, not only your letters but afterwards. Because in my more wistful moments I feel that it is inevitable, but when I come back to earth I wonder if it is possible, so many things happen to we mere humans, especially in wartime.

Sorry I have not answered your letters as I had hoped, I will try again tomorrow, perhaps if I write often my letter writing will improve? I'm possibly off on leave again in a few days time in Kenya, after which about 300 hours flying and if the Gods are good, home – and you dear? That should be around about January, unless the war finishes quickly; what shall we do and where shall we go when it is all over darling? G. night little girl, Joe PS Hope you got the snap.

265 Squadron diary 29 August F/O Pack reports from Diego that Catalina "H" is believed to have been lost while attending an enemy sub, with the possibility that the sub was also lost (the sub was hit but not sunk and was able to carry on causing much trouble until the end of the war - Ed)

Margaret to Joe 30th August 1944

It is some days now since my last letter; I mean to write every day, because so many thoughts in my mind are directly concerned with you. There isn't one day when the thought of you is not the predominating one. But – for a little while – I have been unwell I believe, rather in mind than in body – or perhaps it would be more truthful if I said that the state of mind has been reacting on my physical condition – do you know the feeling? – listless – not caring. It has been only a short spasm but it served to show me how shallow this kind of life is – that we lead – and how much more I want from life.

It's a curious thing – I believe I told you before – that in one sense my life now is a very full one – people I have met in odd parts of the country are always coming to town, there is never a day off when there isn't something to do, and yet, I'm so tired of it. When I'm with people I can be gay and have fun, so-called, and yet at the back of my mind is the wish that they'd go away and leave me alone, and let me be at peace, but when they are not there, there is no peace, I grow restless and miserable, thinking all the time only of my sense of loss, loss of you darling. Dearest Joe, will there ever be a time when I can see you quite close to me – and tell you that I feel? Letters don't, can't, express ones thoughts truly, there must always be something which is left out, something which might make all the difference in the world. Indeed – I could not really express emotion at all – not the feeling of complete and utter longing – so complete and so utter – so fierce in its intensity – that my mind reels with the effort of trying to overcome it. I suppose that sounds like a bit of dramatizing – I don't think I am – one knows oneself well enough by our age to judge ones values, and, much more importantly, ones emotions – please don't think darling, that I'm emotionally unstable – I'm not a silly adolescent. Having imagined myself in love a dozen times I know now that I never have been – until now – when this feeling has lasted so long, in your absence, and has troubled me so consistently – that I know it is not a mere accident but something much more serious which refuses to be ignored. In short – my dear my mind and heart are increasingly conscious, every moment, of only one desire – for you to return – quickly – leaving whatever happens then for the gods to decide, all my love darling, always yours, Margaret

12. September 1944

265 Squadron diary Sept 1ˢᵗ A/S 11.15 (1ˢᵗ) Tombeau bay 0440 (2ⁿᵈ) Tombeau bay

Margaret to Joe 1ˢᵗ September 1944

Joe, darling, unhappiness takes many forms- but far worse than any other is that of sense of loss – isn't it? It may seem a trifle illogical but to go, as I have been, 5 weeks with no word of you – provokes such a deep sense of loss that my days, until a letter comes, will be merely a state of existing in a deep melancholia. It all seems very sad, doesn't it, and darling – it is – I want you back home very much. I suppose many must be feeling just as I am.

Generally speaking, it is strange how the mood of people changes – now it is faith, hope, unquenchable optimism, where before there was bewilderment and a shuddering wonder of what might come next – and you Joe? – what do you feel now? When the end is in sight? I know so little of you, we never had time to absorb each other, to discover all that we each thought and wanted from life. With the thought that the war may soon be at an end comes to me also a feeling of unease, because in my adult life, as in a large part of yours, dear, I have only known service – and war – I can't remember anything I thought or felt before, if I ever was capable of feeling anything at all, then. The thought of changing one's life so completely as we must is not an easy problem to contemplate – or am I merely being a coward? I have dreamed often of the life I should like to live – always – and in that life there is no room for service things or unhappiness, only bright calm peace, and unquenchable faith in the things I love most.

But the stage in between? – that changeover – that period of time – to ease the difficult step to be taken – there are many things I shall never forget about the war- things I shall love to remember – which will mellow with time, and long after will become framed in my mind as exquisite cameos of a time when emotions were precipitated necessarily – a hurried fusion of colours produced mind pictures so truly beautiful that they render one powerless to express delight in them – but leave one inarticulate – and very humble in the thought of them.

The one thing I look forward to now is your return, even though I might see you only once – just that one meeting is all I dream of – to see you close, and talk, knowing you can hear and see what I am feeling, and to hear your voice too, instead of writing and never knowing if you even receive my letters. Letters are too unsatisfactory, they are incomplete, always there may be something left out, which might make all the difference in the world. Perhaps I should be looking forward to a long time hence – planning for afterwards – safeguarding a very precarious future – but for the moment my horizon is limited to a ship, maybe an aircraft, arriving home and my first sight of its precious cargo. A limited horizon perhaps, but made wide and unbounded in its possibility of immeasurable delight. Come home soon, my dear, and meanwhile, write long and often, it helps a period of waiting which is almost unbearable. All my love, always yours, Margaret

Margaret to Joe 2nd September 1944

Another day and no word from you – please don't mind the depressing tone of my letters, but really it is unbearable, not to hear from you. Darling, are you writing? Because if you are not, and if you don't want me to – I'll stop – even though I should be terribly unhappy about it.

The other day I stayed with my father in London and just before dawn one of the buzz raids started. Having once got out of bed it seemed foolish to go back so I went out for a walk and gained one of the most beautiful impressions of my life – just when the dawn broke – for a minute or two – London seemed like fairyland – not real – hard to believe – with a glorious red-gold sun coming up behind dirty grey buildings – silhouetted black as night – and outlining them with a line of fire. The sky was an unearthly colour – not grey, not blue – not anything colder at all – just something like the softest of shrouds – with a warm comforting glow behind. The air was so fresh – and now and then a dark alien shadow would come and go – an early worker bustling off to his factory with no thought of the beauty, strange beauty, of a London dawn – it was almost as though nature was asserting the fact of her beauty – to show too clearly the shabbiness and inferiority of man-made things – but she succeeded in giving to me only a greater respect and perhaps a little more affection for a great city with a personality so great that to live a whole life there, and to say, to pretend to understand it – would be to claim a sympathy akin to that of the gods – who see all – and who amongst us can claim such understanding? I love London, but it wearies and frightens me – it tells me how small and unimportant I am and how little I and my thoughts matter in the great scheme of things. But it tells me too how worthless material things are. It's a strange thing – but to be in London means to me – to appreciate it – but never do I find it so fascinating as when I am away from it – happy with quieter things – and a safer content. Nevertheless – we shall stop – not to see the effect of a dawn – but shall we? Darling when we celebrate – lets go on and on – until we are so tired we just fall asleep – perhaps we shall see a London dawn – it will be a golden one – for me – even if there is no sun – a cold greyness would pass unnoticed – because happiness would rob it of its power to spread gloom. We must see a dawn – please? All my love, Margaret

265 Squadron diary 3rd September 1944 A/S Up 0625 Tombeau bay down 1215 Diego Suarez

Catalina FP 260, with 2 crew members, Joe flew this aircraft often

Margaret to Joe 5th September 1944

The news is very exciting – judging by reaction generally – the war might already be over. Such hilarity – at least as far as I am concerned – not too previous I hope.

The other day, I had a day off – and met some playmates in town – there ensued a celebration of no mean proportions – so enthusiastic was it in fact that I missed the midnight train back to Northwood and they all had to sit with me, the whole night, until the first train at 6.30 next morning – in Lyons Corner House – drinking disgusting coffee and disturbing all the popsies and their American boy friends – who looked daggers at our hilarious behaviour – the waiters loved it and kept up a stream of back chat as they whizzed to and fro – past our overcrowded table. After several hours we had collected hundreds of coffee cups, all stacked on the table, under the table, and all over the place. The waiter begged of us that we might – please miss – use the same cups every time – but that wasn't to be thought of – higher and higher grew the pile – and more and more we laughed – and more and more distressed grew our poor waiter – he was a free Frenchman or something odd, and finally his nerves wouldn't stand it any longer, he came to us almost with tears in his eyes and said, please, he loved us very dearly, we were the nicest people, but he had a wife with many children, all evacuated, and it was wicked the billeting fees and he wanted to buy her some new shoes and " if the cups they break, the bill he pay, and if the bill he couldn't pay, the job he lose – did we see" We saw – one playmate stood up – quite steadily – to our infinite surprise – and made an inspired speech about billeting fees – which included several stories of not too reputable a character – had half of Lyons corner house in stitches and the other half wondering whether to call a policeman. However, finally, when we left, or were ejected I can't remember which – we found a carriage with a horse, supposedly built for two, but, by the time we'd all climbed in – bulging fit to burst – with an old man driving the horse – who carried on a conversation – which required that he turned around every few minutes, leaving the horse to direct himself – and spitting with great gusto in the road – after every two or three words.

However we finally <u>did</u> reach Baker Street Station and to my everlasting amazement I actually found myself on the way back to Northwood all in one piece and not even a ladder in my stockings. However as soon as my ecstatic friends had gone, nature gained her way, and I fell asleep, missed Northwood altogether and went on to the train terminus and found myself quite lost. Ah me. All my love, Margaret.

265 Squadron diary 6th September 1944 A/S up 0550 Diego Suarez down 1150 Kipevu (Mombasa)

Margaret to Joe 6th September 1944

My darling, I've just received your letter dated 24.8.1944 and it has made me quite ridiculously happy. It's so stupid really – one letter – and my whole outlook changed, I walk around the ops room with an inane expression and simply love everybody, everyone is my friend, and they'd think I was mad if I told them it was because one pilot – namely Joseph Pack – had written to me.

Darling Joe, you ask me to tell you if I like you – I can't do that – I don't like you – unless you call wild excitement when your letters come – liking – or the most incredible daydreams at the most inconvenient times – I should describe it – knowing myself now as I do – as rather a most impatient state of being in love – sweet – I do love you – terribly – believe me? You must believe me dear, it's the truest thing I have ever told you – could we have that leave, the one which never happened – together, when you come back? If only we could, the thought of seeing you again – sitting opposite you at dinner, raising glasses, having tea, or just sitting talking – or just loving you, oh Gosh, it makes me happy and miserable in turn – happy because it's so lovely to think about, and miserable because it may be so long before it does happen. I want to be with you, I want to be beautiful for you, for you to be proud of me, I'm very proud of you, Joe dear. If you have done 150 hours in one month – darling – doesn't that mean you are finishing your tour quickly? Please say it does, and please say you are coming home when it is finished, and please, far more importantly than anything, I pray for you to be safe – when you come back I want to be the person you'll see England with again, I want to be the one you'll celebrate with and I want to be the one you'll tell all about Africa – even the unhappy parts –

and you must be the one to hear all about me – even though my troubles are very tiny ones

Dearest – before you go to bed tonight – just imagine for a moment that I am very close to you and whispering all the foolish things I've wanted to say so much – and imagine too that when you wake in the morning, it will be to fresh green fields and the sights and sounds of English country which are so well loved by us both – and the feeling of inarticulate happiness that I know I shall feel when I hold you quite close to me again – and tell you – whilst I can see what your eyes are answering – that all my love is for you only – not a casual love, my dear one, but something which has grown to be a part of my every waking moment and which has stood the test of a parting which has lasted now for more than a year. Write more my darling, your letters mean everything to me. All my love. Always yours, Margaret

Margaret to Joe 8th September 1944

My darling, I've just been visiting Pauline, in Wales, and am sitting in the waiting room at Chester station, waiting for the night train back to London. The station is dreary even on a bright day, but now, when it's dark, and teeming with rain anyway, it is anything but inspiring. However it is enough that I have found a waiting room with a light and am able to write to you.

Altogether it has been a delightful visit, I've done some shopping – the most thrilling purchase of all – is a pair of <u>silk</u> stockings – fully-fashioned – and really lovely. Do you know just what that means? When for nearly 2 years I have – when in mufti – had to wear extraordinary things which don't fit anywhere and look rather as though one might have gone through a hedge backwards – whilst wearing them. I intend to guard them jealously until you return and then wear them with my black suit, the one I'm coming to meet you in.

My brother hopes to be home in October – next month – I'm feeling excited about seeing him again, he's such a darling, and so terribly young – he's 19 – every time I see him now, he's like a different person, growing older so quickly I can hardly keep pace with him.

Darling – I've just been to make sheep's eyes at the stationmaster – my pen ran out of ink and he had a whole bottleful, he laughed and asked if I had as much to write to "him" about as all that. I might have said that I could quite easily spend the whole of every day quite happily writing to you. He would doubtless have thought that here was just another love sick youngster getting enthusiastic about her boyfriend – but he would have been quite wrong – because we are not "just" another couple of people are we? We're really quite unique and very unusual people and nobody could love anybody else quite as I love you, I firmly believe that, and nobody has quite such a ridiculously lovely nose as yours, or eyes quite so expressive or a kiss so utterly tender and sweet.

Darling – how long before you kiss me again? Not long – please? The thing is, I have so much to tell you that is really terribly important, to us both, I can't write it all darling, it would take too many letters, and they wouldn't make sense, you would never get them in order, and in any case, I keep getting distracted when I find my pen saying I love you when all the time I intend it to say something else.

Joe – when you have races over bamboo huts, isn't that really quite dangerous? I don't want you to be hurt darling, even just a little. We can go overseas now, but I shall not go, I'm so desperately afraid that you might come back soon and to be on the other side of the world if you were back here would be the absolute end. Dear – have you any idea how soon you might be coming – I want you to come back so much, it's just so dreadful, waiting. I have no real interest in the friends I have here, except perhaps Pauline, who is really a very sweet person, I think you'd like her, darling.

How often do you get leave? I wish they would post me to Nairobi, could you get in to see me if by any incredible chance I were there? Ah! – what foolishness, to wish for the impossible, far better to wait here patiently until you return and hope fervently that it will not be long. The thing I'm terrified of now is that they will post me away from Northwood, perhaps to the wilds of Scotland just when you come back and I shan't be able to get to you quickly. To know that you were in this country, and not be able to be with you, would drive me crazy. Darling, write long and often, I love you and want the only part of you I can have at the moment – your letters. All my love, darling, Margaret

Margaret to Joe 8th September 1944

My darling, an air letter is not enough to say all that I must say to you. Your letter – telling me what happened at Oban – with Daphne, has made me unutterably sad because honestly I had no idea such a thing had happened. It is not you who can be accused of cruelty, but I, and with every justification.

Darling, before you came to Oban, I knew a man called Bill Martin, he was a Canadian. I won't give you any harrowing details but briefly, I imagined I was in love with him. I knew him in all for about six months, when he was posted, we met on leave, in London, and it was there I discovered that he was a man of the worst type, the casual philanderer. His behaviour and my subsequent enlightenment were almost more than I could bear, he was so hard and beastly that for a long time I couldn't make myself believe that all men were not like that. You see, dear, before I met him, although I had had many friends, men and women, I had never felt anything like the emotional disturbance he caused. It is quite clear to me now that I never did love him, that he just happened to be there when I quite suddenly grew up. However, shortly afterwards you came up with the F.T.U and, almost before I realised what was happening, I was falling in love with you. Directly I realised it I became terrified, that it might happen again, that ghastly disillusionment and the horrible realisation that my idol, to coin a phrase, had feet of clay.

You don't know what awful nights I had, thinking about it all, wishing I could believe in you, and yet, all the time, unable to make myself believe I could. As for the letter, well, you can't have known that I carried your letters everywhere with me, and read them not once but dozens of times during the day and night, always arguing against myself, trying to believe, desperately, that you were different, and that you spoke the truth when you said you loved me, and that it was not just a too rapid growth of false emotion – that can be the only reason Daphne found your letter, and darling, I feel so sorry for her, what a poor starved creature she must have been, to have been unable to resist the temptation to read a letter to another woman. My sweet, I don't know if you ever realised but she was very jealous of me because you were so completely unaware of her. You see – she was quite definitely wanting to know you a great deal better, you were young and clean and, most importantly, such a lovely person. She could, many times, have quite cheerfully murdered me simply because you preferred my companionship.

Darling – how dreadful you must have felt, I could cry for hate of myself, when I think of the humiliation I must have subjected you to. Can you ever forgive me? Then – I told you I wasn't in love with you, if you had really believed me, why then did you imagine that I promised to meet you on leave? I panicked completely and just hadn't the courage to force myself to see that I was being a stupid fool. When you came back from leave, you avoided me, Oh! I can quite understand why – you knew nothing of what was inside me, you didn't know I cried in my room, the first night you were back, you couldn't know that I tried deliberately to bring myself to tell you all about everything, and couldn't, just couldn't!

Then – I went to Davidstow, and finally you wrote, did you ever get my reply? Dear sweet Joe, until your first letter came from Africa, my life was only endured, it alternated between wild parties and misery, but not once, in all that time, have I ever even entertained the thought of another man. I have known many – since – certainly – but they are all quite clearly aware that I do not love them, that I like being with them, and having fun, but there is quite definitely somebody else – that somebody is you Joe.

I didn't want to write this to you, because I could express my feelings, at the time of Oban, so much more clearly if I could talk to you. Some day – soon I hope – we shall be together and then I can tell you everything about me, there is so much I want to tell you my sweet, it can't be written, it wouldn't make sense, but when we talk together about it all you will understand I know. To say any more about it now would only confuse the doubtful clarity of the story I have tried to tell you. Every word of it is true I swear and I think that when we meet again you will believe me. If only you had come to Oban six months before, our lives might have followed a very different course, a happier one my darling.

I do love you, most sincerely. It hurts me sometimes when I think of how long it must be before I can see you and how much time will be wasted in wishing and waiting. For now, my dear, you have all of my devoted and loyal love, there is only you, and will always be, unless you wish otherwise. Even if you don't want it this way darling, you will still be there, in my heart, and anybody else, if there ever were anyone, would be only second best.

You might like to know that I have seen Bill Martin, quite accidentally, since you have been away and, it sounds curious to say this, but it was not until I saw him again that I was quite certain, gloriously certain, that my love for you was very real, and he had absolutely no power to hurt at all, anything, any cheap physical attraction he had inspired, had died completely, I felt free of all that horrid, miserable uncertain attraction from which I couldn't break free. However, now, to me, it is only a bad dream which is almost unbelievable, I find it really hard, when I think of you, to convince myself that I really thought, even for a moment, of a man like that. Be assured of my love, it is a balanced, aware, warm knowledge of the fact that I believe I can identify myself completely with you, that we can, if we wish, be so close as to be one person, and I believe too that with you I could be completely happy, not only in the exquisite discovery of each other, but also in the cold exacting light of the moment after. Since you have been away I feel I have really learned a truer appreciation of things, and of myself, there is little now which remains hidden.

Right in the front of my mind there is always the picture of the way I want to live my life. It presents a very ordinary picture really, but to me it means everything. A house, a little one, cosy and comforting, and children, books, cooking, a garden, walks in the evening, delightful friends to show off my family to, all these things represent now my whole ambition. I don't mean to imply that I'd like to be able to do nothing but rock a cradle or boil an egg, but to establish a solid happiness, and watch it grow, until life is mellow and rich with experience. It sounds rather as though I'm trying to sell you the idea darling, doesn't it? But you know that is not my intention, you know that I am merely being completely honest with you.

Dear one, we don't have to think about people like Daphne, if we wish, our lives can be so full that there would be no room for them, there could be no part to spare for wretchedness, and misfortune, if it had to come, could only be instrumental in binding us more closely together.

Joe – whatever happened in the past, however much misunderstanding there was, now I desire only one thing, that reciprocation from you, which will produce a beautiful and understanding love, which will be little short of perfect. My own darling, I love you, Margaret

Margaret to Joe 9th September 1944

My darling, I wrote yesterday explaining, or trying to explain, something of what happened in Oban, you said you couldn't understand. Oh my dear – if only you were here now, there is so much we both have to talk about. The thought of Daphne saying such beastly things to you is making me feel so unhappy.

Today is one of those beastly grey days, when everything is coloured with a damp depression and people all look blank and disinterested in everything, do you know the feeling of being completely dead, no energy, and no wish to do anything but just sit and stare – at nothing – thinking nothing.

My brother is in London today – he has 18 days leave – I know when I see him my mood will brighten, I'm terribly glad, always, to be with him, he cheers me up immediately we meet. I do want you to meet Frankie, I'm so proud of him, and I know you will like each other. 18 days is a long time, when time is his own, that's when he starts doing mad things. The last time he was in London he was nearly run in by the police for walking across a parapet, a very narrow one, over a river, after he'd had a beer session with some sailor playmates in one of the locals. The policeman called him "sonny" and I think it rather hurt his dignity, especially as he was just home after being on board the Duke of York when she'd sunk the Scharnhorst, or at least she'd helped to sink it. He's rarely serious about anything, least of all about the Navy, of course he shoots lines, who doesn't, but all the time, when he's making fun of the Navy, one knows that really he's terribly proud of it, and simply loves his ship.

It's night now, I am on night duty again, what an effort it was to get back to London by 2100 tonight, especially after drinking beer with Frankie. He tried hard to persuade me not to come back, and I had to try very hard not to give in and stay. He has just told me that he has leave because he is going on draft, I suppose that means overseas somewhere. I just hate the thought of his going, he's so young, and he's had enough war anyway, having been torpedoed twice, and the second time only getting away with it by the skin of his teeth. Oh Lord, this awful war, darling, I wish it were finished, completely, and we could settle down to a decent normal life, instead of wondering every minute if those we love are safe.

There are moments, when I am tired, and I haven't real control over my mind, when the war appears as a madly jumbled merry-go-round, and in all the movement, and jarring noise there is represented death and horror, ghastly frightening colours, which jump into a clear pool of peace and thresh it into a tortured writhing mass of pieces, pieces of souls in agony, and the sobbing despair of those who have lost those things which make life sweet.

I have often wished for a mind and heart which would feel nothing, but just go calmly on, doing that which must be done, and remaining oblivious to all that disturbs the soul, and being always free of the need to decide whether to accept or reject. Imagine seeing a house blown to pieces, and merely observing the grief of he who has suffered, and thinking, for a moment only, how dreadful, and then be able to think of pleasant things, forgetting then and for all time that this had happened. I know what you will say darling, that if one could feel no despair, or sorrow, then also one could not feel joy or happiness. That is true, and perhaps really, deep down inside, I think that those perfect moments of complete happiness are worth all the times when misery is in possession of ones heart, and life seems so difficult. Some day I shall be able to tell you all that I think about everything, it will be wonderful, knowing you will understand completely, and of that I am quite certain. I think I shall understand you too, it seems I have learned so much about you since you have been away, there still remains a tremendous amount to discover, and I am most impatient to begin, will it be soon, dear? Say it will, please.

I'm afraid it's now two days later, I've been spending all my spare time entertaining Frankie, or rather, tagging along after him, while he whizzes from one place to another. On Sunday he wakened in the morning with a shocking hangover and, completely disregarding the idea of food, went straight out and swam until his headache had gone, came back and ate an incredibly large meal, and then started another party. Where he gets his endurance I cannot imagine, perhaps it's simply that he's on leave and having a good time.

Did I tell you we could go to India now? It should be rather fun, but the tour is rather a long one, two years. I should love to go for perhaps a year, and come back just about the same time as you, but I don't want to risk your coming home and my not being here.

Dear – I do hope you don't mind all these plans but, whatever happens, I am quite determined to see you at the earliest possible opportunity, even if you might not want to see me .In your last letter you spoke of the grim absence of letters, darling, I write at the very least twice a week, the mail service to East Africa is terribly bad, sometimes it's a whole month, or even more, before I receive your mail, I can appreciate how you feel, I feel thoroughly miserable when there is no news from you.

I went to Chester again the other day to see Pauline and found something in a shop which made me positively dance with joy, it was some material I've simply longed for, for ages, a silky velvet in deep midnight blue, I'm going to make a housecoat of it, with an enormous skirt, its really terribly extravagant, but I had to have it, and now I have bought it, I'm afraid to start sewing, it looks so elegant.

Joe – do you think you may go on further instead of coming home? If you do I shall just die – really and truly die – with grief. Perhaps I'm being very foolish but, all the time, the one thought, wish, in my mind is for you to come back. I want to explain so much and unless I see you I don't think I can explain, letters don't really help, because one cannot somehow write all that one feels. My photograph is on its way, I do hope it reaches you all right, its awfully risky sending parcels I know, but if it doesn't reach you fairly soon I'll send another *(the photo on page 54 is believed to be the one mentioned here).*

Do write as often as is humanly possible, because I love you, far more than I can describe, and your letters bring you close to me, I read them so often that they are nearly in shreds, if you have a picture of yourself, will you give it to me darling?

Do write, please, all the time, all my love, dear, Margaret

Margaret to Joe 14th September 1944

Darling Joe, Waiting is a horrid business isn't it. I plague the poor postman every day, always asking for letters from you, it's now two whole weeks and no news, I know it isn't very long really but it seems like a lifetime when it means so much.

There was a fairly amusing story in Music hall on the radio tonight – one man was saying stockings were now coming off the ration, the other capped that with the fact that they were going to make them with pockets in – the first man replied with an observation that WAAF, ATS and WRNS had now been ordered to refrain from putting their hands in their pockets, I thought it was quite funny.

The news in France is very cheering, but I still feel we have a hard time ahead before things are really finished.Darling, please don't get sent to the other place, you know where I mean? Because surely you must have nearly finished your tour by now, and they will send you home then won't they?

My small brother, Peter, aged 13, has just started wearing long trousers, did I tell you? I haven't seen them yet, at least not until tomorrow, it will be terribly hard to resist laughing, but I mustn't, he'd be terribly hurt if I did.

Joe – how do you get on with Jack Barber now? Does he still fly with you? Darling – do you remember one night in the mess, I was talking to Jack and he asked you to have a drink. You were awfully grumpy and off hand, I could never understand why. You didn't ever think I gave a second thought to Jack did you? Or to anybody for that matter, except you, and I have already told you why I didn't allow you to know how I felt about you. There isn't one day now when I do not curse myself for being such an idiot, but at the same time, thank God that I have had now the opportunity of telling you. You know darling, I never really thought you'd write to me again, after my weird behaviour, but never really gave up hoping that you would. God was good, not only did you write but you also <u>wanted</u> to hear from me that was almost more than I dreamed and hoped for.

Tomorrow I have a day off, I shall imagine you are with me all the time, getting on the train, the tube, going to the pictures with my brother, having tea, then cleaning up and changing, drinks, dinner and then, when I get into bed I can think of you to the exclusion of all else, its when you are closest. When I'm alone and quiet. I love you darling. Please love me. Margaret

Joe to Margaret 15th September 1944

My darling, I am a fool, several days ago I wrote a letter to you but this previous day I had left my writing necessities at a certain place (they will be returned). Although I could remember Frithwood and Watford I could not remember the rest of the address and in consequence. I could not post the A.M.L. The Intelligence officer could not supply the address of Coastal

Command nor members of the Mess either, there was nothing for it but to wait for my return to base and pray that you had written. You had, thank God and this is to explain the delay. You should get this with the other letter.

My dear little girl, you write so unhappily, you write that you have not received my letters. My darling I do write often and I am always thinking of you, you would be annoyed if you knew how often my thoughts are of Oban, when I knew you. I wanted you so very much then, and now, but now I am frightened because if I was insufficient then, am I still not the same? Because, my darling, you must remember that I am not in the least clever or say the right things, how often have you said to me "talk to me Joe" and not being able to talk to you as I have thought you must want me to speak, well I close up!

My darling sweetheart, I want you more than anything else in this world, but although I know we could always "get along" there are other things almost of equal importance. What the hell am I to do after the war? – That's it. You see sweetheart the thought of you and I is more than wonderful but…?

I have scribbled this after reading your unhappy letter and hope to be able to get it through to mainland before mail day. I love you darling, Joe

Joe to Margaret 16th September 1944

My dear Margaret, I often lie in bed and think of you, think of your letters and how I should answer them. And I find that I can explain myself to you perfectly, in fact I can visualise you and I together, in life, with all thoughts of the war and service life put away, and as you put in your letter, only bright calm peace. Yes I can very easily imagine doing things with you, because from the first time we walked home from the Alex (Oban) together, we seemed kindred in something – I do not know quite what – everything perhaps?

But during the daytime comes reality. I cannot express myself, everything takes a different shape and the hopes of the previous night fade, or perhaps my imagination ceases to exist? I begin to wonder if I could be eligible to fill the other half of your life socially, intellectually, financially, in fact in every way. Eligible is not the right word, but all sensible, or shall I say modern people, look ahead, way ahead, because life can be a hell of a gamble. Or perhaps you do not wish me to worry about such serious matters, in fact I really have no right to.

Like you, in your letters in the beginning of September I am depressed, in fact I am often misery itself. It's the war I suppose, four years in the RAF is too long for any person, it has its moments but I begin to long for a quiet life. Nine to five before the war got monotonous, but the evenings and weekends made such a complete break. The RAF cannot give me those breaks and the luckier of us are just allowed to live.

The reason I am writing this mordant letter is that I get the opportunity to post it on the mainland tomorrow, otherwise I would have spared you until later when I hope to be in a better frame of mind. I shall receive no mail from you for a fortnight perhaps, as I am off again.

Incidentally, my darling, always write to this address irrespective of the address I may write from. And lets both cheer up from now on shall we, it's a bad thing if we both slip down, after all why shouldn't we be happy, the war is almost over, in fact we have everything to live for!! Am I right? Lots of love, Joe PS How many letters have you received this month to date, I have sent four

265 Squadron diary 17th *September 1944 A/S up 0515 Diego Suarez down 1140 Kipevu (Mombasa).*

Joe to Margaret 17th September 1944

My darling, please excuse the scribbled address but I wrote it last night after a small party in the Mess and since ones bed invites sleep (when tight) the letter was not written. Although I dropped off to sleep I fortunately did not lie on this precious Air Mail Letter or my pen.

I expect to be on my way to another command in a day or so, but unfortunately it is in the wrong direction. With luck I shall be back again by the end of the month to collect my mail, it seems a hell of a time to wait!

Incidentally darling I have been reading an overseas Daily Mirror for July which said that there were many tons of overseas mail waiting to be sorted, could that be the reason for you not receiving my letters? Reverting to my forthcoming trip, I am looking forward to seeing the local produce which is supposed to be, or reputed to be, the best in the world, I refer to Indian jewellery. I wish now that I had saved some money instead of drinking it, when I could have bought you something. There are ways and means however, I must find out if the jewellery is all it is cracked up to be; unfortunately it is not possible to mail it.

At the moment I am on the mainland again and have a very important mission. Just before leaving a little black boy from the kitchen came running up to ask if I could get him a hat with a red tassel on it. I measured his head with a piece of string and put it very carefully in my pocket. He went away very happily to sit in a corner and chew a bone that he had previously put into an open-air fire with the rest of the sticks. He is a grand little fellow mainly because he is always smiling and chatters away to all and sundry in a mixture of English, French, Malgashe and Swahili. The red hat makes him an Askari who is a much superior person to the Malgashe native of Madagascar. He calls me "boss".

You must excuse the drivel that you are sure to find in my letters to you, but if you like lots of letters it means that I have to write at lots of odd times and my normal letter writing mood only "comes on" about once a fortnight. I am bound to admit however that writing to you makes me feel nearer to you and gives me a "nice feeling", although my writing ability does not improve.

One of these may be the little boy referred to by Joe.

This Mess has some wonderful records; do you remember that we once planned to have a pub, to which we would only make our friends welcome and we decided to do lots of other things. You even worked out the colour scheme for the saloon, do you remember darling? The music reminded me of that evening, because we decided to buy all the music we liked. That night, or the morning I should say, I realised that you had done something to me and I could not shake you off – I wanted to later. Yes, Margaret sweetheart, I was crazy about you, I did not want to admit it to myself, and I still am. Lots of love, Joe

Margaret to Joe 18th September 1944

Darling, in one of your letters you said you might be back home about January. I can hardly believe it, it's too good to be true. When you do come, wherever you are you must let me know the exact minute you arrive, the very minute, and even if it means deserting duty or something equally drastic, I'll reach you somehow. Oh gosh! – imagine meeting a train, with you on it! The thought of it upsets me completely, just imagine what we shall do, that first time, I shall be speechless, Oh Joe, I can't think, let alone write coherently. You'll step off the train, and quite suddenly, I shall see you, you won't have changed, your picture tells me that, you'll see me then, we'll just say hello, that's all, I shan't be able to say any more than that, then we will get a taxi and go, where? – Café Royal? – nobody there would mind if I kept looking at you quite stupidly, and we'll have a drink, the first for too long a time, and then, no food darling, I just couldn't eat, I know that, then I'd suddenly find my tongue and ask you so much and try to tell you so much, you won't be able to make any sense of it at all, please please don't say it isn't true, make it come true, darling, its only 4 months!

I've written to Audrey today, and have asked her to write to me, I do hope she does. I mentioned that if she is coming down on leave soon to let me know, as I'd like to meet her. If I do go in her direction, I'll make a point of going to see her, perhaps I can wangle a trip up on one off my stand-offs, to stay somewhere near for the night. Norfolk Broads darling? If you like.

Why do you dislike Wales so much? In the North it's very beautiful, or is it the people whom you dislike? Joe – you've lost weight haven't you? Or maybe it's the way the picture is taken. What do you mean? I never had a beery tummy, that's slander, or something very like it, or do I mean libel? Anyway, it's flat now, flatter than yours I bet, you've been drinking enormous amounts for the past year, and I haven't, so there, my little prairie flower.

Darling I should love some Indian whatever you called it, to wear, is it very gaudy? But if you really care to gladden my heart, I should love some kind of material to make underwear, at the rate we're going on now, we shall soon have to go without any at all, or wear red flannel, can you imagine anything worse?

Speaking of Daphne, the thing you mentioned about young Daggs, or not (?), is rather apt, at the moment, since she was to have had a baby, but suffered a miscarriage, it turns out now that it was to have been twins!! And darling – they were young Daggs'. Its really rather sad in a way because although she's not a particularly nice type, Ainsley is really awfully charming, it seems a pity he has to be hurt so much as that, it must have been dreadful for him, don't you think so?

Do I want babies? Of course, dozens of them, all over the place, enough at least for a football team anyway, and maybe even a referee, and daughters too, all pretty, with black hair and naughty eyes, and they'll all of them become famous, and do incredible things, probably so incredible they'll all be shoved in prison, and have to be baled out, but still, they'd be great fun, especially when they were grown up, and married, and then there'd be a lot of new ones, double the number in fact, and a lot of new babies too, imagine, there'd be a positive army of them eventually. Write darling, often, all my love, Margaret

265 Squadron diary *19ᵗʰ September 1944 A/S up 0310 Mombasa down 1112 Port Victoria (Seychelles)*

20ᵗʰ September 1944 A/S up 0150 Seychelles down 1050 Addu Atoll

Margaret to Joe 20ᵗʰ September 1944

My darling, for 20 minutes I have been trying to start writing but there are literally hundreds of gnats in my room and they all seem to like me and concentrate on flying in the very spot where my head is, at the top of the bed, beastly things, I've killed about a dozen already, there are little bits of gnats all over the bed.

How are you darling? I had two letters only 3 days ago but already it seems months since I heard from you. No doubt you have returned from leave now – was it a good one? I hope to go on leave next month for 7 days, and after that intend to save my further leave in case you come home early next year, because if you get some leave we must, at all costs, spend as much time together as possible, that is most important, because if you can bear to have me with you for any length of time, I do so much want to know so much about you, hundreds of things, and I want you to know many, many things about me too. Sometimes I feel I shall burst with longing for you to come home but when I feel really miserable I sit down and scribble little notes to you and afterwards I feel much better. I suppose some people might be aghast at what I write in these little notes, certainly they would reproach me for lack of modesty, in fact I'm not at all sure I could write them to you dearest, but even if you felt a little taken aback, nevertheless I know you would understand. In any case you would find they are always about you so perhaps you might even like them. Joe dear, if you ever feel really inspired why don't you write a really long letter, by sea mail, you write such lovely letters, but I always feel they end too quickly, I've read all the ones you have sent, so many times, they are all dirty and literally frayed at the edges.

Darling – I'm afraid I've started smoking again, I have been so terribly worried about Pauline that my nerves, for several weeks now, have been on edge and smoking seems to make me calmer. But still it's very naughty because, frankly, the reason I stopped in the first place was, as you guessed, to economise financially. You see, dear, I find when I work a long night watch, I was smoking about 40 cigarettes in 24 hours and, apart from the fact that it was too darned expensive I found I wasn't really feeling well. However when I am not watch keeping my consumption goes down with a bang so when we meet on leave you won't have to reproach me. In any case when we meet we shall have no time for reproaches, we shall be far too busy just being gloriously happy. Agreed? All my love dear one, Margaret

265 Squadron diary 21ˢᵗ September 1944 A/S up 0235 Addu Atoll down 1731 Kogalia (Ceylon)

Margaret to Joe 22ⁿᵈ September 1944

My darling, you have monopolised my thoughts all day, it's late now, past one o clock, but still I must stay awake to write. If only I could write beautiful letters, there is so much inside, which I can't express, and which grows and grows in intensity, until I feel that I must tell you somehow, or burst.

You see dearest, all the time I plan, all sorts of things, when we shall see each other again, and where, what shall we say, how will you look, whether I shall look pretty for you, if you will still like me, oh darling, if you didn't, I should be so unhappy, but you will, won't you?

England is very lovely now, it's almost Autumn, today as I left the Mess, thousands of brown leaves crackled under my bicycle wheels, a lovely crunchy sound, the colours were so beautiful too, red-gold and brown, and a gorgeous little squirrel darted across the path in front of me, the poor little thing was terrified, I had disturbed him at some secret and delightful occupation and he'd been caught unawares, when my bicycle came upon him as a terrifying monster, bent, as he no doubt thought, on his destruction.

How lovely to be a creature of the open air, you know that lovely feeling, first thing in the morning, with the dew barely off the grass, when everything is still, and it's cold and bright, to breath in the cold air and feel the blood coursing through your whole body. An animal elation, you might say, but doesn't it give you a feeling of immense superiority, to be young and strong, and to be able to run and laugh and shout, for sheer happiness.

It seems all wrong somehow Joe, to be young and to feel all those nameless intangible desires, which can never be expressed, because they cannot be realised, while there is war and wanton destruction, and worry, and separation, because youth cannot be delayed, can it, it won't wait whilst one is preoccupied. The war has taught me many things, sharpened my appreciation of beauty, and lovely people, but it has also taught me sadness, and many things, which in my selfishness I would not have chosen to have touched my life.

I have such wonderful dreams, of life as it could be, tinged always, even in its darkest moments, with a shining beauty, which, as you say, springs from such simple, but such very big things. Don't you think, if one wants a thing which is so right, and so possible, and if one tries always to make it so, then don't you think it could come true?

After the war, darling, I think we must find a ship, to sail us to places a long way from here, wherever and whenever the whim takes us. To Africa, Egypt, America, South Seas, France, Italy – all the places we've ever wanted to see and know, and if, once knowing them, however slightly, we desire not to further our acquaintance, we shall go, to the next place, or perhaps we shall do nothing of the kind, but go and live in sin in a flat in Bohemian London, and you'll wear your hair long, with baggy corduroy bright red trousers, to proclaim the fact that you are a rotten artist, and I shall crop my hair short, and wear a man's suit, with a monocle, and smoke cigars, and the people will hail us with awe, and say we must be geniuses, obviously, or we'll go and raise pigs? Or any one of a thousand things – sensible, stupid, gay, serious, dull, interesting, sometimes we shall fight – but how wise he was – who said its good to fight, it's so unutterably wonderful to find each other again when anger is spent, and peace again takes hold. We shall fish too, if you like it, and one thing more, can we write little notes to each other? It's a childish pastime which I have never completely outgrown, I simply love writing notes about anything at all.

But enough – to practical things – if it is possible to be practical when I think that in just a few months we may be actually spending leave together, how long darling? Soon? Please?

Write – quickly and often, or else! All my love, Margaret x (for tonight) x (for tomorrow morning)

Margaret to Joe 23rd September 1944

My darling, I think if you realised how much you mean to me you might be a little anxious. It isn't that, because you are a long way removed from me, I credit you with superhuman qualities, or imagine a wonderful you, when you might not want to be at all, no dear, it isn't that, its simply that my ideals, and values have suddenly, and without apparent cause, pulled me up short, and adjusted themselves, so suddenly have they become clear, that never a day passes when I do not bitterly reproach myself for being so blind all the time, in Oban, for not realising sooner, all the things which make life worth living.

Although I have had your photograph only 2 weeks already it is beginning to look rather worn, I pretend to look in my notecase for other things many times during the day, when I'm on duty, and try to appear as though I notice the picture inside merely in passing, but off-duty, it is different, I can gaze and gaze at it, and there is no-one to observe me curiously, or to wonder at my preoccupation.

I feel so restless today, can't settle down to anything, reading, knitting, I'm afraid I can't even write an interesting letter darling, its naughty of me to write when I feel so dull, but it is comforting to talk to you, even if only in letters.

I dream all the time of your homecoming, and never neglect to pray that it might be soon, even January seems terribly far away, it should be now, this minute, even though its nearly midnight, I should die, from joy, just imagine the phone ringing, the orderly telling me its my call, answering, and hearing your voice at the other end.

Darling Joe, do you realise I have only ever heard your voice once on the telephone? It was when I phoned you from (*illegible*) – remember? And asked you to come out to the dance. That was the same day you came into the Ante Room, in mufti, and saw me talking to Soapy Lever by the fire, I wondered what you thought, because you didn't look pleased, you never really liked him Joe, did you? It seems a pity that he must change so much, simply because he is getting married, surely the girl he is marrying wants him as she knew him, not as the completely different person you describe.

That's the extraordinary thing about people, as soon as they marry, they seem to change. If there is any change at all, to my mind it should be for the good. Surely people, when they come so close to each other, that they are quite willing to spend the rest of their lives together, then surely they should be happier, not always anxious and worried. Perhaps I am too much of an idealist, but marriage suggests to me a picture of the perfect companionship, secure in the knowledge of love and trust reciprocated, and if either of these two things is not there, then such a union cannot be a completely happy one, and happiness, regardless of anything else, wealth, possessions, I think, is the most important thing in the world.

Darling, we are to receive a raise in pay this month, if you were here we could celebrate it with great enthusiasm, dearest, lovely Joe, if we don't see each other soon, I think I shall start to drink secretly, to drown my impatient misery. Then, when you see me next year, imagine your horror, when you see, confronting you, an old beery hag, with bleary eyes and a gin-husky voice, leering horribly and breathing alcoholic fumes all over you.Just to complete the picture, I think I must turn up complete with black satin and pearls, and shoes with red heels, my gosh! just imagine, I can see your face if you really found me like that, you'd be quite justified in calling one of our wonderful policemen and asking for protection.

Frankie, my brother, is to go to barracks on Monday, to wait for another ship, I'm keeping my fingers crossed, because very selfishly, I don't like the thought of his going to the next place, as it would appear that he might.

Darling, how about you? Is there a chance that you may be able to stay over here, when you come home, or shall I lose you again? We can't go waltzing off in tents Joe, in winter, we'll have to be content to go and stay somewhere where they have fires, because I'm a very miserable person when I'm cold, I just freeze up and lose interest in everything. In any case, if we lived in tents, I'd have to cook, and if we're to have the grandmother and grandfather of all celebrations, darling, there won't be time!

I think a pub, in the country, where I can wander around in slacks and woolly sweaters, and where there aren't thousands of people to bother us, and you can wear old clothes, and maybe we can even, no maybe not, cycling I mean dear.

Anyway, I'm quite certain that when you do come, I shall be so excited I shan't really know where I am, and certainly won't care very much, so long as you are there.

Are there hundreds of letters on the way? Because my limit of endurance is about 2 weeks after each letter, after that I get moody and miserable, my sweet poppet with the turned up nose, write lots more, all my love, yours always, Margaret

Margaret to Joe 26th September 1944

My dear, I have written a sea-mail letter today, explaining a number of things which could not be written in an AML, since there would not be enough room, I hope you receive it almost as soon as this, because I'm most anxious that you should know all that I have written as soon as possible.

I heard from Audrey yesterday, she asked to meet her in London, but unfortunately I'm on duty, so could not make it, however I hope to be back on a 4 watch system soon, which means more time off, and, probably, a less tired and very much happier Margaret. Her letter was short, since she had already gone on leave I think when I wrote, but very sweet. I think as soon as we do change watches again, I shall try to spend a long standoff somewhere near, so that we shall have more opportunity of meeting.

You must forgive those miserable letters darling, its just been one of those times, for the past few weeks, when its been a little too much, but I feel better now, and I find myself laughing again. Darling – you would be amused to be here sometimes, we have a lot of very old and senior officers, some of whom come down sometimes to talk to me in the Ops room, in fact, one or two have come down so frequently that somebody accused me the other day of having a taste for sugar-daddies – can you imagine me running around with old men with bald heads and corporations? The awful part is that I can say the most dreadful things to them, and they don't realise I'm being rude, if humour is in any way not terribly obvious, and in words of two syllables, they just don't get it, and tell stories, nearly always about them selves, with such heavy and laborious wit, that I know the end almost before they have begun, and the dances! My gosh, talk about the Stone Age, I have always a horror that somebody might start the Charleston, or the old Boston two-step, and Joe, they think they're such gay young blades! At one dance here, some while back, I did manage to persuade an elderly Group Captain to try some jitterbugging, and the sight he presented will take a lot of living down. Judging by the contortions of his body, one might imagine someone was standing by, systematically jabbing him with a red-hot pitchfork, and darling, honestly, his paunch literally <u>bounced</u>! But he loved it, and to my complete disgust, actually came back later, for some more, my poor feet.

However, they are not all such sporty types, some are so pompous and self-opinionated, that I long to stick a pin in them, just to see if they'd burst, I shall one day, the desire is almost irresistible, the least they could do to me would be a posting, and I would welcome that, Rank and I don't agree at all. Its fun annoying them though. All my love, I'll write again tomorrow dear, Margaret.

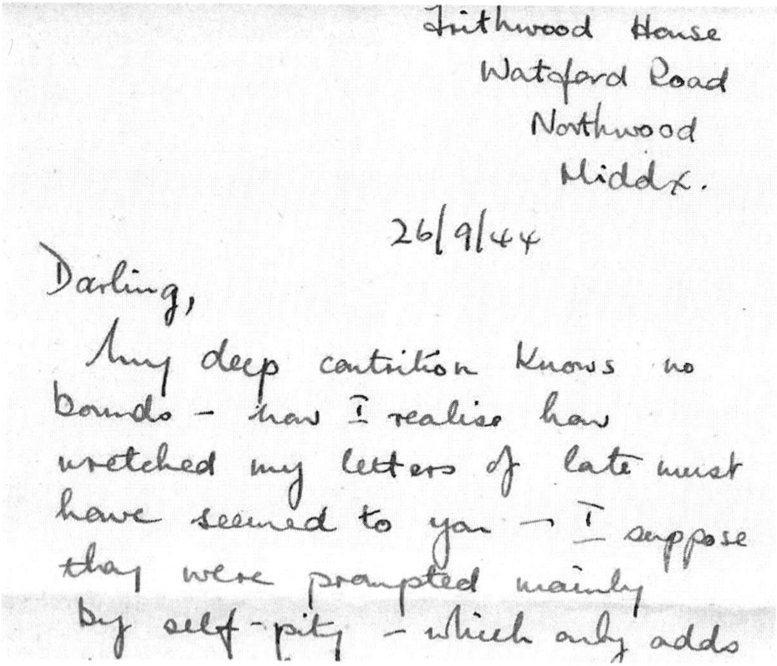

Frithwood House
Watford Road
Northwood
Middx.

26/9/44

Darling,

My deep contrition knows no bounds - how I realise how wretched my letters of late must have seemed to you - I suppose they were prompted mainly by self-pity - which only adds

to my shame, but your replies make quite clear that it's time I told you about myself. It isn't a particularly interesting story, darling, but it is one which I hoped to keep until you came home, because I felt I could express myself so much more clearly in spoken words, than just in bald statement on cold impersonal paper.

You speak of the doubt, in your mind, that you could partner me – <u>socially</u> – <u>intellectually</u> – <u>financially</u> – and you speak too, of whether you have the right to consider such serious matters. Well, darling, lets go through them, and in doing so, emphatically admit that you obviously have the right, most obviously in view of the letters I have written, which are all, with no exceptions, absolutely sincere.

<u>Socially</u> – in my grown up life I have known all kinds of people, some only very briefly, but who have nevertheless contributed to a very varied experience, one which I shall always consider valuable, and by varied, I mean from high society to slum life, which brings me to something which you must know, from the day I was born until the age of 10, I lived, hold your breath Joe! a typical slum life in the very heart of East London, next door to the Limehouse of notorious fame, not only I, but all my family, who, adorable as they all are, to me, are nevertheless quite undeniably Cockney, and, terribly poor. To continue, at 10 years, I somehow, by the grace of God,

gained a scholarship to a secondary school, and was at the same time considered for entry to a boarding school which my parents would not hear of.That, for me, started something new, because whilst studying there, I became aware of the desire to <u>know,</u> about things, my life became quite suddenly terribly narrow, suffocating, and for several years, in my ignorance of true values, I was miserably unhappy, because of that feeling of frustration, that I could see no way of overcoming, except by cutting myself free of all I had known before. This however was for a time impossible, because families are, without doubt, very important, and mine was to me very very dear, I love them all very deeply.

As I grew older I began to realise that my circle of friends were people my parents could not understand, and after a while, just before the war, they abandoned their attempts at understanding why I liked certain people and did odd things, why I spent my evenings reading heavy looking formidable books, and drawing and painting, instead of cultivating the local male population, they would at my going out to have dinner with somebody at <u>night</u>, when, of course, they had dinner in the middle of the day, bless them!

By the time I was 18, I had two sets of friends, all of whom I was very fond, but whom I realised it would be fated to attempt to mix, on a common ground.

In one of my more inspired moments, during this time, I wrote a thing in abstract, on the spirit and degree of happiness reached by a normal average person, it was terribly adolescent and completely theoretical, my mother found it lying around, and having quite unwittingly read it, wondered, I'm quite certain, poor dear, whether her beloved daughter was quite the sweet little innocent she had imagined. I think it was then that the first doubt of my strange friends crept in because until then, they had not realised how terribly far removed from them I had grown. You see – we had formed a habit of gathering in the evenings, all, as we considered in our arrogance, the local and some not so local, intelligentsia, to discuss matters which we imagined must cover everything under the sun, I laugh now, but what fun it was!

To wander off the track a little, all those people, now, are either dead or completely untraceable, they were all older than I, and I was always very flattered when they seemed to want to hear what I had to say.

But the war, and we were blasted from home, and went off to Dorchester, a beautiful spot, where, for a time, I was completely happy, but, much as I adored Mummy and Dad and my brothers, I became increasingly unable to fight the desire to go away, I had to get away, it was imperative, if I were to let my mind grow as I wanted, so, I joined up, and realised, as soon as I had gone from them, two things, first and most importantly, how much they meant to me, and secondly, that to do justice both to them and to myself, I must not ever go back to live with them again, because to do so would mean always an unhappy struggle for each one, trying to understand the other. We are not a demonstrative family, but I know, as surely as though they had said it, that they would prefer that I should not live with them, because I would cause them discomfort.

When I joined the WAAF I was commissioned after a few months and then began new and more satisfying, in a way, experiences, for instance I met people with whom I could feel free, and to whom I could talk on a common ground, not a lot of people, but just one here and there, and once again, I found life held for me the enchantment of warm understanding friendship, with people like Tom Murray and Padre Lake, you see darling, in all my 3 years service, until I met Bill Martin in Oban, I had never once, literally, become aware of physical emotion, it was tragic, for me, that I should have met him at that time, because he only ever did appeal physically, I had no admiration of his character or his outlook at all. So you see, Joe, until I met you, I had never known love in a deeper sense than that of friendship.

Then – Intellectually – darling, darling Joe, I'm not in the least bit demanding in the intellectual sense, I love books, and music, without always understanding, I love to play with words, they fascinate me, and I hope they always will, and I can, at odd moments, express myself averagely well, but only because I have known such vastly different spheres of life, in a sense it has been fortunate, but it can be so terribly discomforting sometimes to possess, as we both do, a sensitive imagination. As with so many very ordinary people Joe, I am the kind of person who dreams of great things, for other people.

And – financially – My dear, in a monetary sense I have always been poor, but count myself rich in experience and, truth to tell, am really rather proud of my history, because I have been so much closer to real life, without veneer and without the smoothing influence of money and honeyed speech than so many people, that I can place such a truer value on things, and see them more clearly, in their right perspective.

I don't think I have expressed myself really clearly, not, anyway, as I would have wished, but at least, now, you know and perhaps understand more of me. I have no real idea of the effect this letter will have on you my dear. When you told me to cheer up and showed so much of the understanding I know you possess my pen began to write of its own accord and needed no prompting to say what it knew it must.

In a most unmaidenly fashion, and, according to the views of the generation of which we are members I must say (most unwisely, which I don't believe) quite plainly that – supposing you wished to spend all your life with me, then I should not care if you had to sell matches to gain a living, if I weren't there beside you, selling them too, it would only be because I should be too busy having babies we couldn't afford, or possibly singing for pennies in the next street.

My dear, I love you, terribly, believe that, and if you ever stop loving me (you might darling!) then I shall simply go abroad, to work, to a completely new life, probably to Australia, or South Africa, where there is no chance of the disturbing influence of a previous life coming to cause unrest. That sounds a terribly sweeping statement but I assure you darling, if I lost you, I should not care ever again for another. I know myself too well to doubt that. God bless darling, all my love, Margaret

265 Squadron diary 27*th* *September 1944 G265 Kisumu to Mombasa*

Margaret to Joe 28*th* September 1944

Today is so heavenly it would be impossible to be anything else but happy. It's autumn at her loveliest. Pauline and I have been window-shopping all morning, which, as usual, has resulted in our buying exactly nothing, but wanting hundreds of lovely things we had no business to buy. Oh darling, I've just remembered, I have a lovely little rhythm for you, hope you haven't heard it.

There was a German Eagle
Who flew one day to Spain
Didn't like what he saw there
So he flew back again
And then he flew to Russia
And met a Russian hawk
Who plucked his feathers one by one
And said "Now walk you ?!! WALK!*

The two Leslies told it last night on the wireless, and the silly story about the young subaltern who went into a shop and said "Er, hev you any pepper?" The bloke said "Why certainly sir, what kind of pepper, red, white, black? We have them all!" The subaltern looked disdainful and said " Well actually what oi wanted was, er, writing pepper?"Don't you love them, Leslies Saremy and Holmes?

Joe, when you come home how much leave will you have? Because, darling, if you have a long one, and you do spend part of it with me, I'll save this quarter's leave and have, if I can, two weeks when you come home. I wish when you do come they would post you here. It's a very selfish wish because I don't really think you would like it, after being with the squadron, but it would be wonderful to see you every day.

Have you received my sea mail letter yet? The one in which I told you the brief and very uninteresting story of myself? Some day I hope to tell you, if you want to hear, not only the brief facts, but things about all that, which would amuse you, some, probably, would horrify you too, but altogether, the whole experience has been quite incredible and there are times when I have to pinch myself hard to convince myself that I'm really a living person, and that all these things really happened to me.

Joe – do you like the theatre? I know you love music, when you come home, we must go to the opera. The theatres in Town are gradually opening now, I shall make an effort to go this week, its so long since I've been and its so convenient to go from here, it seems a pity just to be lazy.

We've been on 3 watches for a little while and until we go back onto 4 there's really not much one can do except sleep and work, because to go without sleep on the watches would be absolutely fatal, sometimes I have come off night duty and stayed up all the following day, but have regretted my rashness later, when I have felt literally like a walking corpse.

You said you had sent four letters this month Joe, up to now I have had two, but no doubt the others will come along, sometimes they get delayed and then arrive in a bunch. Just a couple of weeks ago I was receiving letters written in August, one had taken over a month to reach me. Darling, please don't be sad when you write of the things we can do together, when you come back, its so lovely for me to think about them and, after all, if we both want them enough, they are bound to come true, aren't they? And thank you for telling me to cheer up, I was being very naughty, moaning so much, 3 months is only 12 weeks after all, and that's not _so_ long! Write lots, dear, all my love, yours always, Margaret

265 Squadron diary 29ᵗʰ September G265 flew back to Mombasa

Margaret to Joe 30ᵗʰ September 1944

Darling, your story of the little native boy is simply sweet, you mustn't think it is drivel, I love hearing about all these things, you see, to you, now, it is all so familiar, that you might almost, unconsciously have come to have a slight contempt for sweet little stories like that, but to me, being always among scenes and people I have known always, there is a delightful fascination in them. I only wish that I were there to see and know all that you are seeing now. It seems such a pity Joe, that the white women there become so careless in their behaviour, that's really what it is, isn't it, carelessness, it must be frightful for a husband, if he is still in love with his wife, to see her lowering her standards and being unfaithful. However, I shall bore you, I'd hate you to think I'm a prig.

Of course I remember all about our pub, and I still think it's a wonderful idea. There's a girl, or a woman, here now, who did have one of her own in peacetime, and simply loved it, she ran it just the way we planned ours too, with lovely low rooms, and log fires, and delightful people, if we had one dear, we'd be bankrupt in less than no time, because I just couldn't bear to have people I didn't like, and imagine having drunks and having to throw them out.

Darling, I hope they don't post you to another command instead of sending you home, if they do I'll have to get an overseas posting to wherever you are. I laughed when you spoke of starting to write a letter to me, after a party, and fell asleep, that's so like you, do you remember you wrote one night when you were on leave, and then wrote again very hastily the next morning, apologising for anything you might have said, I couldn't help laughing then, because you so obviously couldn't remember what you'd said, and were probably in a frightful stew about it.

Incidentally Joe, it was then that I first began to feel a little anxious, because I found myself watching for the mail every day, a fatal thing to my mind, then. Dear, the letter Daphne found must have been that one, because it was one I treasured and read a thousand times. It's really a queer feeling, that of wanting so much a person who is hundreds of miles away. But the queerest thing of all is the way it's suddenly affected me. I find I don't want to racket about as I have always done, that doesn't mean I feel dull and miserable, but simply that it all seems such a waste of time, and especially, is it stupid, when, if I do go to parties and odd things, people become slushy and annoying. That sounds like conceit doesn't it? But you know as well as I that some types will become silly over any woman under 90, if her false teeth and wooden leg aren't too obvious.

Do you remember S/Ldr Beeby? At Connel I heard from a cipher officer yesterday that he's gone down to F/Lt and is now adjutant at Oban. Much as I disliked him it's really a little pathetic because he was so proud of his little domain and so terribly much the overlord there. Apparently Roger Curzon and Leoni are not too happy, you know they married don't you? That also is a pity because Leoni was engaged to a perfectly sweet boy who was overseas before she met Roger, and just spent all her time planning their marriage when of course she had to go and marry a drip like that, I'm sorry darling, I know I'm gossiping, but honestly, you remember him, don't you, he is no more or less than a positive drip.

I shall never forget the night when Roger had been silent and antisocial for the better part of a whole year we had an after-Ensa party in the Mess, he astounded everybody and left them gasping by establishing himself very firmly in the corner with an ENSA girl on his knee, it was the blondest, blowsiest and jazziest singer of them all too. It'll be damn funny when Peter opens the golden gates and we all have to answer for our misdemeanours, old Curzon, when asked why, will no doubt answer "Gee Pete, for Lords sake, I had to sow one wild oat didn't I?" Well whatever the torch singer did, or had, it must have had some effect on him, because, shortly after he was rumoured to have spent a wicked weekend with her, he wooed and won Leoni, and in no weakly fashion, she went about cow-eyed for days.

How unkind! Me I mean, but honestly Joe, can you imagine Roger telling his son, the heavy father stunt, among other things, to avoid ENSA girls and to be a good boy, because he knows, by experience!! How terrible the world can be. Gee whiz! I can see him making a positive acre of oats, when he remembers that one!

Darling you speak of drivel, have you ever written such drivel as this? But if you don't mind it too much, I'll write some more tomorrow, and not so much scandal this time. Buckets of affection, darling, all my love, Margaret

Joe to Margaret 30th September 1944

My dear, today I am very happy, exactly why I do not know but I have been thinking about you the whole day. Perhaps it is your letters, I have read them all through again; and again it might be due to the book (Hugh Walpole) that I have been reading, as I have been substituting the characters in my subconscious mind (you see darling, you even interfere with my reading) – Yes, the story is centred around two people in love; and there again the fact that work is at an end out here for us, and the optimistic thought of being home to see you by Christmas or before, might be the cause; the last possible reason is that the lack of activity will probably allow us to go on leave in a day or so, but I cannot work up too much enthusiasm about it.

Darling, today I have had lots of funny thoughts, I feel that I am no longer just one person, but two – both of us- having a friend is so different, I have never felt this way before. It is because you have been very close to me all day long, I have been imagining you with me always, everywhere. Yes, perhaps it's the book, but it has been awfully nice and real, romancing?

Your letters are wonderful my sweetheart, I love every word of them, but from them I realise that you quite often get a wrong impression from my letters to you. In a sea mail letter that I have recently received you tell me, or you ask me, why I suggest in my letter that you are going to marry Sopey Lever? My darling, I wrote telling you that he was about to marry someone but certainly not Margaret Dillon, in any case she is my girl. And surely she has not forgotten a night in Oban when we decided to get married, have lots of kids and keep a pub? And a letter in my possession even went to the extent of expressing her willingness to have enough kids for a football team, and if it were not for this setback, (this letter suggesting that she was not sure of her man), there would have been a further letter despatched on my return, pointing out that all the best people play rugby these days, not football, which game would require a further four players to make up the fifteen, and what did she think?

Darling, if only you knew how frightened I am of loving you. I fell in love with you at Oban but you would not encourage me. Now that you want to know me, I know how deeply and hopelessly I shall want you, and if your expectations of me do not materialise the consequences would be disastrous – for me. I am silly aren't I. Love, Joe

PS I wait in vain for your photograph

13. October 1944

265 Squadron diary October 1944 "The enemy did not put in an appearance during the month of October and Squadron activities have been directed into operational training" (there is no record in the squadron diary of any operational flights for Joe in October although there were 5 training flights).

Margaret to Joe 1ˢᵗ October 1944

Joseph, light of my life and flame of my soul, to thee I would come clad in garments of flowers, sunflowers, and upon thy head I would place a crown of immeasurable beauty, protesting the while my undying love, and if perchance thou didst not return my burning passion for thee, then would I drink bottles of bloody whisky and weep buckets of bloody bitter tears, until I was but a shadow of my former self, and then would thy heart be touched, and then it would be too late, because I'd probably be dead from dipsomania, or don't people die of that? Anyway, you'd probably strut around with a chest like a pewter pigeon, and murmur sadly, "Ah yes, there lies a woman who died for love of me, telling lies? well, if you don't believe me, I'll show you the empty bottles of whisky she knocked back when I told her to buzz off! See this black eye? That was through the blasted sunflowers she chucked at me, the trouble with her was, she had no idea of the size, or the weight of sunflowers!!" Darling, lets go and eat apples in the garden of Eden sometime, only we'd better forget about the fig leaves, it would be altogether too cold wouldn't it?

I hope you are back from your trip by this time, and have collected some, at least, of the many letters I have written. The sooner you are back, the safer I will feel, from the chance of your staying there, and not coming home. Which brings me to something I've wanted to say, especially when I wrote you the outline of the good old life history, darling, if, at any time, you feel differently, even in the slightest degree, you must please say so, a change of heart is not so terrific really, it happens to lots of people, and if it happened to you, I should understand, and not question.

But what fence jumping! And egg-counting! Let us discuss less sober things, my chicken (I think that's a compliment in French, but I wouldn't be too sure) let us away to follow the will-o-the-wisp of fancy, and frolic, like the lambs, in the sunlit glow of freedom, or deep in the heart of Texas!

Darling, I hope you don't mind, but once, when you had a haircut, you looked sort of surprised, from behind, like a sheep, wot's just been shorn, I have a feeling I'm quoting somebody there, but honestly, that's just how you looked, except that sheep haven't dark hair and nice friendly brown eyes, that screw up into a laugh, and clever looking hands, did you know you have nice hands Joe? They're strong and fine, and look as though you should have been a scientist, or a musician, imagine!

Joseph Packoffsky, world famous pianist, one performance only, book your seats now, nothing less than 30 guineas. Maestro Packoffsky has to be in Paris tomorrow, New York and Rome, and then <u>Moscow</u> (pronounced with a low growl at the end, to indicate the severity of the climate – Note: care must be taken to ensure that it doesn't sound like a shiver)

Or – Lady Shoveoff cordially invites you to cocktails at 7 on Friday, to meet Jose Pac, the famous scientist, Monsieur Pac has been actively concerned for some years with research in the subject of the crossing of roads by chickens, it is his considered opinion that if a chicken hadn't attempted to cross a road in the first place, there wouldn't have been so much ado about nothing.

Tripe? Certainly, with or without? (onions)

Which reminds me, before the war, a woman cleaned her dress with petrol, BEFORE THE WAR I SAID! And put the used spirit down the lavatory, well....her husband came home from the office and found it necessary to visit the toilet immediately, he was smoking a cigarette, which he threw, also, down the lavatory, the next thing his wife knew was a colossal explosion, and upon looking out of the window, she saw her husband sitting at the bottom of the garden, with the lavatory seat round his neck. When she asked good heavens what had happened, he replied pathetically he really didn't know dear, it must have been something he'd eaten.

And now, my sweet angelic (?) darling, I must answer the clarion call of duty, I'm on night watch and work awaits, somewhat impatiently. Love, darling, Margaret

Margaret to Joe 2nd October 1944

Darling, it's a queer thing but the urge to write to you comes at the oddest times, this time its right bang in the middle of a difficult piece of sewing, which I know dashed well I shouldn't put down, but nevertheless its <u>been</u> put down, and now it probably won't be finished for another week. Tonight is the last of my first break from work for 2 weeks, tomorrow brings work, alas!

Its October now, time is passing rapidly, dear, but not rapidly enough, I'm simply dying to hear from you, now that I've told you all about myself, among all the people I have met in the last four years, only those I value, and they are very few, know anything about me at all, its strange that people never seem to be curious about one, at all, ever. I suppose it is because the numerous acquaintanceships one is bound to form develop so rapidly there is room only for superficial interest, beastly thought, that of merely flitting around and never taking root, it must be horrid to be in the service all ones life.

Curious that I should have told you about my early friendships the other day Joe, because only a day or so after I had a letter, which, judging by the crossed out addresses has been following me around for ages, from one of the lads of our old gang, he's in the medical corps apparently and he gave me news of one other boy who is in the Indian army, It still doesn't help me to get in touch with either of them, because upon enquiry, I discovered that John, the man who wrote, has also gone overseas and nobody knows where. John would amuse you darling, he's the type who saves the world, you know, good works and all that, actually he's awfully sweet, much older than we are, about 34 I think, and quite charming. Harry, the boy in India, is also older, he's a little surly, but interesting. When I knew him he was quite determined to become a priest and although quite obviously, in view of his ambition, intending to keep well clear of the feminine influence, he did just tolerate us (us being some 10 or so girls who were members of the old would-be intellectuals).

However, the ambition faded, he's now engaged to somebody hardly known to any of us, and who, as far as I can see, will make him a perfectly good wife, but who has absolutely no imagination, so how much changed he must be I can only guess.

How naughty to use up nearly a whole letter talking of people you don't know! Forgive me darling, I'm sure, really, you would enjoy knowing them. John mentioned too a girl who was the most conventional creature, who suddenly, for no reason at all, dyed her hair black, and now she can't go out in the rain, because the dye runs and makes black streaks all over her face, its dreadful, because she has a job and has to stay away every time the weather's wet, the thought of her haring madly through the streets with a streaky black face is too much for me, I give up. I'll write again tomorrow dear, all my love, Yours, Margaret

Margaret to Joe 3rd October 1944

Darling, its early morning and a day nearer your return, wonderful! Last night the wireless was giving a programme especially for people in French-speaking places like Mauritius. When the announcer spoke the name so casually, I could almost imagine you were just round the corner, for a moment it was a glorious feeling. They played a new song too, one which we must add to our collection, its called "The first few days". Among some of the junk these songwriters turn out, there is sometimes a gem, and this is one, its so true to life. Because for thousands of people the first few days of reunion will hold unbelievable joy, and so it will be for me darling, quite unbelievable.

The day after tomorrow brings another 2 day break and that will be the last rest we have for another two weeks, I am going to see my family, it should be great fun, because Peter, my 13 year old brother, has just started to wear long trousers, no doubt he is rapidly developing now, a standing in front of the fire principle, you know, hands in pockets and tummy pushed out. He's most amusing, writes delightful letters, and calls me commodore. There's another little boy too, Stanley, he's 11, and he's the King ruffian of ruffians, and can express himself with his eyes better than anyone I know. If I take him chocolate he devotes himself, for the length of my stay, entirely to my comfort, like fetching slippers, bringing cups of tea, or getting his feet mixed up in my wool, or sitting on the arm of my chair, and constantly distracting me with unanswerable questions – but - if I don't take him chocolate, I can expect the worst, like being jumped on, and having my hair ruined by wrestling, and being told that I am not a devoted sister, and suffering menacing scowls from unexpected dark quarters.

Peter is clever, he got himself a scholarship, just as Frank and I did, and is getting on awfully well at school but Stanley is one who'll probably be a rugby player or something, his teachers say he's bone lazy and prefers to play Red Indians in the playground rather than do sums, and who can blame him? Perhaps he'll be a great explorer, and astound us all. The pair of them scrap like anything but if anybody else attacks one of them the other goes to his rescue and beats hell out of the attacker. Stanley, at the moment, is keeping a very important diary and when he allowed me to read it I had to exercise the greatest self control to prevent myself bursting, because all the entries refer to fights, and whether due to his imagination or not, I don't know, but the odds appear always to be against him both in numbers and size and age of his opponents. Time for me to stop darling, until tomorrow, all my love, yours always, Margaret.

Margaret to Joe 4th October 1944

Darling, I've decided on another record, its called "Long ago and far away", and its all about an individual who dreamed a long time ago and a long way away about something, but they are not quite certain what, until now, when it's quite obvious that they dreamed about somebody who has just popped up beside them, and in whom are combined all the qualities, earthly and unearthly, which this other individual has ever dreamed about, makes you think doesn't it?

There's another one too, I'm not quite certain what they've called this one, but it would appear to be in the form of advice given to a small child – Quote – he can do one of several things, he can be a pig, or he can swing on a star, he can only swing on a star if he learns his lessons, he can be a fish, or he can swing on a star, he can be all sorts of things, or he can swing on a star, and so it goes on, personally the thought of being a fish, or a pig, or a duck, or a something else, I should imagine would be an enthralling idea for a small boy, especially if by so being he could annoy grown-ups.

To increase my discomfort when I was listening to this thing the girl who was graciously rendering it suffered acutely from the loss, I imagine, of the roof of her mouth, and also a complete inability to sound the letter "R" the result I leave you to guess. One of the airman clerks was describing to me the other day his bewilderment when, having spent 3 years in the wilds overseas somewhere, he returned to England and heard for the first time the thing called "Mares eat oats" – you know the way its sung Joe? He said his wife first of all left him staring fascinated at the contortions of her face and the strange sounds issuing from her mouth when she was singing it, he was so taken aback he was left speechless, imagining she must have been most industrious in his absence and learned some obscure language, he was, needless to say, thoroughly disillusioned later, to his complete disgust. I wonder what changes you will find when you come home, it'll be most interesting to see because there must be some, and we can't possibly notice them here, they are too close to us.

I had great fun yesterday making chocolate fudge in the hostel kitchen, first of all it wouldn't set, and the orderly and I were in tears laughing at the complete and utter failure of our efforts, the wretched thing was consistently wet, in spite of our placing it in draughts in all sorts of odd corners to freeze it. However last night when I came off duty I cooked it again and the orderly is keeping me informed by phone this morning of its progress, the latest news I have from her is that she'll have to sharpen the knife to cut it, it's set harder than we bargained for – ah! But such is life, I suppose the next thing will be broken teeth when we try to eat it. Do you mind if I have false teeth darling because I'm quite determined to eat some of it, if only to justify cooking the beastly stuff. All my love, yours always, Margaret

Margaret to Joe 4th October 1944

My darling, this is the second letter today, it's because you seem to be very close, more than usual, I could almost imagine I might see you at any moment. This morning whilst on duty I got out the map and looked at all the places you might have been to – I found Mauritius and all the surrounding islands, and even went across to India, that's an awful long way from here darling, I pray you really will come home soon. Darling Joe, if, oh gosh! Damn these ifs, Joe when you come home, and its all quite finished, lets go somewhere new, like Australia or New Zealand or South Africa (or, as I asked before, are you tired of Africa?) and do something really different. If we haven't any money, we can live in a tent, and we'll be unusual tramps, and we'll be so happy everybody else will want to do the same thing.

I'm in my room now and the wireless is on again, it always plays something which reminds me of you, now there's a programme called " In a sentimental mood" – it's got me nearly in tears, literally. Its so silly, I used not to go off into daydreams and get all sentimental but the silliest crooner can set me off staring into space now. We must have "These foolish things" in our pub darling.

Joe – I showed your picture to a friend of mine the other day and she exclaimed, "My goodness he looks naughty". She said it was the way you laughed, are you naughty? Now they're playing "Smoke gets in your eyes" – oh gosh! It's too much for me, I can picture you sitting opposite me, listening too, and smiling, ah me, isn't it funny, I can't imagine you as a civilian, not flying, and not being thousands of miles away, now just for a moment, I can't imagine myself as a civilian either, not having to do night duty, or signing passes, or being addressed as Ma'am. We've really grown up in the service, you and I Joe, haven't we? I wonder if we'll make good civilians? I somehow think you'd be rather a nice citizen, for want of a better word, or do I mean a nice neighbour? That is – unless you persist in habits like rolling home in the early hours and driving cars into trees as you did once on leave – remember?

I suspect that of us both you are the more balanced one darling, your letters cheer me up, do write and tear strips off when I get miserable, it does me oceans of good, for the last few days I have been back in my old form again, people are beginning to laugh with me again, I must have been insufferable for a little while. Bye for now my darling, all my love, Margaret

Margaret to Joe 5th October 1944

My darling, the orderly told lies, the fudge was perfectly good, I've eaten far too much and although I won't have to wear the threatened false teeth to be quite frank I feel very slightly sick.

A most amusing incident occurred the other night, Joe, I have told you often that most of the officers in the Mess here are terribly senior, a G.C. is almost beneath notice. You can imagine then the atmosphere of the Mess, very sombre, well, apparently somebody had a bet on a horse, and it won, the bloke concerned was a W/Cdr, a positive nonentity, he started celebrating directly the bar opened and became more and more excited as the evening progressed, finally he was seen to throw open the Ladies Room door and invite everybody to have a party with him, that was all right, but his appearance by this time was somewhat startling, he was minus collar and tie, and tunic, which he'd taken off because of the heat and when attempting to find it picked up one belonging to the bar orderly and put it on. Not noticing the difference in extremely lit up condition – well! – the bar orderly was an LAC, and the P.M.C. is an Air Commodore – I leave you to guess the rest.

Your letter from Ceylon has just this minute arrived, my dear, you don't still doubt what I say? Its all true, every word of what I have said, I love you and every minute makes me more certain of that, I can't tell you how or why I'm so sure, I just am, I can offer no explanation of why you seem so much a part of me. Everything about you seems so familiar, your letters seem to strike a chord inside me, I always understand what you must be thinking when you are writing, and I think you understand me too, not many people do darling, not many people know so much about me so instinctively as you. When I wrote those unhappy letters to you, you replied exactly in the way most calculated to do me good, you reminded me that we still have many happy and wonderful things to discover, you are so right darling, its almost ridiculous, we shall discover all that beauty together Joe, of that I am convinced, because I know, instinctively, that we feel the same about things, I know that you dislike ugliness and sordid things, so do I, and suppose we have no money? What difference will it make? Happiness, if measured in terms of wealth or possessions, is a poor thing, we shan't need money in that sense darling, because we are both too happy by nature to worry about such things, don't lets think about them, I can assure you they will never worry me, I have had many friends Joe and can't ever remember that the wealthiest among them was also by any means the happiest.

The happiest person I can remember is a girl who works in a factory in East London and who earns an incredibly small salary but because she never thinks of it, neither do any of her friends, the kind who last a lifetime, and those are the only ones worth bothering with after all, aren't they? Believe me darling, you have all my love, yours always, Margaret

Margaret to Joe 5th October 1944

My dearest, I felt I had to write more today, the letter I was writing when your Ceylon one arrived must have seemed so patchy to you. You see, darling, when I read it my mood changed so completely, it made me feel so frightened, the fact that you doubted me even in the slightest, you must believe how much I love you, sometimes when I am just lying in bed, dreaming, I want you home so much that it hurts, and I can't sleep, how can I describe to you how much you colour my whole life?

I go to dances, I try to be gay, and all the time I dance I half close my eyes, trying to imagine its you I'm dancing with, I imagine too that when its over, you'll come back with me and we'll talk of the people there, and you'll kiss me goodnight, that's the hardest part of all, sweet, to know I can't hear your voice, touch you and hold you, all the rest is easy, I just have to close my eyes and I can see your face and my imagination does the rest for me, but the dream doesn't last, when I open my eyes you are gone, but more and more I find less need to will you closer, because you are there with me all the time, sometimes I find myself not doing things because I feel you wouldn't like it, and other times I feel so happy because I know you will understand the things I do, and why I do them, it's a beautiful feeling darling, to be so sure of your understanding that I can be completely natural.

You have me excited too Joe, what is it you have brought from Ceylon? Do tell me. Darling, for Christmas I going to send you a large framed picture, it's not perhaps an imaginative present, but, short of coming out to you myself, that is the thing which will let you see perhaps how much I want to be with you. I should like to have sent it without telling you, but in case it doesn't arrive I'd like you to know so that I can perhaps send another. I've used the word "perhaps" 3 times in the last few sentences which shows that my brain is moving too rapidly for clarity, there is so much I want to say, but dare not, I shall wait until you come to me and then say all that is in my heart.

Have you received all my letters dear? I've written seven in about 5 days, I try to write every day, because I hate the thought of there ever being a mail day for you with no mail from me. Dear lovely Joe, if you come home next year, I shall be quite stupidly happy, but darling, if you have to stay longer, or go to some other place, I shall wait for you, even if we are both old and grey by the time you do come back, be happy darling, love me and know that I love you too, with all my heart and soul, and it will last, always, or even longer than that, believe my words, words seem futile, but until you come, they are the only way I can show my love. Bye for now dearest, yours always, Margaret

Margaret to Joe 6ᵗʰ October 1944

My darling, It's nearly midnight, the wireless, a faithful companion, as you will have gathered, is playing Hawaiian music, soft and enchanting, it brings to the mind a lovely picture of lazy beauty, a gorgeous scene of blue sea and velvety sky, and stars like gems, framing an unbelievable moon. Although such things can be seen in so many other places, to the non-travellers, like me, Hawaii must inevitably be tied up somehow with blue sea and a full moon, you see the power of advertisement! When we start our street corner match selling we must certainly advertise darling, make people match conscious, we'll be millionaires in no time at all.

I suppose you must be back in, or shall I say, you are at "home" again, by now, don't go off on these trips too often dear, because its just possible that on one of them they'll keep you there and you are quite far enough away now without going further. Darling, is Jack Barber still flying with you? I wonder what he thinks of Daphne's marriage, its funny to realise that she's been Ainsley's wife now for a year, it all happened so suddenly that I can't really believe, even now, that it really did happen at all.

Joe – you have never said whether you received the picture I sent, its quite a small one, maybe it's lost, I hope not because the larger one which will come about Christmas will not be such a good one, or shall I say, that was terrible, but this one will be even worse, false modesty!

Pauline's mother, you would have laughed if you could have seen us, after dinner, Mr and Mrs Vickers and I sat by the fire, Mrs Vickers was knitting and so was I, by the end of the evening I felt so domesticated and aged I could not recognise myself, we talked of operations! Of all things, and of course bombs. As I left the door of the flat to come back to Northwood I felt at least I should have a bath chair and a fond grandchild to wheel me down to the station. I was asked if I knew any new stories and had to place great restraint upon myself to try to sort out which ones I couldn't tell, believe me, because honestly Joe, I just haven't the first idea what civilians think about or what kind of stories they like, the ones I know are none of them strictly drawing room and I know I should be ashamed to admit it. Ah me! I feel we shall make very odd civilians some of us. Do you think they will call us "ex-servicewomen"? what an awful thought, whenever I hear that term I always think of a great big wench with a terrific bosom and about 3 chins, charging down the main street corners and running clubs, you know, hearty all girls together, and don't let the side down, can you imagine? I think I'd almost rather be the dissipated old hag with bags under her eyes and black satin with red-heeled shoes, that I described in an earlier letter. Take very good care of yourself, my sweet, you are a very important person and January is not so very far away now, I love you, all my love dearest, yours always, Margaret

Joe to Margaret 7*th* October 1944

My dear Margaret, I am doing as you suggest and writing a sea mail letter, just a few lines at odd moments. This first addition (sic) may not be very successful as I am sitting on a veranda and the rain is dripping through the palm leaf roof onto my papers. The strange thing about this letter is that I wrote an A.M.L. yesterday, and well, damn it, I have never done such a thing before in my whole life! – what are you doing to me?

Yesterday I went into Mombasa with the express intention of buying some little things to remember Africa by, when I got home I could not decide on anything however, although two beautifully carved elephants heads caught my eye, I will go again and beat him down. Everyone buys elephants in Africa, the country is full of them.

I did buy Audrey a little handbag, mainly because it is made from lion skin, it is quite nice. The best and most expensive bags were made from Zebra skin, very silky (brown and white stripes) but I wondered if a lady would appreciate it? Do write and tell me if you would like me to get you something of that description, the only difficulty is, it would probably not be possible to send it by mail. The cloth you asked me to get is difficult, since it is imported, and cannot therefore be sent by mail. But I may be able to work something. When I get to Nairobi I intend going through the native shops with a fine toothed comb and get those things that attract me, I am already looking forward to showing them to you. I hope you like them darling. The shopping must be done before I get the taste of the demon alc. However because this will probably be my last trip before I am "on my way" – wistful thinking?

Nairobi 9th **Oct,** There are lots of things I want to tell you darling, the most important is, just in case you are not absolutely certain, that I love you more than anything else in the world and quite certainly more than anyone else and I want to always be able to love you, in fact to be your man. Since leaving the "Horseshoe" where I have been drinking brandy with some Pongoes (do you know the term?) I have been looking forward to subsiding under my mosquito net and writing to you, because I feel so very near to you when I write, dear – may I call you that?

In spite of what Blondie said (the girl who almost had twins) I want to tell you lots of things that I shouldn't – I hope you get the gist of this and really do not mean to say things that are not nice about Daphne. But, darling, please, I want to live with you always, I only want you to be nice to me, love me a lot, and tolerate me. I loved you so hard at Oban and you are making me love you again, much harder, so, darling little girl, there is nothing for it you will have to marry me won't you, it is the only thing – please. My elder sister has married a man who drinks an awful lot and she claims that man speaks the truth when he is drunk. That may not mean a thing my darling, but I am a trifle tight now and write things I would not write when sober, but please believe me they are so very true. I remember very clearly when I pointed out to you (this was at Oban) that I could not say clever things at the right moment (we were drinking at some place) you told me how relatively unimportant it was. And I know that night (I really knew it before) how grand you were, and darling, during the following days I was to understand you so perfectly.

I remember you now with Padre Lake and lots of friends and I know that I loved you wherever you were, with friends or alone. And again I marvel why a person so charmingly lovely should also be beautiful too – it rarely works out like that, so many charming people are seemingly gifted to cover other apparent lack of charms. Please let me be the only one to hold you tight and love all of you, as I used to. The next time I shall be so very careful with you, because it is so different, you love me too, now. I would like to write and tell you how, how I long to hold you, both of us belonging to one another in every possible way, as only we two can love one another, darling, but there are so many reasons why I should not. It has been my misfortune to censor many letters of men to their wives and girlfriends. Most of them seem to drip everywhere about love and so on, it usually seems very unreal and artificial, they have probably been out here a good while. Let not your boyfriend follow their example.

As you may have guessed the leave has begun. Bill and I were due to leave Mombasa from here by train at 16.30 yesterday. 13.00 witnessed us at the Mess bar, Mombasa, fairly tight together with a few Fleet Air Arm "bods". A chappy with three rings suggested our going to Nairobi with an Air Arm kite which was leaving in 10 minutes. My next really conscious moment was seeing six cases and a large and fairly tight naval pilot standing near a two seater Defiant. The three of us arrived in three individual pieces, strangely enough, and we all said nice things about one another, being by now sober, but the whole thing was a little, well, you know... The 75-minute flight saved Bill and I 17 hours on the train, although we had to sleep on the floor of the officers club each in company with a large stomach of bad beer which is all this war-exploited town can provide.

Tomorrow I will spend the whole day persuading myself to send this letter because I may decide that it may make you angry although really my darling I write very sincerely, as a matter of fact I am quite sober now. There is not much room left on this page so I will stop tonight but feel I should point out that I love you much more than you think I do – yes.

Brackenhurst Friday 13th (in bed) Writing to you is so very difficult because I am apt to forget what I have already written in letter cards. I told you about Brackenhurst I think. I am getting in some tennis now, and am secretly thrilled to find that the old torso is getting back to normal again, in fact I feel quite fit. Between you and I Margaret, your boyfriend is quite proud of his physical being.

Brackenhurst is believed to have been the holiday venue for officers. Joe and Bill Graham, Joe's navigator, were the only officers in his crew, the NCO's would have had their own holiday place.

The people here, I believe I mentioned, are a well-practised bunch of snobs who love scandal of any description. Those folk with little money do not exist in their world and, although some of them are clever, they have very small minds. In the company of friends everything is "perfectly lovely my dear" or "absolutely divine" and they all "purr" beautifully to order – but they are all cats anyway. However I am being entertained almost gratis "one must do something to help those poor, poor boys my dear" and we shall be needing lots of money soon – right? Lets not ever become affected in any way my sweet, you and I, we can have lots more fun loving everything and everybody.

This is believed to be Joe at Brackenhurst

Part of this letter appears to be the work of a small boy not yet in his teens. A wise man would not risk his girlfriend by sending such a letter. This particular one thinks that his Irish sweetheart should know what a hopeless person he is, so he is chancing it. She will find out these things sooner or later – so what!

She has been known to be crazily lovely herself at times and, damn it, why should not a fellow write when he has been drinking.

Which reminds me of another point that entered his beer-sodden brain on the night of Oct 9th – if this woman of mine continues to end her letter with Yours always and such things as that, she will be taken literally and that will be that, and perhaps in years to come she will find herself with a son or a daughter, as well as a husband – you see the danger? And this husband will be much more trouble than the kids.

It is your fault that I write like this darling, it is because I love you, always your, Joe

Margaret to Joe 8th October 1944

My darling, night duty again, I really like watch keeping, it makes the time go very quickly, although for me it still doesn't pass quickly enough.

Joe – what do you do, all the time when you are not flying? I try to imagine but it's such a strange life you are living now, and in such different surroundings to these, it's almost impossible to judge. To travel and see all the different customs and scenes of other countries would be marvellous, but just recently I have come to realise a great love for English countryside, its so clean and beautiful, and all the people who have always lived and worked there seem so much part of it, to take the people from their places, and leave the country empty, or to put the people in a town, each would be tragic, I'm sure our lovely country would be less beautiful if it did not know how well-loved it was.

Today I found an old copy of Men Only, there was an article written by a man who loved Kent, your home county, he described the fruit trees in blossom and the effect such a scene had on some American visitors who were so taken aback by such fresh beauty they were quite silent, for the first time in the narrators experience. I wish I could paint all these things, not just reproduce the colours, but to express the enormous surge of emotion they provoke.

One of the loveliest memories I have is the first sunset I ever saw, at Oban, do you remember how heavenly they were Joe? And sometimes they were reflected on the Mess windows so that instead of one there were two or three suns setting on darkened windows, and the colours in the sky were quite breathtaking. I remember describing to Judy Read one day how I felt about things like these and I was horribly disappointed when she replied in a matter of fact voice "Yes they are rather pretty" Pretty!! I ask you – how can such a word describe beauty like this? Nevertheless, I think Oban has had some effect upon even our materialist Judy – because she has twice been back on leave, and as all the people we know there have gone, it must be the place which draws her back.

Tomorrow is Monday, I almost always hear from you on Mondays, all tonight will be spent in hoping, for 9.30 tomorrow, and for the postman to bring that which means most in the world to me, next to your homecoming.

Darling, your picture is getting terribly worn at the edges, I feel that it must without doubt be afforded the protection of a frame fairly soon or I shan't be able to keep it any longer in my notecase. It's an awfully little part of you to have but if I hadn't it now, I should feel completely lost. I told you it wasn't possible to meet Audrey on her leave darling, because of watches, but have written her, and will certainly go to see her on one of my long stand-off periods, when they start again. All my love dearest, yours always, Margaret

Margaret to Joe 9th October 1944

My darling, I thought all my air mail letters were used up and then quite suddenly found this very crumpled one in the pocket of my raincoat, I suppose it must have been there for weeks, since I rarely use the raincoat anyway.

The hoped-for letter did not come this morning but I am away now until after tomorrow's post so have merely postponed the eager anticipation. No doubt I shall sound terribly naive and adolescent when I say that it really is wonderful to be able to write you every day, but I do think it is, considering how far away from me you are, it's a comforting thought that wherever you are we need never be out of touch. Writing to you now is a big part of my day, Nancy, my roommate, has been away for 3 weeks, but much as I like her, I do like to be alone when I write to you dear, and she came back today, I think I must go each day and lock myself in the bathroom, practically the only room in the house where one can be quite alone. Imagine the confusion you will inadvertently cause among 20 odd women with me in the bathroom staunchly refusing admittance to all comers and determinedly writing at great length.

Darling, have you received any sea mail letters recently? I like writing more than an AML will hold, that is the reason I write them. This will be a very dull letter because I'm terribly tired having been on duty all night and now find I cannot sleep, even now when its 5 o'clock and I have been off duty since 8.30 this morning, can't imagine why, overtired no doubt. I wish you were operating over here, I should know what you were doing every day then, and would know when you were in or out, but still it isn't long now darling is it? I loved your stories about the natives, do tell me some more, I want to know all about everything which interests you because I'm sure they will interest me too. Did you get the hat with the red tassel? I do hope you could, or there will be a very disappointed little darkie about somewhere. And how about your leave? Will you be getting it after all Joe? A lot of your 300 hours must be done by now, will it still be around January?

I'm home just at the moment, my small brother has made me some coffee, it strangely resembles a cup of tar, I hesitate to drink it, but he's watching very closely from the corner, so in the cause of tact and diplomacy and for the sake of peace and quiet, I risk severe poisoning. Ugh! It's simply ghastly and I have to look pleased! Write lots dearest and say you'll be home soon please? All my love sweet, yours always, Margaret

Joe to Margaret 12ᵗʰ October 1944

My dear Margaret, It is a strange thing but whenever I find myself alone I want to write to you but that is not the only time that I am thinking about you. I wish you were here now, dear, this Kenya is very lovely. I am on leave at Brackenhurst which is a spot about 30 miles east of Nairobi and the house at which I am staying is surrounded with lovely gardens.

Another picture of Joe at Brackenhurst

The flowers, English flowers, are wonderful, the birds are singing and there is green grass everywhere, there is blossom in the fruit trees too. There is a crisp tang in the air and all around are high hills covered with green vegetation – although near the equator this part of Kenya is 6000 feet above sea level making it cool.To me this is heaven and it makes me feel very homesick.

The people whom I am staying with are very kind but extremely highbrow and I do not know anyone. I could find some friends, or at least make some acquaintances, but as yet, I feel I do not want to, I want to go for solitary walks alone with my thoughts, perhaps you think me foolish, I probably am. There are some tennis courts nearby, perhaps later on I will find someone to play with, do you play tennis darling? And I have often wondered if you play bridge too? There is a hotel quite near with a wizard bar and log fires (in the evening) – yes, I have already been in – pity.

My mail may be spasmodic as there is no place to post it, even Nairobi is difficult. The base P.O. is holding your mail at Nairobi for me and since leaving Madagascar I have already had an A.M.L. – your letters are wizard. Yes darling, we will spend lots of leave together if humanly possible. I should get 3 weeks and ought to spend about a week of it at home, how I am looking forward to it although the thought scares me a little.

You were with Pauline when you wrote and I do hope you had a happy time together, are her problems solving themselves? Have you seen or heard from Audrey? Mum tells me (very secretively) that there is a romance in the air, he will have to be good because Audrey is my favourite sister. Goodbye for now my sweetheart, love, Joe

Joe to Margaret 14ᵗʰ October 1944

Margaret sweetheart, I feel almost apologetic about writing to you so often, it seems that I write every day. Roaming around the countryside makes me think of you, perhaps doing the same in Wales, although no doubt you are now back at HQ. To me you are always very feeling as your last letter portrays you. As to how you are looking I can only guess, as I have only seen you in service dress, which is a little severe. Do you ever wear slacks darling? I imagine you in your costume, I am sure you look your best that way but I shall get a big thrill when I see you in a dance frock. Actually I don't care a damn how I see you as long as I see you soon, in fact soon is not soon enough, I want you now.

If we are able to spend say 12 or 14 days together how shall we spend it? It depends on the season I suppose and it will probably be wintertime. We could spend it in London, go to lots of theatres, have lots of parties and see lots of wonderful things, in fact make whoopee the whole time - would you like to do that dear? And again we could go out of London and spend more time really together, it would be more difficult to fill in the time as there would be fewer dances and parties and things. What do we both want out of this leave dearest, please wire and tell me, you can put into words those things that are often a mixed jumble of thoughts in my mind, so write and tell me what you think, please.

We two individuals will have to adjust to quite a new way of living after the war. The RAF to us both is our lives; 4 and a half years for me in the service is almost the only grown-up life I know. It has given me lots of fun and has made me realise what wizard people there are in the world, and what it has taught me is beyond my power to write.

Nevertheless service life is a little unreal, lots of important things in peacetime seem to become unimportant and it is almost unnatural – the war makes it like that. I wonder how you feel about these things?

Sorry about the serious note my darling, now that I have read through my letter I realise what a failure I have made of what I wanted to write. Your man is far from perfect, darling. Love, Joe

Margaret to Joe 17th October 1944

My dearest, It came – after haunting the Mess all day, trying not to look as though I were waiting for the mail, I gave up and went to bed for two hours before going on night duty and then – when I got up late and had not a minute to spare a well meaning but not very wise cipher type said there was a letter for me across in the Mess – well! – needless to say, caution was thrown to the winds and across I sailed, and of course took over my watch late, I could hardly explain that the importance of my letter quite exceeded any other thing in the whole world, even a war!

Darling, your talk of coming home is very cheering, I'm keeping as many fingers crossed as is humanly possible, and, just as you do, spend literally all my time dreaming. Can I bear you? Oh my dear! – can I bear you, come home soon, you will see how much I want you, much more than I can say in a letter, and your lovely description of the evening spent with Bill and the S/Ldr bears out an instinctive feeling I have had for a long time, that we shall, if we wish, be terribly happy, intuition you might call it, do you believe in a woman's intuition darling? I do – especially when my intuition absolutely refuses to be silenced and troubles me insistently with a conviction which grows until really it becomes so firmly rooted in my mind that I realise with a shock that it has become, in my inner self, an established fact, and a very necessary part of my life, this dreaming of what I wish could be.

But darling sweet, to be a little practical for just a moment, you must tell me quickly if you have yet received my sea-mail letter telling you something of myself, my childhood, I know it isn't really important, not to our two personal lives, which belong to us alone, and which, quite secretly cannot be touched by other people, but on the other hand dear I love my family very dearly and they, if we belong to each other finally and completely, to be frank, if we marry, and darling I must be honest and admit that I do want to be yours - then – they must become part, even if but a small part, of our lives – and Joe I'll try to make myself clear about this, they and I for some time too, have lived the kind of life which is so different to perhaps the one you have known, that perhaps it might be a little difficult for you to understand them.

Don't mistake my meaning my darling, I would not ever allow my family to influence my feelings for you, but if we are to spend our lives together, you will see dear, won't you, that first of all you must know and accept all there is to know about me. But in spite of, or maybe because of, all that I know, so surely, that if you really want me, we can be two very happy people, I think I know how well we could manage our lives darling, and I think perhaps you do too, even if, as the conditions after the war might indicate, we may even have to sell watches to enable us to be together. To be with you always would be not a condition which I would have to bear, but one which I could not bear to be without. All my love my dear one, yours completely, Margaret

Margaret to Joe 18th October 1944

My darling sweetheart, it is late and I must tell you that I have been to a party during the whole of which I have wanted you so badly that it is almost too much to admit even to myself. There was a man there who looked at me in such a way, the way in which I want only you to look at me, because it is only to you I can allow it and, my darling, it is only to you I can answer. I imagined all the time that the person beside me was you, adorable you, and when I accepted a mug of beer, I said thank you, but inside I added "darling", and the person who lighted my cigarette was really you, but he didn't know it.

Joe, my sweet darling, its next day now, I'm afraid the party last night proved to be just a little too much for me, I fell asleep whilst writing to you and now, looking back, I'm really rather ashamed to see how much space I've wasted of the letter. Last week I was able to go and see Pauline, since an old Oxford was going and the pilot kindly offered me a lift, and, even more fortunately, I was able to fly back again, this time in an Ansan, rather amusing really, because the pilot of the Ansan thought I had never flown before and watched me with great interest, no doubt hoping I'd be sick. He also suggested I should sit up in front instead of the Sgt. Navigator, I declined with thanks, I have a shrewd suspicion he intended me to wind up the undercarriage, and I'd been caught that way once before.

It was a wizard trip back, there were really far more bumps in the train going out to Northwood than in the air. I wish they'd let me fly, even if only for a little while, maybe until I grew tired of it, as so many pilots seem to be. Joe – I've been thinking, darling if you are likely to be home fairly soon, I think it'll be better to save my Christmas present for you until you come, and I can give it to you myself. The thought of actually seeing you soon is a very wonderful one and one which I almost dare not believe. Is there any more news yet dear? (did you have a good leave?) Write soon, all my love, yours always, Margaret

Joe to Margaret 18th October 1944 Brackenhurst

Darling, Yesterday I went into Nairobi and found five letters from you awaiting me at the Base P.O. Sweetheart they made me wonderfully happy, I did not know mere words could have such an effect on me. And strangely enough I now look forward to writing back to you, it is because you almost appear in person while I am writing. I will not answer your letters now.

There are four Italian P.O.W's working here and I got quite a kick out of taking their photograph the other day. They insisted on putting on their No. 1's, shaving and so on and I am getting them each a copy to send home.

The four Italian Prisoners of war.

It seems so wrong that they should have worked on the gardens for two whole years and yet they are very happy and seem wizard fellows. One year seems a hell of a time to me, and I have been free, almost, thank God they will not keep me out here for more than 6 months more, and it had better be less. Your picture when it comes will help a lot dear.

I am having quite a good leave, the people where I am staying are a little more human now, I believe I have made them that way. I spend most of my time playing golf, but the shortage of balls is difficult. The little black Jo-Jo's (caddies) run a black market in balls and on losing a ball one is liable to have the same one sold back the following day, perhaps by the caddie who lost it! I humour my boy by giving him an occasional cigarette and it has made him almost honest. I was amazed to find that Brackenhurst is 7300 feet above S.L. and 36 holes a day is very tiring, in fact I am scared to play the highest hole for fear of passing out through lack of oxygen! – pause for laughter – sorry, do you play golf darling?

There are two honeymoon couples living at the hotel, they are the butt of many jokes, although everyone is secretly envious of them. It is quite a spot for a honeymoon as the guests live in separate little cottages, beautifully furnished, each with a lovely log fire at night and separate bathrooms, does it appeal to you darling?

Audrey has written and is madly happy. Her boyfriend came home with her on her last leave and I believe she is engaged, she seems awfully young, I do hope everything will be OK because she is a sensitive kid, I should not like her to be hurt badly. Bye for now, dear, shall be writing again tomorrow, Love, Joe

Thinking of Oban reminds me that when I met you there I was never quite at ease. And I know now it was because when I met your friends and acquaintances I felt like an outsider, who would soon be leaving and really had no right to butt in. It will be grand when we can both have the same friends and know the same people, I wonder if you realised how I felt at Oban? I am a strange person and suddenly find myself going shy and reserved for no reason at all.

I am awaiting your sea mail letters with great interest telling me of Ireland's most amazing phenomenon, Margaret Dillon, the girl who when she thinks about herself just has to laugh! Darling, your humour is wonderful, I envy you, it is one of those things that make you so lovable to me. When I get your letters, probably around Christmas time, I will despatch to you by return, a complete unabridged version of how one, Joe, of country fame, left it at quite an early age, worked hard, to find about 10 years later that he was in the RAF and had got absolutely nowhere, in fact they have not even given him his two rings which are due.

Your brothers must be grand kids, I wish I had a brother. You must feel quite parental towards them with your 23 years? I was amused at your first efforts to make fudge, you will have to do better than that you know. A magazine cover I saw gave food for thought (?) It showed a young couple (arm in arm) looking up at a notice board on which evening classes were being advertised. The pictures left everything to one's imagination.

So you want to go to Australia or South Africa, well well, we shall have to talk it over, what a difficult woman I have to please. Perhaps we could afford Europe for a couple of weeks but would that be far enough for you? It is a good thing I realise my responsibilities!!! – Ah me, yes I am saying it now.

You may gather that I have been trying to answer your last letters, or at least letters you wrote a month ago. I, too, find myself not doing things that I would have done if I did not know you. Whilst in Nairobi we usually find ourselves girlfriends to dance and flirt with, because we see none for months. But I have no inclination what so ever. And there are lots of other little things too. I have learned to play squash too, only because I knew you played it – silly is it not? I bet you look funny playing squash, lots of love, Joe

Margaret to Joe 22nd October 1944

Darling Joe, how inadequate letters are! And how foolish to dwell on platitudes of that kind, but then how true that particular platitude is!

This afternoon I went to bed in preparation for night duty tonight and in that hazy moment between sleeping and waking I thought of all that I wanted to say to you, but when I sit down before my letter I find there are no words to express all those lovely disturbing things I feel, indeed, when I remembered all the letters you must have read from me I can't help thinking they must be very dull for you, perhaps I never shall be able to say all that to you, but darling, I think somehow I shan't have to say anything, you will know, as surely as if I could tell you in words.

Tomorrow is Monday again, the start of another blighted week for the poor postman, who is becoming accustomed to a fierce-looking WAAF Officer coming upon him suddenly from behind unexpected corners and demanding mail in a threatening voice. Do you know, I've just noticed that although our handwriting is not really similar, we print almost identically, it might almost be a letter from myself I receive sometimes when I see the address. But I couldn't write to myself all the sweet things you say. If it were possible for me to judge you impersonally, Joe, I should say, to quote a Canadian phrase, that you were "nice people", and darling, from a Canadian that's quite a compliment, I mean an impersonal Canadian, <u>but</u>, it is really quite impossible for me to see you from a detached view because I love you too much and feel you too close to me.

Joe – it is fortunate that we are so much alike in some ways, because we are darling, have you noticed? Tomorrow I'm going to see my family for two days, I wish it were you, for two whole days, away somewhere, just we two by ourselves, dear sweetheart, it makes me very happy to think of you, but oh dear, I get so very impatient with waiting, it's very unreasonable, because even now you may be home long before I dreamed even in my wildest moments.

Nancy, my roommate, has just been posted and they've put a newcomer in my room, it's all very difficult, because Nancy and I were used to each other, she was a terribly sweet person, and understood my "thinking moods" perfectly, always having the tact to leave me severely alone when I wanted to write or just daydream, but alas! the comforting presence of Nancy is now a thing of the past, and instead, a large person with big feet insinuates herself into my thoughts and demands my attention quite determinedly, and I don't know her well enough, or like her enough, yet, to tell her to beat it. The first sight of her person, which really is very large, opened my eyes just a little wider than usual, but when she appeared one day attired in a voluminous dressing gown in PALE PINK, it was almost too much for me, I hope my gasp went unnoticed. Here's where you call me cat, which I shouldn't mind so long as you say you love me in the same breath. All my love, dear one, yours always, Margaret

Margaret to Joe 23rd October 1944

My darling, in one of your letters some weeks ago you mentioned that you still hadn't received my photograph, just in case it has not even yet arrived there is enclosed some tiny miniatures, I do hope they get to you. Is there any more news of home posting dear? This year is very short now, it seems incredible that in a month or two I might actually see you.

I'm at home at the moment and feeling just a little disappointed, Frankie, my sailor brother, has been home for one day, unexpectedly and had to leave early this morning, so I just missed him, but he has left word that he may be back again in a week or two, so there is a chance that I may see him then.

Joe – these little pictures are really rather weird, I had no make-up on and was photographed literally in the raw, I happened to be passing the polyfoto section in Selfridges some while back, and the idea seemed rather fun, so in I waltzed, the result leaves me wondering whether it was really wise, but still, I want you to have some kind of picture, and at the moment, having sent you the only decent one I had, and it not having arrived, these funny little things are the best I can do. Please don't mind them too much, I'm saving, or rather I intend to save a decent one which is being done, to give you when you come home, it may be better to save it darling, because if you are likely to come soon it may pass you on the way, as it will certainly not be ready for at least a month.

Are you well dear? + happy? No more sad moods? Mine have had no chance to rear their disturbing heads because pressure (line!) of work has been too entirely absorbing, I should be quite happy to work like a black until you come home, with time off to dream about you every day, work helps to quieten the longing for you which never in one degree lessens. All my love darling, yours always, Margaret

Margaret to Joe 25th October 1944

My dearest, you ask me to try to express what we both want from this leave of ours. For my part darling, first and most importantly, I want to be with you, have you completely to myself, for as long as we can possibly be, I want to give you the opportunity of knowing all there is to know about me, because, Joe, really you know very little of my life, which has been, in many ways, not an ordinary one. Sometimes I have a feeling, no doubt it comes to everybody at times, that there are big and wonderful things I can do, I think we could do these things together, we both have a vivid imagination, whereby ideas are born, it remains only to have the courage to carry them out. I don't mean that we should attempt to build wondrous careers, or be famous, or anything so <u>ordinary</u>, but just, oh well, I can't explain clearly, that must be one of the things we'll talk about when we go on leave.We could spend part of it in London and be quite mad and then go off to a quiet place and talk deep and serious things, really and truly.

I heard from Audrey, but she hasn't written since she returned from leave, if your news of a romance is well-founded she'll have no time, dear, to write to people, in any case you'll be home soon, we must meet her together then perhaps she'll bring her mysterious romance along, we could have a sort of whoopee party, that's an idea Joe, lets do that? I've an awful lot of drinking time to put in with you Joe, just to celebrate, because, still, I so rarely drink I've almost forgotten the taste.

It's sweet of you to ask about Pauline, yes, fortunately everything is clear for her now, except for a rather horrid memory, she has nothing to worry about, except to try and forget the wretched man, who has subsequently proved to have a most doubtful record with women. It's had a queer effect on her though, she's quite suddenly almost hard and slightly unapproachable, no doubt she will adjust herself when her emotions have had time to get back to normal, but I'm still surprised, I should never have imagined Pauline to become embittered over anything, but I suppose the experience was no ordinary one, I'll tell you all about it someday, Joe, it has an aspect which I think might amuse you slightly.

I must tell you all the shows which are running and you can tell me which ones you want to see, darling, as soon as you know anything definite will you please let me know somehow, by cable if you can, I want to know the minute you actually move, I might even know you are here, somewhere, before you can get in touch with me, and Joe, directly, absolutely the first minute you can get to a phone, will you send me a wire, its safer, but if you can get to a phone I might be in and the number is NOR 2200 EXT 178 or 247. Remember, please, I must know the very minute you are here. Put the number in your inside pocket somewhere and please don't forget will you? All my love, darling, yours always, Margaret

Joe to Margaret 27th October 1944

My dear Margaret, it must be almost a week since my last letter, so long ago in fact that I cannot remember if you know of my recall from leave. Anyway it happened, the Gods decided that I should do a training course of one week and rather than take one of the many idle crews from the squadron, recalled us. Needless to say no one has taken any interest whatsoever in the course – fair enough? Fortunately only four days of the leave were lost and we have all returned looking very fit and feeling quite a lot better mentally.

I have bought some Indian embroidery work, unfortunately it is only a yard in width but it looked pretty and I bought it, what it could be used for I leave to your imagination, it is an Indian sarong. If I send you a few odds and ends in a parcel could you hang on to the things that you will not want until I get home? I will write and tell you all about the contents after I have sent it, I am allowed only one 8lb duty free parcel a year and most <u>non</u> duty free parcels are eligible for 100% duty!! Damned pity.

Darling, my hopes of returning to you change almost daily, so I will try and give you the set-up (as much as I can without being court-martialled) and you can work it out yourself. You will appreciate that work is finished here for obvious reasons and the yellow gentlemen do not come this way. But there is always a possibility of something turning up while Jerry has ports. Query number one, how long will he last? When he finishes there is no reason for us to stay unless we go east. But obsolete household pets are of no use to anyone therefore they must be sent home – get me? At the very worst I will not be here for more than 18 months which is exactly 6 months from the time you get this A.M.L.card. There is rather more to the story than this my sweetheart but perhaps you form your own ideas from these pointers. Personally I am still favouring January in my optimistic moments and I pray God it will be soon. How about getting one of your sugar daddies to post me to U.K.? – lay on the sex appeal or whatever it is you get 'em with. Lots of love, darling, Joe

Another picture from Brackenhurst with an interesting swimming hat

Margaret to Joe 28th October 1944

My darling, I've had a distinct feeling all day that I shall be seeing you very soon, there's no reason, apart from the news you have given me, except possibly wishful thinking, I've been thinking all the time, you see, of our leave, and since your last letter, mentioning that we may be able to have two whole weeks together, I have asked the Senior Plotter here if I may save this quarter's leave, and have two weeks at very short notice, and Joe, it's all right! – I shan't believe it until your voice really tells me on the phone, or a letter from inland, and I actually assure you that I'll meet you at a certain time, and a certain place, and that we shall stay here or there, for this long or that, darling, I'm just a little frightened too, its been such a long time since we met and there is so much to explain isn't there? For <u>me</u> to explain I mean.

Joe, do you think the first few days we are together we could be really gay, and just not talk about anything really serious, except just that it'll take me many days to become, or at least it'll be many days before I stop pinching myself, and probably pinching you too, my dear one, to make sure you are real, and then, oh! Gosh – what point is there in measuring such a leave by days, it'll go so quickly, but two weeks! We mustn't let anything happen to stop it, we just mustn't!

You know I have the most exquisite dreams, about you, I'm losing a lot of sleep over them because they come to my mind so overwhelmingly, and the thought of dreams like these ending is a loathsome one, I wish I had no need of sleep, I wish too that I could write them all down, I have tried, but my pen fails me here, to express such things would need a truly great writer and it seems pure impertinence for me even to try, darling, darling I love you, I wish so hard that we shall be happy, I pray too that when you see me again, the feeling I know you had before, will not have lessened and that in your face I shall see what I hope to see.

I'm rambling, but you remember how you described your confused thoughts? – that is how my mind is now, all the time, with only one clear thought, you know what that is darling, but I can't tell you too often, I love you with all my heart and although I want many and varied things, quite badly, none of them could ever mean anything if I couldn't have you – and dearest Joe, do you know just how much I want you? Judge by the un-ashamed admission, shorn of any vestige of maiden modesty (?) if such a term could possibly be applied to the female gender of our generation. By the way sweet, I don't play bridge, you must teach me, and the dance frock, can you possibly wait until, anyway, some time hence? In our, or at least <u>my</u>, companionless state pretty clothes are things to dream about, but as soon as it can be done darling, it without doubt will be, for you. All my love dearest, yours always, Margaret

Joe to Margaret 30th October 1944

My darling, today I am very sorry for myself, in fact I am living in morbid self-pity and my only hope of sympathy is from you, dear and you are not here. Yesterday I returned to Madagascar and within 3 or 4 hours of landing lost my wallet. I am not usually careless but these damned silly shorts have such hopeless pockets. Normally I get drunk and do not worry about such things, but darling I have been trying so hard to save money and my last month's effort just disappears into thin air. It is hellish disappointing because money is quite important to me (us) now.

There was a letter awaiting me on my return in which you asked if I had received your sea mail letter and you made some references to your folk, which I could not understand. Your letter will probably arrive about the end of November. Please do not worry about anything sweetheart I am a very easy person and if necessary can be very flexible. The only possible thing I can think of, for your doubts, is that you are RC and I am C of E. But is that so serious? I shall look forward to writing and putting your mind at rest, we must let nothing spoil the happiness I am sure we can enjoy together.

Whilst at Mombasa I met a Canadian friend (a radar nark) and he was leaving for Cairo and UK. He asked if he could take anything home for me, knowing that I had bought odd curios for my people at home. The result is that a box of odds and ends is now on its way to you dear and perhaps you would send part of it home, but let me tell you what I have sent.

This fellows name is F/Lt Maltby by the way. There is a leopard skin bag, I thought you might like this, for when you are in civvies, and a small lion skin bag that I intended giving my sister's child, Sheila. I have sent the Indian stuff I told you about in a recent AML, do exactly what you want with it, the size is so awkward it will probably not make up into anything. The little dog was so beautifully made I had to get him, I have his brothers and will send them sometime. The two ivory heads on ebony may not make the trip in one piece, I think they are wizard things, we may have someplace to put them one day, and the dogs too. The tortoiseshell buttons from the Seychelles islands may look OK on something, if you do not want both sets, perhaps Audrey could do things with a set. On second thoughts hold everything, I will take the little bag when I see you and the other things you will not want, hope you like everything. Maltby hopes to be in UK by the end of November. Lots of love, darling, Joe

Margaret to Joe 30th October 1944

My own darling, time is passing quickly now, it's only 7 weeks to Christmas, shall I see you before then I wonder?

Today brought one of those minor upsets which can bring one's soul down to a grey drab existence, which seem to drain the mind of all joy, that's how it was, until with happy persistence the thought of you pushed itself to the fore of my mind, and with a mental shake, I could laugh at myself for dwelling upon such unimportant and joyless things, and so, when my "cross" returned, I faced her cheerfully and with a mind not darkened with dislike, and darling, she returned my smile and everything was all right again.

I wish it was possible to take from life all hate and unworthy things, there are such lovely things which could keep them out, but, this adolescent rambling again, forgive me dear, but you do stand for so much that is happy in my mind, and the thought of you is a sure cure for so many stupid moments. It seems such a pity that so many people now see things in such a distorted light. In a place such as this where there are bound to be gathered a number of people who have seen much of service, and war, the most obviously disillusioned, and also the most obviously inspired are bound to stand out very clearly, and really its very hard to find any people who are truly sincere in motive, conscious or unconscious.

I was talking one evening to a WRN officer here, she was bemoaning the fact that nowadays she could drink indefinitely and it would give her no kick at all, and went on to remark quite seriously "What the hell have I to live for if I can't drink?" – darling, can you credit this in a woman of 31, young, attractive, a good if completely unused brain. I can't, but then my life quite suddenly has become exquisitely full, with thoughts and plans centred around we two, Joe dear, please don't worry if I think about you too much, if you knew the amount of pleasure it gives me, you wouldn't mind at all I know.

They have been playing some Ink spots records tonight, we are going to have lots in our pub aren't we? All the nicest and most familiar ones, you know, maybe, and whispering grass, and every night about this time, I think just now the fat one is my favourite, especially about this time, its just after nine, the wireless is on faintly and the most beautiful log fire is burning in the grate, darling, what is it about a fire which brings things to such peace, it's this time of day, by the fire, when you are closest to me, I can imagine you almost sitting near me, so near that if I reached out my hand, it would find yours, I could say something, and imagine your voice answering, soon we shall do all these things, don't you somehow feel, as I do, Joe, that we can find peace together, not dullness, but sure happiness, as well as gay excitement.

Frankie, my little brother, knows about you, Joe – I think Audrey must be close to you, just as he is to me, and he wants to meet you, I do hope you are home before he leaves the country, I want you to know him so much.

I'll write again my sweet tomorrow, my letters to you have been sadly neglected for the past week, simply because we are on short watches again and time has never been enough to fit in necessary mundane things like washing etc. I can't do you justice in between washing smalls. All my love darling, yours always, Margaret

14. November 1944

265 Squadron diary November 1ˢᵗ A/S up 0400 Diego Suarez down 0920 Port Victoria. F265 struck a reef at 0845, aircraft written off, no one hurt. Crew returned Diego Suarez 9ᵗʰ November (this is the 3ʳᵈ aircraft written off – Ed. The following 2 letters must have been written before he took off, and the letter dated 6ᵗʰ November was after the write-off but only refers passingly to it)

Joe to Margaret 1ˢᵗ November 1944

My dear Margaret, it must be about a year ago when I saw you disappear from view in a southbound train from Oban. What a send off you had? I do not know quite why I came to see you off because I was trying to forget you then. For no reason at all I felt self conscious and foolish and very much out of place with your firmly established friends. And when you had gone it seemed that I had lost something that could not be replaced although not seeing you around the Mess to constantly make me miserable was a relief. A few days after you left I too travelled south and left 'Batten on the 7ᵗʰ Nov and quite truthfully I was very happy to leave, there was lots to keep my mind occupied. Let us hope that our next parting will be <u>very</u> different and <u>very</u> temporary, right now the thought of meeting you is very frightening, I am sure we shall both be distant, but not for long!

Madagascar is the same as when I left nearly a month ago, although the monsoon wind has stopped for a while. My leave is in the very distant past especially the coolness of it, as it is summer here now, and one gets wet with perspiration, just sitting. My extreme low spirits touched zero when apart from losing my fountain pen and wallet I awoke the following morning to find that the mice had been at the "other" dog! I nearly wept. These disappointments are being slowly ousted out however and I am living again. You must be rather curious about the dogs that I have told you about, in fact you might even think that I am now completely round the bend. But really my sweet when you see the one I have sent you will want to put him on your dressing table and leave him there, but he will be lonely without his "Cheeta" brothers.

We here are now thinking of Christmas due probably to the Christmas cards that have been distributed. I do hope you get better shifts for Christmas, I am always feeling that you are working too hard dear. Don't overdo it, complain or see the M.O. or something, it would not be unpatriotic, there are so many people doing nothing. I wish I were able to look after you, Bye for now darling, Joe

Joe to Margaret 1ˢᵗ November 1944

Margaret sweetheart, I must write to you tonight because it may be almost 14 days before my next letter to you will be on its way, as I am going on detachment; your letters may not reach me for a fortnight too. The radio is wizard tonight, I am sitting almost alone enjoying it, the rest of the Mess being below the bank at the open-air cinema. Old Churchill is a little disappointing suggesting that the European job may not be over by the end of the year, lets not agree with him this time?

The little Malgashe boy did not get his hat when I returned from the mainland, do you remember? He came running up to my hut quite early in the morning as soon as I was awake and asked me about it. I had to tell him that the shopkeeper in Mombasa had sold out and, as he looked disappointed, gave him a pair of my worn out black socks that I had. The socks apparently were almost as valuable to him as a Fez because he went away quite happily. When I see him now I ask why he is not wearing my socks on his bare feet, he finds it quite a big joke – but, damn it, when he smiles I do too! I have asked him to get me a crocodile skin, but will be away in the morning before he arrives.

There has been quite a lot of talk between the officers in the Mess about going east with bigger and better kites, some of them almost want to go. Searching my mind I find that I too would like to find new adventures and see fresh countries eastward if I had not that burning desire to go home. And my only reason for wanting to go home is you, darling, and I shall not want to come back, in fact I will not as I will have completed two tours. It was quite a shock to me when I realised you and you alone was pulling me. It will be nice to see my Mother and folk of course but there is a big difference – now.

Darling, do I usually remind you that I love you on the first of every month, because it is the first today. Please God let me be with you soon, Joe

Margaret to Joe 2ⁿᵈ November 1944

Dear Sweetheart, your new snap gave me a big kick, in fact very soon it's going to be as worn as the first one you gave me. You look very tanned darling, and awfully fit, quite a he-man in fact.

The news of Audrey is good, I expect she is longing to show you to her man. How old is Audrey, Joe? Darling, will it really be another six months? It seems such a long time, but still, it will give me a little time to get some pretty clothes, I do want to look nice for you Joe. It would be nice to go to far places with you, but really and truly I don't care where we are, it would be absolutely wizard to be stationed together for a while, I warn you Joe, I shall pester you for the monopoly of your time, for a little while, until you refuse to do it anymore, you'll have to write or phone every day without fail, will you promise to let me know the minute you arrive in the country? And, Joe – if you land up somewhere in the North, please meet me in town, on your way home? Even if its only for a few moments, oh gosh! I wish with every bone in my body it were now, this minute, it's pouring with rain, but if you were here I should run, bareheaded, all the way from here to London if necessary.

I'm afraid golf is another of the things I've been too lazy to learn too, will you teach me? And what do you mean by suggesting I'd look funny playing squash? Although, as a matter of fact, now I come to consider the matter, my legs are somewhat comical. By the way, darling, I believe my elderly admirer (do you remember? – the G.C. with the cow-like expression?) has at last been shaken off – Nancy – my ex-room-mate sent a friend of hers up to Command with a message for me, and I had a noggins with him in the RAF Mess, the dear old faithful saw us making mild merriment and, Joe, believe it or not, he took umbrage, and my life once again is free and there is no longer the need to look cautiously round corners before turning them.

Is it really only a year since you went? – but Joe its more than a year since I saw you, and believe me dear one, it seems 10 years at least, I wonder if you will find me changed? I feel I must have changed quite a lot darling, since Oban. Do you know the clearest thing in my mind about the people who bid me farewell on the station platform was a thought which came to me when I saw you coming along with Jack Barber, that you didn't look well, each time I looked at you, you turned your head, and never said a word, and as the train moved out, I could still see you standing there, with that white look on your face, and no smile, were you feeling ill darling, or were you still just a little sore with me?

Come soon Joe, there is so much time and so many things to make up for. All my love, darling, yours always, Margaret

Joe to Margaret 3rd November 1944

My dear Margaret, Once again I am in the Seychelles and this time probably for a long stay. There is nothing wrong with that except for the fact that mail may only be fortnightly, or even longer, on the other hand frequent calls by odd A/C may improve the situation. This drivel about mail might seem a little unnecessary darling, but it is so important to me, please forgive me.

It would be wonderful if you were here with me. The Seychelles is a group of volcanic islands in the Indian Ocean, the type of tropical island one reads and dreams about. The hills rise almost sheer from the seas and are covered with very green trees intermingled with coconut trees. There are little birds to be seen, vividly red, green or blue and the flowers are magnificent. The local town, like all native towns, is something of a shambles, but the native is a good type and hardly smells at all. It differs from others insofar as the people all wear clothes, European clothes, but no shoes of course. The women are <u>always</u> dressed in very clean and usually white dresses and they wear wide brimmed straw hats, which went out of vogue in England about 12 years ago.

This evening I went out sailing in the harbour, it was wizard, you would have loved it dear. The water was very clear and the bottom looked fantastically beautiful, it being coral and like the birds in the hills the fish too were of many colours. Cloudy Jim and I returned from our trip just as an almost full moon began to silhouette some small islands out to sea. Darling, I must be sentimental because the scene was so lovely that I wanted you to be with me and enjoy it too. Can you imagine it, the moon at the side, the terrifying black mountain ahead with twinkling lights on it, the fireflies darting over the surface of the water and a barely audible swish of the boat going through the water, otherwise silence.

This may be the boat trip Joe refers to.

Our honeymoon must include a moon, little girl, and lots of water, but not a large town, please? It does not really matter providing we have one another I guess. Lots of love, darling, Joe. PS Will try and get another letter off to you tomorrow... because the mail leaves the morning after.

Margaret to Joe 4th November 1944

Darling, its just 2.30 in the middle of the night, night watch again, I've just finished wading through a whole pile of work and my eyes are being most difficult, refusing to stay open. I had my hair cut today, not very much shorter but just enough to take it above my collar, just in case one of our beringed jobs gets ideas, I should not like to be shifted from such a convenient spot now that you are so soon coming home. I shall post this tonight darling, as soon as its written, so please forgive if its badly written and perhaps a little abrupt, its only because I really am very sleepy, but still must talk to you before I go to sleep.

Joe – you never told me much about your bomber command life have you? I often wonder about it, because I haven't the faintest idea of what kind of station a bomber one would be, it must be quite different to Coastal, will you tell me when you come home? You did write a little about it once, when you were home on leave, but I want to know lots more. Joe dear, I don't know if I mentioned this before but if you happen to see Soapy Lever again you might like to mention to him that a friend of his, by name Hugh Sheldon, is stationed here and has been trying to trace him (Soapy). I expect your leave is finished by now, but still, every minute brings you nearer home dear and your homecoming.

I'm going to get my head down now, dream with me darling, if you can bear to dream of yourself, because mine are all of you. Good night, dear sweet Joe, I love you very much, all my love darling, yours always, Margaret

Margaret to Joe 5th November 1944

Darling, I'm at home today and at the back of my mind, all the time, I can't help wondering how this love of ours is going to work out. It has never occurred to me before, because, you see, until I realised how much you meant to me, my plans for a future life after the war were so very detached, and far removed from the life of my people, but now, when every moment of my time is subconsciously spent in planning to be with you, I can't help wondering just how they will affect you. After all darling, I have known them all my life and understand them well, and quite truly love and respect them, but it would hardly be fair to expect you to see them as I do, I who have known them all my life, and you, who have not even met them. However, when you come home, during our stay in London, we shall see them, and then darling, I shall know.

My sailor brother is home this weekend, he may be going away in several weeks, its so sad really, because since I told him how much I think of you he is most anxious to meet you. Almost every time we meet he has some girlfriend problem he wants straightened out, and this, dear, at 19! – although it's hard to believe he is so young, as you would agree if you knew him.

My fathers young sister, she's 28, it seems silly to call her aunt, is to be married in two weeks, her fiancé is just back after <u>3</u> years abroad, one year seems a lifetime to me.

Darling, in your picture you seem to look a little older, have you changed very much, I'm rather afraid I have, but perhaps it's because I've grown quieter and don't waltz around so much.

I suppose marriage is a gamble, but just like you, it's a gamble I consider worth taking, and in a my case, I want you so much that I honestly wouldn't say no even if my reason told me it was all wrong – which it quite definitely doesn't, everything about you, to me, seems right, the feeling that you understand and would know my feelings about things, and your ideals too, the things you want, are just so like mine that it <u>must</u> be right. Oh Joe, whatever we do, whether it comes out right or not, I love you quite terribly and if I lost you it would break my heart. Keep on loving me darling, I need you more than I have ever needed anything in the world. All my love, my dear, your always, Margaret

Margaret to Joe 5th November 1944

Darling, I got your letter today explaining about the chances of coming home, I want to see you desperately, you know that, but Joe, dear, if we are unlucky and you have to go on further my love goes with you, and I don't care whether its another ten years, I'll just sit and wait until you come.

Its funny, darling, but in the anteroom tonight some of the WAAF were talking about the different types they had met in the service and for no reason at all I suddenly thought of Daphne and the mean little thing she did, although to you it must have been an awfully big thing, and as I sat and thought about it I saw more and more clearly how terribly hurt you must have been, Joe, how could you bear to write to me again, believing that I had done such a thing? – and how could one human being do such a despicably mean thing to another? When you told me at first, I was so completely taken aback that it really didn't register at all, but whenever I think of the immeasurable harm it might have done, I shudder, and thank heaven you were sweet and good enough to tell me about it, and to have believed me when I told you the truth, that I honestly didn't know your letter was there, even doubted that it had ever been there, in the Mess, as Daphne had said. The only reason I mention all this again is because it might so easily have caused me to lose you forever and, dear sweet Joe, when I think of that I put the thought away from me as being too dreadful to contemplate.

Joe – this parcel you told me about has made me quite excited and terribly curious, what is inside? – and darling, directly you have <u>any</u> idea at all about coming home, even if it is only a hunch, please let me know, because I want to know whether or not to send the second photograph, it seems so risky darling, you have never had the first one have you? However, as I told you, I have sent off for another decent one and it should be ready in about four weeks, have you had the little ones yet dear? Mummy says she thinks they are awful, but even so, at least they look something like me, which is more than one could say for most pictures, which I think suffer considerably through too much flattery.

However, if I'm going to work on my sugar daddies to get you home, then beauty sleep is indicated. Good night my darling, all my love, yours always, Margaret

Joe to Margaret 6th November 1944 Seychelles

Margaret darling, this detachment here at Seychelles has proved disastrous. The treacherous coral reefs have already taken their toll, the result of which is yet to be known. But the trouble is the opening of the local hotel at

11.00 hours and with a gang from the squadron – well I leave everything to your imagination. The scotch beer costing 3/6d a pint seems to matter not at all, and this midday session continues later at the Mess, two or three hours sleep and the party goes on, it is the fourth day now. Fortunately we are breaking up tomorrow, I am hoping to go back, I miss your letters darling.

Please excuse this one letter, Toto but I am a little sodden mostly with bad South African brandy and although cold sober, my head is far from clear. I should not really write to you now but when there happens to be an A/C carrying mail bags to the mainland I feel that I should be letting you down if I did not get something off. And I do love writing to you Margaret, you know that, but sometimes I feel a chronic hopelessness, you and England seem so far away as to be impossible. England does not matter too much, I can live without my home country, but not without you my darling. When I receive your letters I take on a more normal attitude towards life but without you then life falls flat. Sorry about this self-pity but you mean so much to me, I love you so very much.

Please is your photograph on its way? – I must have a picture of you, do you think you could send me a snap in an Air Letter Card? Your letters are never opened. Write often darling sweetheart, your letters are all that I have of you for a few more weeks…and then..my thoughts make me tingle! Always yours, Joe

Margaret to Joe 9ᵗʰ November 1944

Joe darling, for the first time in many months I have had a really lazy stand off, just sleeping and sitting listening to the wireless, sewing, its been so restful and lovely, especially as we have a roaring fire inside, and outside it's cold and the leaves are blowing about, making little swirling pools of brown and gold. In a short time I have to go down to the village to get some air letters, this is my last one, I can hardly bear to leave the fire, the wireless is playing Forces Favourites, at the moment it's the Andrews Sisters telling us about a place called Massachusetts, and I am sprawled on a low chair, in slacks and a frightful old polo-necked sweater, if the Squadron Officer comes in, no doubt a none too friendly glance will be directed at me, but I couldn't care less, anyway, she ought to be thankful I've just had my hair cut simply on her account, and having a haircut is something of a major ordeal, for me.

Darling, when you come home, how long will you be here? Will you have to go abroad again? I wish I hadn't changed my job now, I might have been able to be stationed with you, but even so, miracles do happen, maybe we can do it anyway.

Joe, I've been thinking about your dance frock idea, maybe I can make one, what colour do you like? By the time you arrive here Joe, all the theatres should have some awfully good shows, several new ones have started only recently. Its too bad you aren't here now, before the winter really sets in, Autumn weather for our week in the country would be absolute heaven, even if you couldn't bear my ropey old slacks and sweaters, but it doesn't matter in the country darling, does it? – if you could possibly look as ropey as I, they'd probably think we were millionaires or something equally incredible.

The hostel cat has deceived us cruelly, here we are, believing we have been harbouring under our female roof, for the last three months, an invaluable tom cat, who keeps away the mice, and now, to our utter and complete horror, we observe that said cat is about to produce offspring, we are very hurt, and not slightly disgusted, it doesn't even look like a female cat, or at least, that's what the people who know these things say, and now it moans around the place looking extremely sorry for itself, and nobody knows what should be done about it, however, write many letters darling, without letters I am lost. All my love darling, your always, Margaret

Joe to Margaret 10th November 1944

Margaret my darling, I can now sit and write to you with your photographs on my knee, yes, I received them yesterday, darling they are wizard! Sitting here with a glass of Guinness by my arm and looking at this wee picture of you makes a perfect setting for writing to you. Although I thought I knew exactly how you looked dear, 14 months from you had distorted my memory, you cannot know what these little pictures mean to me!

Like you my life is now full of thoughts and plans for the future, our future. I get a hell of a kick out of it and would love to tell you of the silly things I think about. I am vain enough to dream about life with you darling. But my dreams soon veer to our meeting when I get home and I feel almost frightened, frightened at the thought that something might happen to prevent it, frightened that when we meet again, something might go wrong. You mean everything to me, dear, I know just what you <u>could</u> mean to me and I know that I could make you happy too. The reason I even worry about the outcome of our love is that I have always been a pessimistic type of person and for the last ten years have been trying to live down an inferiority complex.

Damn, I did not mean to get serious in this letter, I am always wandering off that way! Yes, we must leave the last part of our leave for that, and the first half, whoopee! Gosh, this thought of London with you all to myself, darling! You were going to teach me something when we were together in Oban, remember?

That kid sister of mine is engaged, what a shocker she is! Apparently Jack may be going out East when this thing starts in earnest and they think that there is no point in waiting for the end of the war. Mum thinks that they are rather young but Dad has taken a fancy to Jack and thinks there is no point in waiting. Audrey and Jack have vague ideas of marrying in June or July, wouldn't it be grand if we were engaged? We must see if we can put up with one another first – give me a chance!

I must tell you a little story. While at Seychelles I saw several chickens chasing a green lizard. Seeing me, the lizard ran towards me and stopped within a foot of me and the chickens would not follow. And there it remained with half of its tail off and part of a leg missing, looking up at me. It was very pathetic, I should have killed the lizard. All my love, darling, Joe

Margaret to Joe 11th November 1944

Margaret to Joe 11ᵗʰ November 1944

Darling, there is just one more mail and then no more until Monday morning. In a short time, but not before the postman has been, I must go to bed, to sleep before night duty, and I have all my fingers <u>and</u> thumbs crossed for just one letter, what are the chances darling?

You asked in one letter how Pauline's troubles were sorting themselves out, well, apparently she's managed to clear up the whole thing, I think you can guess how, and is now feeling absolutely wretched about the whole thing, but she'll be happier in a short time, when she's had time to forget all about it.

In a couple of months or so we are to start attachments to stations, an attachment usually lasts 3 weeks, I hope and pray you don't arrive whilst I am away, but, Joe, the duty Plotter at Command would always know exactly where I was.

As a matter of fact I've often wondered if there might not be something in the sugar daddy idea, but darling, quite honestly, I'm not quite certain quite how much "sex appeal", as you call it, would do, I suppose holding hands might not be too unpleasant, but if they become really amorous, I should probably do something quite drastic and get you landed in the Pacific for the duration, my gosh, I shudder at the very thought. In any case I believe I could stand a sugar daddy just so long as I kept my eyes shut, but they might not take such a good view of being with somebody who appeared to suffer permanently from sleeping sickness.

Last week there was a most amusing American here who informed me he thought I was "It", I'm not quite certain whether he was being complimentary, but felt rather like a cross between a seventh row chorus girl and Mae West, and wondered if I ought to start chewing gum frantically whilst doing something queer with my mouth, you know, the old nasal out-of-the-side of the mouth, "Come up and see me" etc. However, I thought the best idea was simply to fade very gently away, while I was still under the impression that the remark was not meant unkindly. So, remember Joe darling when you come don't tell me I'm "It", unless you can also tell me what our dear American friend meant by it, it has a most extraordinary psychological effect upon my sensitive (?) feelings, I think I'd almost rather be called a buxom wench.

No mail came, so here's waiting for Monday, all my love darling, yours always, Margaret

---

Joe to Margaret 15th November 1944

Darling sweetheart, I have just received the two sea mail letters from you written on the 8th and 9th of Sept, the ones about Oban remember? Darling it was lovely of you telling me about everything, it made me feel very happy about some things, and "we two" as we are now, seems almost feasible instead of a wonderful dream. Gosh, its wonderful having you to love, to look forward to you and make fantastic, no _real_ plans for the future, but I am cheating, I dream about them _now_ and I have three tiny little pictures to help me, although I used to dream before I had them.

Margaret, sweetheart, I will not answer your letters now because last night when I crawled under my net I thought of the things I wanted to write you and they came so easily but now there are lots of distractions.

Darling, did I tell you about the slippers I bought for you at Seychelles? I know you will like them. The woman who sold them, whipped off her shoe for me to show that they would fit. They will look nice with _the_ costume, because they are mostly black (I'm crazy to see you in civvies) The material for the nick-knacks you wear underneath is not forgotten dear, I may be able to get some parachute silk through, would that do? Or would you squeak? Maltby, who is bringing the first consignment, on all accounts, had a quick trip home. He may even write to say Jambo, might even ask to appear in person and you would like him darling I am convinced, although he is not the man who leads the party.

I have been fortunate enough to pick up a Penguin book called the Cherry Tree by Adrian Bell, you would love parts of it, do try and get it, I like his book because I understand and appreciate it all, his characters are real. But if you should read it don't get worried little ToTo I shall never be a Farmer. And whatever the Gods decide for me, damn it, it doesn't really matter because we shall be together. Did you know I love you? J

17/11/44 Joe promoted Flight Lieutenant with effect from 1 November 1944 (this is just days after writing off his 3rd aircraft on 1st November!)

Margaret to Joe 17th November 1944

My darling, I have been neglecting you badly this week, its all because one of the Plotters went sick and left us on three watches and, bang in the middle of all the muddle, I had to get a cold, and spent several days being extremely sorry for myself. However, just like a cold, it has cleared up just as the watches have also cleared up, so everything in the proverbial garden is lovely, except that I do miss your letters darling, I know you can't help it, because you told me you would be able to send none for two weeks, but alas! two such weeks might be almost years when one has grown into the habit of post watching.

We had a session this afternoon of discussing plans for a discussion group, you know, like the things we had in Oban, and having gone only because I was expected to, and having also decided to say absolutely nothing, I held onto my self control until finally I just couldn't bear to listen to the damn-fool remarks people were making any longer and started talking, imagine my horror when I found that everybody had stopped talking and I felt a battery of eyes turned upon me, the attempt to slide down in my chair and disappear gently from public view failed miserably and the next few moments were spent in parrying words with all and sundry, sharp and telling blows coming in rapid succession from all directions , however, once I fairly got my balance, I sat up a bit straighter and managed to answer more or less coherently the critical, if not always constructive, questions of my attackers, heigh ho! Such is life, I intend to do one thing and then do the exact opposite, you'll have to watch me like a hawk darling, if I promise you steak one night you'll probably come home to find fish, or if I go out to buy some stockings, I'll probably come back with anything but stockings – but I'll try so hard to be practical, and sensible, and if I get the temptation to sit down and write stories when I should be doing something else, I'll exercise all of my will power and be frightfully stern and then probably you'll think I'm about to throw a fit or something equally dreadful and just become absolutely petrified, but if you ever find me just a little too much to bear, just remember I love you darling, and then you'll forgive me, won't you? Write as soon as you can, Joe, all my love darling, yours always, Margaret

Joe to Margaret undated postage-free RAF Christmas letter "Greetings from East Africa" assumed to be about mid November 1944

GREETINGS from EAST AFRICA

F/o S.T.PACK 136647
265, SQUADRON.
EAST AFRICA COMMAND

My dear Margaret,

To try & write something seasonal six weeks before Christmas, & in a hot climate, presents difficulties.

I would wish you a white Christmas, but it'd be dirty & slushy in town, but I can wish you lots of fun & parties, many presents and a sincere hope that you will be home at least some of the time. Darling, us both pray hard that we spend our next Christmas together, somewhere, in fact anywhere — but together.

When I think of Christmas and all that it means, my thoughts go back to my childhood days. My Christmas began to grow on me when the shops began to brighten and I would give serious thought to finances because everyone <u>must</u> have a present This would be followed with numerous secret lists (with costs) and my sisters and I would mention quite casually, so very casually, any particular thing we wanted, knowing full well that many ears were waiting for just such a remark. The buying and hiding of the presents was always most thrilling and they would be packed and repacked in coloured papers and a Christmas card slipped inside.

Carol singing with the village choir on Christmas Eve began Christmas proper. Later I gained proficiency with hand bells and would return home, pockets stuffed full of nuts and oranges, feeling very tired, very full, but very happy. Getting home late gave me the opportunity to put my sisters presents on their beds while they slept, ready for the morning, but sometimes they would only be pretending to be asleep.

Damn silly thinking about these things now, but rather pleasant. Christmas Day mornings I shall always remember. Everyone so very happy, trying not to like one present more than another for fear of hurting the other's feelings. And Dad and Mum pretending that their presents were things that they had wanted more than anything in the world. Later the Christmas morning service with carols, the church having in some mysterious manner become gaily decorated overnight. And the turkey, Christmas pudding, threepenny pieces and.......Sorry about all this sweetheart darling, this is not much of a greetings letter, all I can really do is to send you all my love and hope you have a whacko Christmas. Bye darling, Joe

Margaret to Joe 18th November 1944

> Darling,
>
> This morning its simply ghastly outside – blustery + wet + horrid – just the right sort of day to stay in by the fire – but I can't – I have a flight of airwomen – who are literally the bane of my life – they find out where I am – it doesn't matter where – + pounce upon me with passes – + moans – + lord knows what else –

one's lost a pair of gloves, another is undergoing 7 days CC and her husband has suddenly come home on leave and she still has 3 days to do, another has jaundice, and so on, ad infinitum, and now, just because the hostel is really warm for once and again, just because it's a shocking day, they have to have a dance, and I have to stagger round the camp demanding P.S.I. money from people and smiling sweetly at NAAFI women, when all the time I should like to swear at them, especially the one here who has false teeth which don't fit properly and every time she argues or gets excited, they slip!

I had a letter from Pauline today, she seems to be getting over her nasty experience quite well, I must remember to tell you all about it darling when you come home, there's a lot which I can't tell you in a letter, quite apart from the fact that I'm quite fond of Pauline, the whole thing was to my mind a perfect study, a cameo, of human nature.

Darling Joe, I wonder where they will post you when you come back? I suppose if you are not going to do another tour, it will be to a training station won't it? I think I must go back into Admin, where there might be a chance of being stationed with you, or at least somewhere near. As it is at the moment Joe, the job we do here is the only one of its kind, which means we are without doubt here for the duration, which is really most convenient for me whilst you are away, but when you come back you might be stationed miles away and I want to be as near you as possible.

I wonder if your friend Maltby will have any news of you, I hope its possible for him to come up to Coastal, or at the very least to write, because I want to ask him thousands of questions, the most important one you can guess, I wonder if he will have any idea? Now I must venture forth into the storm, mount my gallant steed and hop away to get weaving, this wretched dance. Bye for now, all my love darling, yours always, Margaret

Margaret to Joe 19ᵗʰ November 1944

Darling, I was really awfully sad about the loss of your wallet, but I believe I have now written two letters and not mentioned a word about it, I can't really imagine why because I can feel exactly as you must have felt when it happened, but I'm so happy now that you feel better about it, in any case please don't worry about money darling, it doesn't mean a thing to me, in spite of its apparent importance, we have no need to worry too much about it, there are many other things of far greater importance, in any case Joe, there never has been a time in my life when I have had a lot of money, and quite frankly have never coveted it.

There are times when I think of being with you that it seems it would be wonderful to be able to wear lovely clothes and look beautiful for you so that you would be proud of me, but still, I can look at least quite decent, and anyway, that's the only reason I should want lots of money, and I don't particularly admire a woman who wishes for nothing but pretty clothes. I have been raking round darling and have heard from several people of decent places to stay in the country, some of them sound simply lovely, but perhaps there is a special place you want to go to?

Darling Joe, I'm so impatient to see you, the time is not so long now, sometimes it is incredibly difficult to imagine seeing you in just a few months, and other times it is almost too much to bear just waiting even that short time.

The larger photograph I promised you is terribly long coming, I expect its due to the Christmas rush, darling, it will have to be a flat parcel, is it worth sending to you now? Let me know if you can, soon, and if you think it's worthwhile I'll despatch it directly it reaches me.

I hope to see Frankie tomorrow, he has just finished a course and may know by now whether he is bound for far places. I believe I told you that Margaret, my young aunt of 27, was to be married this week, its been postponed for a week, fortunately for me, because I couldn't have gone today, her fiancé has been in Ceylon for 2 years, shore-based Navy!

I wish to goodness it were you here instead, nasty thought to express, but human. All my love darling, your always, Margaret

Margaret to Joe 21ˢᵗ November 1944

Dearest, it is so many days since I last wrote, but your letters came in two batches, and somehow I had to wait until they had all come, and I had the complete six. You are an absolute brick Joe, I just honestly didn't know that any human being could be so utterly sweet. Its incredible, darling, that you understand about me so completely, you might almost have a secret light which could see into the deepest and most securely hidden recesses of my mind. I have told Mummy and Dad about you and they have seen your pictures. Darling, its really quite wonderful, I have a fair amount of respect for my father's opinion of people, he's not an easy man to deceive, and he's really liking you tremendously, even before he has met you. I asked him if it was maybe because he knew that I was in love with you, and he replied quite honestly that he would never allow himself to be prejudiced by my feelings for you, but he just had a feeling that you were, to use his own words, a decent bloke.

The parcel came yesterday dear, its absolutely thrilling, my bag is beautiful, Mummy raved about it, I'm quite sure little Audrey will have hysterics when she sees hers, its too sweet for words. The sari and buttons and the elephants heads are lovely, thank you so much darling. I will save them all until you come home, and then you can take whatever you intend to take home for your people.

I have just received your latest letter, its certainly an indication that you have no illusions about my domestic ability, which, I must admit my sweet, is at the moment absolutely <u>nil</u>, mainly because I have spent the larger part of my grown up life as a very spoiled WAAF officer - but do not grieve! – you may suffer very violent discomfort in the way of indigestion and other odd things, like holes in socks, for the first seven years, but old married people assure me that the first seven are without doubt the worst. I love you darling, Margaret

Joe to Margaret 21st November 1944

Margaret sweet heart, Yesterday I received four sea mail letters from you, wizard letters, if a trifle old, they were written in August and September. I looked hurriedly through the mail for something that might evolve into a photograph, but it was not to be, your miniatures are filling the breach.

If this letter is not too cheerful darling, it will be because I cannot throw off that fed-up hopeless feeling. There is no reason for it, except lack of work perhaps, and wanting to come home so much, and perhaps that is not all, let me tell you about it.

During the last 10 days I have been putting up a series of blacks. The first happened at a party in the Mess. There were visitors present, everyone tight, the C.O. was balancing a glass of whisky on his head, and I had to be the person to knock it off with a bottle cap. He (the old man) caught me squirting a fire extinguisher at some of the lads that night. Shortly afterwards I was having fun with a Cat and made a hole in it. The C.O. got me off a court of enquiry that time (*this is probably a reference to the write-off on 1st November - Ed*) The next party I had to break the only table in the Mess by standing on it, I had to mend it the next day, but it is now very rickety, that also displeased the C.O. My last big black was a couple of nights ago, several of the squadron with the Win.Co went to the officers club in a nearby town to eat and drink. The joint is owned and run by the French (*Madagascar had been a French colony before the war*) and at the height of the jollification, in trying to hit one of the boys with a mangrove, missed him and hit a plate glass mirror about six feet high. But darling, you should have seen it fall, first about a foot of the top fell off, then another piece of it waivered and toppled, and then the final crash! – wizard.

The French woman who runs the place went mad, tearing her hair and, pouncing on the guilty mangrove, placed it in front of the Group Captain who had to be there. He, needless to say, was not happy about it and came over and told us to ease up a little. Our C.O. was even more annoyed and later enquired as to who and why. The next morning he banned me from the club for two months (it is a terrible place, I was not sorry, we very rarely visit the place) but then worse was to come when he barred me from our own bar for two whole weeks!! It is not safe to do secret drinking, because the C.O. is on the wagon himself now, and would smell my breath.

And all this, little girl, so that you will understand the mood, it will improve and I will write nicer things to you, your boyfriend seems to be cut out for a permanent F/O! Will try again tomorrow, darling, lots of love, Joe

Margaret to Joe 22ⁿᵈ November 1944

Darling Joe, your letter about your sailing trip with Cloudy Joe (is that right?) is too lovely for words, you make me want so much to be there, and the thought of a honeymoon with you and a moon and, oh! Gosh, thousands of things, set me off dreaming, such dreams, I came out of my reverie to find that I was shivering.

No darling, not a large town, but a quiet place, lovely and peaceful, where we can be quite quite alone, with nobody at all to bother us. Joe you mentioned that your present attachment would be a long one, how long exactly do you mean dear? And does that mean that it will be even longer before you are home? One good thing is that I am almost certain of staying here for the duration so at least you will have no difficulty in finding me if you arrive unexpectedly. Have you any more news of Audrey's romance? Do you remember showing me her picture last year? You were very proud of it, I think she must be proud of you too.

I'm going into Acton to see my aunt today, poor thing, she's been terribly ill, and naturally a most active person, is now almost completely confined to sitting in a chair and having things brought to her, she's only 38 and apparently the doctor told her the reason for the sudden collapse of her heart is that she has been too active, an extraordinary thing, a will which can make a body do more than it is capable of, to such an extent that it simply wears out, and at such an incredibly young age.

Its so queer darling, I sometimes can't see into the future at all, just as far as the first time I see you, and then a blur, it's not surprising really, when every moment is taken up with longing for just that moment.

The thing which gives me a little anxiety is the thought that you might find me changed, because I have changed, I can't say how, but I just feel so different to that person of a year ago, the only conscious indication I have myself is that there is the desire for less movement and excitement and more of a warmer quieter environment and, darling, I feel older, please don't mind, I might even look older.

The other day I met an old friend who said there was a very definite change, and, darling Joe, please don't mind too much will you, but he said I seemed more <u>mature</u>, of all dreadful things! But don't worry my sweet I shan't start discussing deep and serious things or looking <u>prim</u> when we meet, in fact you know, I shall probably look quite stupid for just a little while. I love you, darling, yours always, Margaret

Joe to Margaret 24th November 1944

My darling, now that I find myself in an almost human mood I must whip you off a quick letter or you will wonder what has happened to me, you might think I am on my way home or something.

Sweetheart, I have been loving you a lot during the last three or four days, wanting you a lot too, but have been as miserable as hell, God knows why, probably due to my "dry" week.

Last night having returned to the Mess a little tight, the C.O. relaxed his restriction and insisted on my drinking buckets of gin, what a party we had, my shirt went for a burton. Not a bad fellow this C.O. it is a pity he is one of the 40,000 of the Transvaal, not his fault I guess. Have lots to write to you but have not time to think it up before the mail is closed. So you are "It" are you, well, well. I guess it's all right by me, but if any of those God-damn Yanks try (anything) just beat them over the head with something hard.

Darling I must tell you about my sister's kids. There is a particular one I love so much – Ann Delia or Andy, a wizard kid, about 3 and a half. She told her mother that she (her Mum) would die before Nanna (my mother). When asked why she said "because Nanna has not stopped growing yet". My mother is quite short. She also said "if I eat hair will I grow whiskers?"

Lets have some niplets, darling, but not yet, lets have some fun first – OK?

Sorry about this letter, will write lots in about 2 days time. I love you, Joe

Margaret to Joe 25th November 1944

My dearest Joe, the more I see of other people the more I want you, it's bad for me, because if it goes on like this I shall begin to be completely anti-social. Every time I find myself standing in a crowd, I wish you were beside me, I want to stand close to you, and when people aren't looking, hold your hand, to feel you warm and close. It's funny darling but I get a tremendous kick out of watching other people because you are so much nicer.

Margaret, my juvenile aunt, was married yesterday, she looked simply beautiful, in white satin, with very large lovely white flowers, and on her hair, tufts of white feathery flowers, with a voluminous veil flowing out behind. Ted, the boy she has married, looked very smart in his navy uniform, but awfully nervous, poor thing. Margaret is such a darling, she has promised me that I can be married (when I'm married) in her gown and veil and I was so thrilled I wished you were there so that I could let you see how lovely they were. When the ceremony was over everybody gathered in my grandmother's flat (in East London, darling) and did all the usual things, my boy cousin had brought his crew down (he's in Bomber Command) and they proceeded to make an awful racket. They had to catch a train at some weird hour and everybody had a dreadful time trying to get them off. It was all great fun though my grandmother cried, but we all expected her to so nobody really minded, she always cries at weddings and funerals, even if the people are not hers. When I think of that gathering of people now, I marvel at the number and variety of types. There was a different accent to be found in almost every part of the room. Mainly cockney, because you will know, if you have had my "life confessions", that my family are all the old Bow-Bells listeners, or at least, even if they have never heard them, they will claim an undisputed priority upon ownership.

Frankie has 16 days leave, we've almost ceased to be afraid of the threat of far places for him, he's had so much leave in the last 3 months, but this time might be the last, so I'm taking 7 days, last quarters leave, to be with him. I shall still be able to have our precious two weeks darling, even if you come home before the end of this quarter, because the Senior Plotter here says I can have this quarters leave and also bring forward next quarter.

Joe, dearest sweet, I'm 24 next February, it seems too incredible, we're both getting older very quickly darling, but it doesn't matter really, does it. Tell me I shall see you soon, all my love darling, yours always, Margaret

Margaret to Joe 25ᵗʰ November 1944

This morning was one of those times when things are a little difficult and I grew more and more sorry for myself and, as usual, began to wish you were here, so that I could be comforted, but when I really thought about you, and realised how very lonely and unhappy it must be for you sometimes, I felt ashamed of my self pity. The thing I find most incredible is that you never grumble about anything, even when you lost your wallet, you merely reproached yourself. I do want you to know, darling, that I have some idea of how you must feel, at least I have my family here, to console me if I'm tired or upset, and it must be ghastly too when there is no mail for you. I try to write every day, Joe, if I can. The other day I was sleeping in the afternoon, before night duty, and dreamed about you, it was a wonderful dream, so wonderful that when I woke and realised that it _was_ only imagination, all the glow went and I felt unhappy for a long time, until this morning in fact, when I began to be ashamed for being so utterly selfish. If ever you do feel terribly unhappy darling, do write and tell me, because I shall understand exactly how you feel, and it will help me to realise how small my own grumbles seem when compared with the ones you must have sometimes. Shall I continue to address letters to you as before, Joe, or if your new abode is to be for some time – static – shall I send them to you there?

I saw my sick aunt yesterday, her illness seems to have had a most extraordinary effect upon her, it's made her talk more than she ever has before, and believe me she was no mean talker. Yesterday I arrived there at about 5, just after tea, she started talking then and literally didn't stop, except when she slept, until 10.30 this morning, when I left.

I walked down to the bus in a complete daze, and quite exhausted, I think she had asked me, roughly about a thousand questions and didn't bother to wait for an answer to any of them. How my uncle can sit for hours listening and never saying a word is quite beyond me. I promise solemnly darling, that if I ever find myself nagging at you, I'll go straight out and kick myself hard. It won't be long now Joe, before I see you again, when I do, I shall die of happiness, although there wouldn't be much point in your going on a honeymoon with a dead wife. I love you so terribly darling, and want you so much, you cannot come to me too soon. All my love, dearest, yours always, Margaret

Margaret to Joe 28th November 1944

Darling, I think my mind is quite definitely slipping, I always address my letters to you before writing them, and this time, I addressed it to Flying Officer M.E.Dillon! – how the postal people would have sorted that out I don't quite know, but fortunately I noticed it directly it was written, hence the blot on the front.

Darling Joe, does a week without a letter seem as long to you as it does to me? Even though you might have had three last week, as I did? And three such lovely ones too. You wrote one of them whilst suffering a hangover from South African brandy, but it too, in spite of your apology for writing whilst in a distinctly delicate condition, was a lovely one, you told me you loved me and wanted very badly to come home, and darling Joe, you can say that drunk or sober and it would make me happy, but I hope when you do come home, you will say nice things when you are sober, mainly, because when you see me without the softening glow of "nectar" you will see me, dear one, without illusion, and if you love me then, then, Oh! My goodness, I'd better not continue on that theme or the censor will blush for my lack of shame. Dearest Joe, I have expressed that thought very badly, but when we met in Oban, the short time we spent together was in rather a queer and slightly hectic atmosphere, wasn't it?

I often wonder what you must have thought of me that first night you came, and Judy and I had drinks with all of you. You looked rather hard at me several times, a little disapprovingly I thought, I remember thinking at the time that you looked awfully English and just a little unapproachable, little did I guess then that you were the one to occupy my thoughts to the exclusion of all else for so long, but, soon darling, it won't be just the thought of you, it will be the real you, alive and near, oh darling, it will be soon won't it? Take care of yourself dearest, God bless, all my love, yours always, Margaret

Margaret to Joe 29th November 1944

Darling sweetheart, its awfully late, but I've just come in from a party and I had to tell you about it. I was on duty till nine anyway, but was dragged in as I was leaving the Ops room. The most incredible and most unnerving thing about the whole party was that there was a man there who was exactly like you darling, your eyes, and build, and even the way he danced. It was all too completely unbalancing for words, as you can imagine. Coming home, alone!! Made my imagination run riot, the night is so beautiful, clear and warm, and a full moon, and little woolly clouds all over the sky, oh gosh! Joe, the thought of walking home with you and kissing you goodnight was almost too much for me, I'm almost ready to cry now, but when you are here, sweet, imagine all the time we have to make up for! Imagine too, that we need not be any more than a few hours away from each other, and imagine too darling, 2 whole weeks when we can see each other all the time, hold hands any time we like, and I can kiss you really and truly, instead of just dreaming it. I do hope when we meet, and you see me again after all this time, Joe, that you'll still feel the same, I can't think of what might happen if you don't.

When I look back over the last 12 months I realise they have been very lonely ones, I never was lonely before, a crowd of friends was enough to keep me happy, but when I began to miss you, and I had to admit to myself that I really had fallen in love with you, they were not enough, I'm still just as fond of the few real and charming friends I have, but its awfully difficult to make the effort to see them, when the only person I want to see is you.

Last night (its morning now dear) the party really was great fun, but all the time I wanted to get away, to dream over your picture, to make you come closer to me, to write down that I loved you, and all these people are so superfluous. Darling, I could send you something for Christmas, but if you may be coming home at any time, it will probably miss you won't it? I try so hard to say how much I love you, but it's so much I'm inarticulate, I shall say all these things to you when you are close to me, and darling, when you are with me again, I shall never let you go. Bye for now my dearest darling, all my love, Margaret

265 Squadron diary 30th November 1944 A/S up 2130 Diego Suarez down 0515 Grand Port, Mauritius 2nd Officer to W/Cdr Louw DFC (Joe was 2nd Officer probably to prove he could still fly after his prang at the start of the month)

15. December 1944

Joe to Margaret 1ˢᵗ December 1944

My darling sweetheart, you poor kid, why did you ever for one moment think so seriously of what you have written as if it could possibly make any difference whatsoever to we two. Darling, I know you so much better now, understand why you are you – and I love you so much as "you" and would not have you any other way. And what a relief to know that your folk are human, I shall be able to be just me, and not try to put up an unnatural good show when I meet them, because we are just ordinary people too

I was brought up among country people and understand them so well, just as you understand and appreciate the folk you knew when a kid. We understand their philosophy and I for one often wonder if they are not happiest for it. As for being poor we too are far from rich, and have lots of uncles and aunts who are really quite poor, but happy because most of them live in the country.

And again, you will understand and like my people too, they are just simple honest country folk, you will get quite a kick out of my old man's country way of talking!

Oh darling I love you more (if that is possible) for everything about you, in fact everything that is you, and had you not been Margaret Dillon of the Dillons, London, you would have been different, and I should not even have known you. The thought of you and me tackling life together is perfic ! because it will be quite a new life and adventures for both of us. I dare to think that we fit in so well if we give and take a little, one to the other, our lives could be a perfect union.

The reason for my very hopeful enthusiasm is brought forward by your letter, dear, but let me tell you about myself too, and you will understand. I feel that you have made so much more than me out of your life, and I envy you.

All my love, darling, Joe. PS I do hope you get the letters that I am writing, together

PPS Did you get my wire, darling?

Joe to Margaret, undated, four letters in sequence follow the above one

My darling, this letter really follows on from the one I wrote from Mauritius yesterday. My ability to express myself is very limited, especially when compared with yourself, dear, but I will try to tell you about myself to the best of that ability.

Life in a small village with no railway, two busses a day and 10 miles from the nearest town, is, as you can imagine, extremely rural. Apart from a few "upper class ", the vicar and the schoolmaster, the inhabitants 10 and 12 years ago were of a type, knowing little of the "outer world", just honest simple country folk. My people were of this rural stock and for that reason my three sisters and I, living so far from modern England, suffered disadvantages. I, for my part, realise that although I was way behind other town boys in my thirst for knowledge, in my teens (due to my being country born) know there is something in my blood that can only be born thus, and I value it.

My mother was a farmer's daughter, a lovely person. There is something in her nature everyone loves, the baker boy and the people who almost own the village, she lives for other people.

Dad's father was a drunken bulldog type of person and so scared his children that they grew up meek and strange. Dad took over his father's decadent business as local building contractor because Pack senior had drunk himself into debt. Keeping this debt very quiet the old man quickly married Mum, and by her perfect management and self-denial they can now boast a small capital. Dad still does small bomb repair jobs although he has to do most of it himself as there are no labourers but when the war is over he will return to his labours.

It was Mum who insisted on her children going to a secondary school, and what a battle it was, because to Dad it was a waste of money. She even used some money her father left her to pay for it. And when we left school there was nothing for it but to go away from home, if we were to get anywhere. Poor Mum, to be left alone with Dad after working so hard for us all, but Mum's happiness is made up by being angelic to others.

I went to a technical school, cycled about 12 miles a day and for all that it was not a good school, I have suffered since. On leaving school I had not a clue what I wanted to do, in fact had no ideas how high a person such as..........

Joe to Margaret, next in sequence

....myself should aim, you know what I mean, Prime Minister or engine driver, and there was no-one eligible to advise me. When I did leave home (I got work in an industrial town in Leicestershire) I had to begin to learn about things that my home life should have taught me, so you see darling I started life a little strangely too.

Three months in this dead end job (I marvel now at my common sense) and I knew enough to leave. Rather than face the humiliation of going home and for local people to say "I did not think he would stick it" (no-one from a village goes so far from home on leaving school that he can only get home twice a year!) I wrote an amazing number of applications and eventually got a job as junior draughtsman in a large engineering drawing office. It was a wizard opening and after holding the job down easily for a few months, JTP began to realise the possibilities of even he. Yes, it seems damn silly to me now, and I am wondering whether you will be interested or should I say – why I am telling you?

Anyway, then I was in Loughborough just beginning to live. By living in very cheap lodgings with another chap it was not necessary to ask my mother to send more money each week and for several months had 2/6d a week to spend, which was not much at 17 years of age. It was at Loughborough that I joined Toc H (it cost nothing) and learnt so much from some of the members. Why two or three of the fellows should choose to befriend a shy, silent, spotty youth from the South is something I shall never appreciate, but they did, and I was a worried kid sifting and sorting out life. (*Toc H was a charity committed to building a fairer society by youth mentoring, individual and family support. Its history is interesting. It began in 1915 in the First World War when a Belgian gave a house for a British soldiers club but it had to be regardless of rank. Above the door was a sign "All rank abandon, ye who enter here". The house was called Talbot House, which became TH, which became Toc H because Toc was the army signalling code for "T"*).

But it was a friend in the drawing office (he was about 40) who changed the course of my whole life. He was a grand fellow, very sound and spent hours giving me gen on my work. He had a craze for designing things and I told him about my home life.

To make a long story short, by his influence and logical reasoning I decided that my career lay in building, there were so many possibilities and although I was well set for life in the Midlands, I went home. I know now that his advice was good, in fact even now I know that there is no work I should like better.

But when I got home, Dad, in his strange way, tried to teach me about building construction and by working damned hard at night I learned a lot.

I drew Dad's plans for him, helped him in hundreds of ways, tried to modernise him, tried to make him take.....

Joe to Margaret, next in sequence

....bigger jobs, but I should have known before I began, it was hopeless. He had this complex, had no guts to try anything new, no ambition. And so we fell out more and more often, he is a damned difficult person to get along with. Thus after having left school almost 3 years I realised I was getting nowhere fast and told Dad he had had me.

For the next 12 months my mother's little nest was again depleted while I studied as an articled pupil with the local surveyor and passed an examination of some small importance. On the strength of this I got an appointment (appointment this time!) with an important firm of Consulting Engineers in Westminster, where I worked with engineers, few of whom had qualifications below BSc (Eng). But I was getting somewhere at last, and worked hard to pass my A.M.I.C.E. The war came and 25% of us had to go and with the war my last chance of a successful career in engineering went with my job. My next 9 months were spent in the Borough Surveyors

Office, Dagenham and I did some important worthwhile work, only because there were no service engineers available. In August 1940 I felt such a worm that I joined the RAF to become a pilot, and could hold this old head up again. The job at Dagenham is still available for me after the war but I cannot earn much money without passing my finals and I have now decided that that is impossible after 5 years in the RAF.

This dope on my so-called career is possibly boring to you, it is important to me of course and you should know about it too. But there are other things and I think I shall come out on top in the end. Money in itself is not important but it is a matter of personal achievement, and there is you, too, now.

There is a little more of my life to tell you about and that is about life in the RAF. A year after joining I was made a Sgt pilot, my speech was not quite right for a P.O. in '41, or my school. After some excitement in '42, the Gods decided to give me one, probably because I had just about completed a tour. While converting from Sunderland's to Cats I met the most exquisite girl imaginable and for a while she allowed me to know her. We were to part however, she to another station, me to East Africa, where I pine for her. About 3 months ago my tour out here was almost completed, but the work stopped so I just wait.

You might as well hear about the....

Joe to Margaret, last in sequence

....rest of the family now.

These sisters of mine have been getting married. The elder, Gladys, who became a secretary, married her boss and now has four wizard kids you know about. The next one (another Margaret) married a boy from Derby about a year ago. Recent embarkation leave has sent Meg into crazy happiness and she awaits the end of April. My last and youngest sister you know about and I do hope you have met her. At the moment she is too full of her Jack to write regularly to her brother, but who could blame the kid? If you should meet her, write and tell me if you think she is like me, she is supposed to be the spitting image.

And that, my darling, is the very sketchy story of us, and me. I expect I have failed to impress on you the points I wished to point out to you. I am apt to start writing something and forget what I was leading up to, or go off onto something else. Your active pen makes me envious

We Packs are a strange mixture, we are always striving to get somewhere, somewhere better, always appreciating the better things in other people, always lamenting our own deficiencies, and somehow other people seem to like us, thank God for that. My sisters are just the same, Glad a little less so perhaps, but they have not an inferiority complex as I have.

I hope I have not bored you with all this about myself, you will at least gather that my financial future is not as solid as it should be at 26 ½ years of age. And you must know my sweetheart why your long letter of a month ago meant so much to me, we both have our ideals, and they are unusually similar. And what is so important is that we both know life and people and that, darling, means so very much.

I shall look forward anxiously to your letter after you have received these 6, I wonder if they will make you feel as happy as your letter made me feel? As soon as I received it I sent a cable to you, but was told a couple of days later that the service had been suspended for Christmas. Christmas will be over when you get this I expect, the months are slipping past dear, it cannot be long now, keep loving me please, I love you more every day and have been thinking about you for four solid days and dreaming of you at night. Always your Joe

265 Squadron diary 3rd December 1944 up 0122 Mauritius down 0700 Diego Suarez 2nd Officer to W/Cdr Louw DFC (still proving himself as second officer)

Margaret to Joe 3rd December 1944

Darling, yesterday I had two letters, the first for two weeks, did you know that I have heard from you regularly every week for months now? Some times there are three. All the orderlies in the Mess know that I wait for airmail letters and when I am on duty they ring me to say they are there. Your last two were simply lovely, dear, they make me so happy, darling Joe, I'm so sorry you've had a spot of bother but when I read your account of the club incident, and then the table, and the C.O.'s glass of whisky I couldn't help being very amused, because I can imagine the whole thing so well.

Joe – please don't have fun with Cats, I can't bear the thought of it, I've seen the results of quite a lot of fun with kites, and it would just tear me apart if anything happened to you. I'm sorry darling, I don't mean to say things like that in a possessive sense, to bind you to me with that kind of sentiment is the last thing I should care to do, but quite apart from the fact that my whole life is bound up in you now, you are far too decent and nice to go out for a reason which is anything less than worthwhile.

In any case darling, how about our Rugby team? It can't be done solo my sweet, and I haven't the slightest desire to produce a Rugby fifteen with anybody else, you see, they've just got to have turned-up noses and wicked eyes, otherwise the whole idea is not worth considering.

I'm at home on leave today, until the 10th Dec. Tomorrow I'm going to get some shoes for <u>the</u> suit, black ones. Darling, when the leopard skin bag comes I shall try to get a collar to match, to make me look very rich, just to fool people.

Oh by the way dear, I have some pretty blue velvet to make a new dress, I think you will like it, it's called midnight blue, ring, or silk velvet, it shines as the light catches it, do you like blue? I thought of having an evening frock made of it but it's so pretty I shall want to wear it often when you are home, so it will have to be a short one. Darling, I do want to look nice for you. I'll write again tomorrow, God bless, dearest Joe, all my love, Margaret

Margaret to Joe 4ᵗʰ December 1944

Darling, it seems ages since I last wrote but it really was only yesterday. It's queer, but when I am at home, away from service surroundings, you seem farther away from me, and I feel the urgent need to write, more and more, so that you will come nearer, and enter with me into a sphere which you have not known, and to understand it, to know why and how much I love and appreciate it.

Darling, have you had, among my sea mail letters, one describing my family, or perhaps mainly myself to you? – because, until you know all that, I shall not be really easy in my mind. Perhaps when you do know everything it will all seem quite inconsiderable to you, but you must tell me what you feel about it.

When I told you about Bill Martin, it was because, for a little while, that small bit of my life affected us both so intensely, but that too was something which now seems so small that it might never have happened at all. However, darling, this, that is in my mind now, is different, because, in spite, or perhaps, shall I say, whatever our life will be together, and I think it will be a lovely, gracious, joyful life, there is still this essential part of it, this part from which I grew, and which has, unknowingly, sewn into my heart the seeds of a deep affection and respect for it.

Its all so awfully confused really, but you will understand dear, because one of the many things we have in common is an imagination which colours things very vividly, and so you will understand when I say that to visit my home, which is still in the East End slums, and I think, probably, will always be that of my people, is <u>always</u> a stimulant to my mind, to visit the local pubs and to drink a beer, with old dock workers with rakish caps over one eye, and to hear Cockney voices asking how I am, and where am I stationed now, and to know, when I go out, that the old sailor behind the bar will look up from what he is doing to wave a smiling goodnight, and if I haven't been in for some weeks, will most certainly ask where I am, that is all so colourful and cheering, darling, I love it.

I love you far more than anything else though, Margaret

Margaret to Joe 5ᵗʰ December 1944

Darling Joe, I've just been reading your last letter again, the one all about your beautiful blacks, I wish it were possible to reproduce a helpless giggle, because every time I read it I can't help chuckling more. And if you're permanently to be a F/O, what fun, I shall have to do something about a black or two, and dip a ring, then we shall both be the ropiest one-ringers (permanent) in the RAF.

I try to imagine the expression on your face when you saw the mirror falling in pieces to the ground, and doubt very much if among the emotions registered there was sorrow, you wicked thing!

I can see you will take a wee bit of handling, Joe my sweet, I bet you would take a huge delight in ruining a brand new permanent wave. No doubt Audrey could express fairly well just how provoking you could be, but never mind my darling, I have always had brothers to cope with, so here's to some fairly well matched scraps. Incidentally, following the thought of permanent waves, that's one thing, or at least one level of promotion, you'll never have, my little chicken, because I never have them! I'm going to the dressmaker tomorrow to have the new blue velvet made up, I hope its finished by the time you come home.

Darling, I do hope Maltby doesn't try to get in touch with me this week, whilst I am on leave, or if he does I hope he leaves a message for me, because I would like so much to talk to him, he can tell me so many little things which, although they may seem unimportant to you, really mean so much to me, when ones people are so far away, and, dear Joe, you are my people now, do you realise that?

It sounds awfully final and binding, just saying it like that, but you know darling, that there is no tie, up to now, which you cannot break if you wished to, and the only final thing about us is that we have both said that we love each other, and that fact Is enough to make me wait forever, if need be, for you to come home. Write lots darling, all my love, yours always, Margaret

Margaret to Joe 6th December 1944

My darling, one more day of leave gone but one day nearer your letters, I know there will be something for me, there's a feeling in my bones.

Frankie has just told me about a friend of his, a Sgt. Navigator, who, with his whole crew, has been posted back to U.K. by mistake, bang in the middle of a tour, by mistake darling! Oh my gosh! If it were only you, except that they may have to go back again and, once you come home, I shan't ever be able to bear letting you go again. By the way, dear, I know you must be frightfully disappointed about the second photograph not coming, but, Lord knows what's the matter with the photographers, its over 2 months now since I sent for a copy and there's absolutely no sign of it yet. However I shall be going into Town next week and will most certainly give them a piece of my mind.

It's heavenly here today, even in the crowded and scarred streets of East London, people are so absolutely marvellous, it's hard to believe, even with my own first hand knowledge, that many of them have been bombed from their homes, time and time again, have spent nights in crowded airless shelters, with the fear of death beating on their minds, fear expressed in a grin and "have a cup of tea".

Just think, darling, of the tremendous, unconscious courage of people who, with no display of heroics at all, just carry on working, and marrying, and having babies, and having fun too, laughing, never thinking of those things which experience has taught them may happen to them at any moment of day or night. I have a depth of feeling for our servicemen, and some of the women, but to these people I could never express just how much I am inspired by their courage, unconscious, uncalculated and instinctive. I have never loved my own family more than when I saw them, and sometimes even now see them, under fire, literally, and hear their very enlightening opinions of war, and anybody who isn't on our side. All my love, dear one, Margaret

Joe to Margaret 6th December 1944

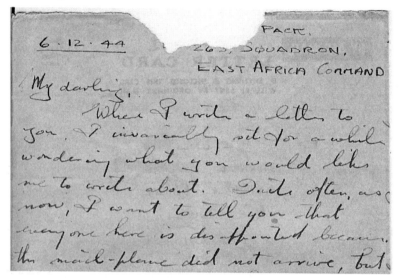

you do not want to know about that. Again I want to write about my hopes of leaving for U.K. because it is always on my mind, not to get to U.K. but to see you, I should have liked to go to the Far East, if there were no you. You must have tired of reading about that too. Then so many of my letters try to explain what a hell of a wizard kid I think you are, and how much I want you, but that too must get a trifle monotonous. Then often I whip through some of your letters and little things strike a particular, pleasant chord such as " running around in old clothes looking untidy", you wearing slacks and a jumper, are you a sweaters girl, darling? Gosh, I bet you look wizard in slacks, I have often thought about you in slacks,

I remember seeing a person in a blue blouse and slacks on the golf course at Brackenhurst and thinking how much like you she looked, and we can pop into little country pubs in our untidiness and talk to the locals, in fact play them at darts. Another letter tells me that you will try so hard to be practical and sensible and will not sit down and write stories when you should be frying sausages for our dinner! I see many meals in the local fish and chip shop!

But you must write Toto, I have wanted to ask if you had ever written a short story. What a problem you will be, I visualise going to work with no breakfast and holes in my socks and all the neighbours will be sympathetic and I shall be the only one to know how lucky I am to have you for a wife! We must set one night a week aside for the sole purpose of getting tight, pay night for preference and we shall have to eat bread and cheese and welsh rarebit alternately until next pay day. We shall be such a strange couple that nothing will be certain from one day to the next, except one thing, loving each other, Joe

Margaret to Joe 7th December 1944

Darling, it's mid-morning, Frankie is still asleep, having exhausted himself with a session of skating last evening, he came in looking absolutely done in, limping quite badly, and saying with great enthusiasm that he'd had a wonderful time. In the afternoon we went to see Carmen Miranda in "Greenwich Village" – much as I admired her naughty and provoking ugliness the first time I saw dear Carmen, she now has the power only to bore me, even her accent is irritating, if one hears it more than once. The one thing I still do admire about her though, is the extreme design of her amusing hats, they really are quite unbelievable. In one scene she wore an enormous one made entirely of very large sticks of peppermint candy, and in another, a cage with a canary in it, reposing in the midst of a bed of rubbish, on top of her head, all in such bizarre colours that when I emerged from the cinema into daylight outside, my eyes felt as though they were being danced upon by gremlins with hob-nailed boots. What a wonderful life for an escapist though, to be able to lose oneself in a character brilliantly gaudy, portraying falsely, with a secret chuckle inside, cheap emotion and tawdry sentiment, to look up with swimming eyes into the adoring gaze of the hero, and think " Oh God, there's a suspender gone" or "What foul stuff has he put on his ruddy hair now?"

Imagine the self-discipline, to convince millions of cinema fans that you are crazy about somebody who hates you, privately, just about as much as you hate him, or her. Imagine too, the delight in secretly sticking a pin in him, during a tensely dramatic scene, and see the murderous threat in his eyes, and to know he can't do a damn thing about it, great fun, or is that sadistic?

Anyway, I promise not to stick pins in you, old sock. All my love darling, yours always, Margaret

Margaret to Joe 8th December 1944

Darling, just two more days of leave, today and tomorrow, and then back to the grind again. I don't mind going back so much really because if one is watch keeping time goes very quickly, and the quicker the better as far as I am concerned. The last month has gone in a flash, so quickly that I often have a feeling now that you will be here soon, sooner than I can possibly realise. It's a queer feeling being at home again, for 7 whole days, after so long, it is a long time since I have stayed any longer than two days with my people. I think they find it a little strange since Frankie is here too.

My smallest brother is impatiently waiting to post this letter for me, so I'd better make it fast, do you mind? Frankie and I went to see "Dragon Seed" yesterday, a Chinese story of courage and endurance, during the Japanese invasion, terribly dramatic and intense, as I supposed it would be, with Katherine Hepburn as the star. Do you have up to date films darling? You did mention an open-air theatre in one letter, does that mean it is not in darkness? How else could they show films except in a darkened room?

Just at the moment there's an unholy row going on – Stanley, the baby of 10 – is employing anything but noiseless tactics of the guerrilla kind in stalking the dog, who thinks its all great fun, and is having no compunction in expressing her delight at the top of her voice, she's a little mongrel, with not the slightest claim to any ancestry at all, let alone any aristocratic distinction. My father and Frankie are discussing in the most audible of undertones the merits of woollen underwear, and they think I can't hear them.

Stanley is getting restless now, he's issued an ultimatum, the letter has to be ready within one minute, or else!

Well here goes darling, it's a nasty scrappy little letter, but I've talked to you for a little while, Bye till tomorrow, all my love dear one, yours always, Margaret

Joe to Margaret 11ᵗʰ December 1944

Darling, when you receive this Christmas will be over at home, I do hope you have lots of fun and not too much plotting. The V.2.'s must be rather worrying to you, they are certainly damned worrying to me, I cannot even ask you to be careful because you get no warning of their coming. *(the V2's or doodlebugs or buzz bombs were pilot-less flying bombs with one tonne warheads that were guided by a gyroscopic automatic pilot, they were fairly indiscriminate in what they hit. In all 1100 were launched against England, 500 of which fell on London. After the war many of the German team who developed them went to the USA and laid the foundations for the Apollo moon rocket space mission)*

Do tell me when you write if you have been getting any in your area dear, the information is not censorable, not that I have ever had an A.M.L. censored – received one I mean.

I wonder if you have got my parcel yet, I realise now that the bag I sent you is a major boob. How can you wear a leopard skin bag without a leopard skin coat? – or can you, I think not, and even if you would wear a leopard skin coat, which I doubt, how could I ever afford one? Or will you nag me until I get you one? There is an easy way out and that is to give the bag away or perhaps I can get a skin so that it can be fixed on gloves and cuffs, but my ideas are probably ridiculous anyway. Tell me what you think about it.

Thinking back about your little worry, the one that caused me to whip off six quick letters, I can now get a smile out of it, because I was worrying about the self-same thing! You are so splendid in every way that I was sure you were from a very important family, important in the social world I mean. And although I thought I knew you enough to think that you would not worry too much about it, I was a little anxious, we can now both be assured.

When I write again I hope to be able to give you something a little more definite about coming home – don't get too hopeful darling, there is always the possibility that I shall have to do the full term, which is four months from the date you receive this letter.

Keep loving me darling, you can always rest assured of my love for you, I will try and write you more letters than I have been writing. When your mail arrives my black mood softens and I can write to you, but in between, this place is getting me down. Love, Joe

Joe to Margaret 13th December 1944

Joe to Margaret 13ᵗʰ December 1944

My dear Margaret, if my letters seem to be less interesting (although I cannot ever imagine them ever being interesting) perhaps losing a little "something", do not worry in any way darling, I am really always the same. Such things as environment, latest rumours, mail from you and from home all have their effect. Of late I have been in quite a bad way, self-pity no doubt, I imagined that because I had been on O.T.U's, F.T.U.'s or operations since Sept '41, I was damned unlucky to be a F/O and to be made to stay out here. The C.O. thought I was getting a little marbish (?) and asked me what was the matter. After saying some quite nice things, he said that he may send me home at the end of January, but would promise nothing. With that I have managed to snap out of it. He may think he did it by tickling my vanity, but he is quite wrong, he does not know there is a you dear.

You know sweetheart I often think of going places with you and being with you a lot, in fact even living with you. But I rarely think of the other side of married life. That of course is a very silly thing to call it, because there are not two sides, it is all one. And when I do think of it, the whole set up improves 100%- to make 200% - because to live with you would be absolutely wizard, I know that, as I already know you so well, but to live with you in the real sense would be, or I should say will be, exquisitely delightful.

I cannot imagine any girl, decent girl, really wanting to sleep with a man. Most females are so feminine that the thought of sleeping with someone who might make those noises that some men make before and after sleeping must be repulsive. Surely many newly wed's dread all that, to begin with anyway. The sexual side of married life is quite important I suppose (horrid word sexual) something tells me that that side of the picture will sort itself out all right with we two.

My powers of expression are extremely limited and I have not written quite what I wanted, perhaps I should not try to write my passing thoughts? But in 1944 there should be no closed books between people such as we, in fact between you and I Toto, I am going to try and dream about you tonight, it thrills me to think about it, pity imagination can only go so far. A severe rep in your next letter, darling? Love, Joe

Joe to Margaret 15th December 1944

Margaret my darling, today I received four letters from you, lucky me. They, like all your letters were wizard! They told me that I had to be careful or there would be no rugger team, about your local "pubbing", to think that my girlfriend appreciates and understands a smile or a goodbye from an old sailor behind a bar, who is probably a trifle grimy, is "wacko" because it means that we are sentimentally understanding people together, and I used to think I was original in that respect! And you also told me in your letters about the Margaret Dillon of 1945 in civvies.

About this rugger team idea we had, well Toto, I have thought of a better plan, I do hope you like it. You know of course that you have a natural flair for writing, well, why not you write and earn lots of money and I stay at home and do the cooking? I am quite handy with the needle too and scrupulously clean in the house, I am not too certain about the babies but am making enquiries.

Oh yes, and re the local, you must try and improve your darts darling, because now that I know you like locals, you have had it old girl, you will literally be pulled around to the odd little pubs I like because I am silly enough to think that you will like them too. And if you do not throw a crafty dart we will lose so much beer, that you will have to write all night long, and you wouldn't like that, would you? Sorry darling, I can assure you that I am blushing in shame.

And the visit to the dressmakers, when I think of what is to come later, I long for the native system on some islands here. A man can have as many wives as he wants if he can supply them with one sari every year! Lucky people! But seriously my darling sweet heart, I get a big kick out of your dresses, costumes and things, please be feminine Toto, most of the time. How about a picture of you in slacks, if you have one, I guess you look wizard in them!

Your big picture has not arrived yet, it will have to come quickly for Christmas, there are only about three more mail days.

Do you like wine coloured jewellery Toto, you know, odd things hanging here and there for special occasions? I love you darling, Joe

Joe to Margaret 18th December 1944

My darling, what lucky people we are out here! Yesterday the Padre had a parcel containing about a dozen copies of "Woman's Own", sent by his wife, with the result that the whole mess, from the C.O. down is reading them –

silence reigns (sic)!! The most interesting page is the last one, where a woman endeavours to answer the problems of her many love-lost correspondents – what a woman! – but "she" might be a man of course. The Padre needless to say, is very pleased with himself, he probably thinks that he has at last got us reading a better class of literature.

As one wit suggested, five more shopping days to Christmas, how the time flies! It will be nice to get '45 started, my outlook on life changes with the year, sort of cleans itself up, becomes more optimistic, do you know what I mean? What a huge imagination one needs to even hazard a guess at our lives twelve months from now. It is rather nice trying.

I shall soon be getting your letters telling me of your Christmas celebrations, how I would have loved to have been with you darling! By being in an alcoholic stupor most of the time we will have our moments I expect, but the mornings – oh what heads and stomachs. I will write you detailed accounts of what goes on little girl, if I had your ability I could make it interesting, because we always have lots of laughs.

Poor old Aud has had her commission, I am very sorry for her sake, because I know it will worry her. She coped with all the questions at the A.M. Board but was nervous the whole time which is not expected from a WAAF Officer I guess.

I still pine for your picture dear, the big one, perhaps it will show up for Christmas, what a perfect present! We must start a photographic diary  when I get home, you know the kind of thing, pictures of places we visit, people we meet, pubs that we stay at, our first squalling half-pint job, with groups later on of course. Underneath the date, and remarks, what do you think Toto, a good idea? Bye for now, darling, love, Joe

Joe to Margaret 20th December 1944

My dear Margaret, yesterday our squadron leader left the squadron and there was the expected party. We put him to bed at about 2 o clock in the morning and he left by air at first light. A signal has just arrived asking for the other half of his kit, but it has disappeared. The highlight of the evening was our Padre *(photo on left)* getting roaring drunk (the first time ever) and murmuring incessantly "this is the one thing I had to guard against, drunkenness" Later he was very ill, he could not apparently guard against that either.

This leave-taking from the squadron usually has its thrills. A month or so back my navigator *(Bill Graham)* was posted, and he was still very drunk when he arrived 10 minutes late the following morning to catch the BOAC 'plane. The authorities were a little peeved, even more so when he could not find his ticket. They at once sent a car post haste to the BOAC office to get him another. Forty minutes later when the returning car hove into sight the flying officer triumphantly produced his original ticket from a small inside pocket, the ticket pocket as a matter of fact. The C.O.'s remarks went like this "What held BOAC up for an hour, shall have to send a signal and have him reproved, damn good show, wasn't it" – all of which probably does not interest you in the least, darling, but today has been a bad day in lots of ways apart from a mild hangover, so I thought you might like an AML filled up with something rather than no AML at all.

Did I tell you about the Christmas cards that I sent out more than a month ago? Assuming that my Flt/Lt must be in the bag by Christmas time I sent them out as F/Lt J.T.P. and now it seems probable that the all-important gap of a month plus, is not going to be for a while. Quite funny but it will take a lot of explaining!

And there is something else I have been meaning to tell you for quite a while little Toto. The longer I stay out here the more money we are worth, because about £17 a month is now being put into my bank and none being drawn out, truly amazing, yes?

How much money will we need to get married with, after we have de-cided we can put up with one another darling? Love, Joe

Joe to Margaret 21ˢᵗ December 1944

Darling sweetheart, now that there is little flying for me, little to do other than watch the days slip past, you are in my thoughts more than ever before. And (like you) I find writing to you brings you nearer. I have to admit that I am a sentimentalist, I love romancing in my thoughts on those wonderful things that can happen to us and, God willing, will. The big day, our day, or should I say, our fortnight, is still a long way off. Strangely enough the thought of our meeting is not quite so frightening, now that I know you so much better through your letters.

I wonder if happenings here will interest you. Last night after all Mess members had retired the W/Co returned with another W/Co and G/C feeling like a party and promptly awoke my navigator and myself and two other fellows. We dressed and with the promise of free beer joined in. After about an hours solid drinking we awoke our pianist and began singing, later waking two of our soloists who appeared in dressing gowns. That is really all there was to it, we retired at the first flush of dawn – 0430 – but the whole thing seems too damned silly, it cost the C.O. a fiver. Since waking this morning the rain has been coming down in torrents without stopping. We are cut off by road and the complete camp is a quagmire. Everyone is sitting under those places where the water is not coming in and the floor is almost completely covered with water. It might sound rather uncomfort-able to you at home but we do not worry, it is of no use anyway.

The limited news of the German counter attack is of great interest. I am daring to hope that it will prove to be the last major battle of that war, it seems highly probable, although news is being withheld. The thought of living at peace is quite beyond my conception, imagine no hat or flannels for weeks on end!

As a letter this is rather a mess but there is yet hope, Bill and I have located a table for our bedroom and if we can stick it my letter writing will be done without distraction. Bye for now darling, always yours, Joe

Joe to Margaret 27th December 1944

Darling, yes it is through at last, substantive too, so it cannot be whipped away from me for any number of blacks. Had it been through a few months earlier I had every chance of an A/S Ldr – there were several going cheap, but I have had it once and for all now, so what anyway?

It is quite a relief to be getting back to normal after the Christmas festivities. They came well up to expectations, more so perhaps and everyone is quite happy to leave the alcohol alone for a while. On Christmas Saturday we had the first dance ever at the Mess. The females were well in the minority of course, a few frogesses, a couple of nurses and several jobs of varying colours, not too pronounced, this being an officers (and gentlemen's?) Mess. The best joke of the evening was the story that went around that Lofty (who is a tall black youth working in the Mess and has never been known to smile) that Lofty had given in his notice to the P.M.C. because F/O Bishop (a giggle type) had invited his wife to the dance! "Bishop's black" gave us quite a laugh.

The dance was quite a success. The day was fine and in consequence we were not flooded out. The "dance" of course was really a blind for a first class drink, concluding, when the ladies had left, with a singsong. Our four boys arrived in their best clothes and looked really smart. Exactly why they decided to wear shoes I do not know but they were extremely awkward and thoroughly frightened when they saw the Christmas decorations we had stuck up.

Did you have any parties darling, do write and tell me all about them. It seems ages since I received your last letters, actually only a week. I love you darling, Joe

Margaret to Joe 27th December 1944

Darling, I'm up in Wales again with Pauline, and wanting you dreadfully, I do hope you will have some good news for me very soon darling. Have you been hearing more regularly from Audrey? I expect she is quite used to the idea of being engaged now.

Dear, I can't remember whether I thanked you for the sweet dog in my last letter, he really is a darling. What shall we call him? What a pity his brother was chewed by the mice, I can feel exactly the way you must have felt now that I have him and see how adorable he is. Joe, my dear, I feel absolutely dreadful about the photograph, it still has not returned from the photographer and I wanted so badly to get it to you by Christmas, you must think I am very careless and neglectful, but really dear heart, I am so upset about it, I suppose the first one I sent has never turned up has it? Now I don't know what to do, you'll probably be home before it gets there, but if I don't send it, it may be months before you get home and you just won't have a decent photograph of me all that time. You tell me which I must do darling.

I wish you were going to be here for the New Year, it would be wonderful to start off the New Year together. Coming up on the train I travelled with a young pilot who was going home without any warning to his mother at all, from overseas after four years. He was so excited and happy I really envied him. Darling sweetheart if you walk in on me unexpectedly like that I shall just pass completely away, please try to cable me darling, won't you?

Back to the grind tomorrow for a couple of days and then I'm going home for two days to see Frankie who <u>still</u> has not sailed, he certainly is lucky, I hope it continues like that for him. Write lots my darling, I love you, Margaret

Joe to Margaret 29th December 1944

My darling, it is hard to visualise you all at home trying to keep warm while here the temperature is between 95F and 100F all day long, in the shade. At night I lie on top of my bed, without a stitch, perspiring everywhere. It must be wizard to be out walking on a frosty day and feel your blood tingling all over in a glow. My blood stream can now be best described as a thin alcoholic trickle enabling me to walk small distances. Rain is becoming more frequent now however with its consequent sticky cooling effect. Millions of tiny shoots are appearing giving a welcome relief to the bare brown earth and the rocky mountains. Soon, say in about four weeks, the camp will be overrun with vegetation.

Christmas Eve will always be a pleasant memory. The bar opened at 10.30 and we had a snack for lunch without getting off our stools. Later several of us piled into the C.O.'s car and he drove us to various army and other messes. At a Pongo mess one of the more flippant 2nd Lieuts poured beer over my head which of course cannot be allowed by the RAF, so I pushed him over quite a high wall. That nearly caused a fight. On the way home we had to stop the car for half a dozen geese which would not get out of the way. We hopped out but could only catch one which we brought back to the Mess and named Scruffy. He is a grand chappie but prefers to live outside of the mess now.

With Scruffy we have Hooby the kitten and a small chicken which sat on one egg for weeks and hatched it so now we have chicks too. During Christmas they were all running around inside the mess and an oldish American turned up from God knows where, a civilian. He went around putting out his hand to everyone and murmuring sadly in his drawl "I am

Doc. Stewart". We were tight without exception and he was sober. I have wondered since what he thought of us all and our farmyard, he is to lecture on British and American relations, or something.

As you can imagine this is a crazy place, most of us are "around the bend", do you know the term? Cheerio for now, Toto darling, you know I am always thinking of you and shall always want you, love, Joe

Joe to Margaret 31st December 1944

Margaret my darling, yesterday I received your telegram, it was awfully nice of you to send it, it gave me a nice warm feeling inside and I could not stop myself smiling and feeling really good. But apart from that it was a relief to know that you were OK because I had not received any letters from you for a while, and the God-damn V2's are a worry.

There is a lot of disturbance in the Mess tonight and I find it difficult to concentrate. On such occasions as this I can only think of such things as "I love you darling" to tell you, which must get a trifle boring to you. But to try and put dreams and plans into words and a constant yearning that goes out from me, for you dear, is beyond the powers of my pen. You will have to accept it, tell me that you do when you write darling, please?

I nearly got a trip to Durban but another fellow is going. I will ask him to get you some stockings dear, I expect you have difficulty in getting them, the size and colour will have to be a guess. Pity I am not going, there are lots of things I would like to have got to take home with me. The big day seems as distant as ever, nothing seems to happen these days but keep your fingers crossed for the end of January. Keep writing sweet heart, I will send you a telegram if there is any news.

Lots of luck for the New Year, lets make it our year, all my love darling, Joe

16.   January 1945

Jan 1945 OBE awarded to Wing Commander "Fats" Louw (photo, right).

Joe to Margaret 2ⁿᵈ January 1945 Tulear

Joe to Margaret 2nd January 1945 Tulear

My dear Margaret, I must admit to myself that I am worried about you. Until last night when the third mail plane arrived with no news of you, I imagined I was but now I am sure. You see darling you have been writing so regularly for months now and no mail from you spells something wrong. With luck I shall be away from here in a few days and if I have another disappointment on my return, will wire you.

Of all the things that might prevent your mail from reaching me I can only seriously consider three. The first is that you are ill, the second that you are a casualty – God forbid either of these – and the third that it has been held up in transit. I just cannot entertain thoughts seriously of – another boyfriend, something in my letters that you objected to, or any of those silly things that do upset lovers, I feel that we two are above all that. Sorry about all this dear, how I shall laugh when I am presented with a large bundle of Northwood mail on my return! You have grown on me, you know, just how much I realise when my one means of communication stops. When I remember how I thought of you at Oban and my conception of you now, I realise how very intimately I have seemingly got to know you. To think that fourteen months ago I was one of your many casual friends and that I now have the audacity to look upon myself as <u>the</u> favoured one, it makes me a little frightened sometimes dear, does it help to show how much I love you? Yours always, Joe

PS An Aussie friend of mine from the squadron will arrive in London soon and have told him to look you up, hope you do not mind, you will like him. Name John Pinkard.

Margaret to Joe 2ⁿᵈ January 1945

Margaret to Joe 2nd January 1945

Darling funny sweet Joe, you are truly delightful, your letters are absolutely perfect. I have just received two written on the 20ᵗʰ and 21ˢᵗ Dec – and you ask how much money we shall need to get married, <u>when</u> we have decided that we want to marry each other. Have you already decided then darling?

Your way of reasoning, dear, is most of the time very clear and sensible but just at times, you are utterly and charmingly illogical, and your letters are things of joy and I shall keep them forever, even if you decide you <u>don't</u> want to marry me. Seriously, dear one, I honestly have no idea, I hadn't really given much thought to the practical side of loving you. Getting married, in as much as the actual ceremony is concerned, can be either inexpensive or expensive, depending on the number of people you want to be there and the way you want the whole thing done. But Joe, just so long as somebody says that we are well and truly married, and that you belong to me, I don't care if we are married in a barn. In fact I'd really rather like us just to be very quietly married (would you mind a Catholic church darling?) with just our own people there. Then, as far as anything else goes, a house etc, there isn't very much we can do until we are both out of the service is there? Unless I start having babies right away I shall have to stay in for some time yet. Darling sweet, you know how I should love to have babies, but I do agree with what you said some time back, that we might wait just a little, at first, because I want you completely to myself, at least until I have begun to believe that you are really home again, and really have a chance to make you believe how much I love you, it's a tremendous amount darling.

Joe, I have told you something of my family. They are really dying for you to come home, I want you to see something of them when you are on leave, will you darling? The unfortunate thing is that there is nowhere to stay at home, so I have told Daddy that we shall both stay somewhere in London, so that we, or at least, I can take you to see them, it only means getting from one side of London to the other. It is absolutely marvellous of you to save so much money darling, but don't for goodness sake ever worry about it, it makes no difference to me whether you have any money or not, we'll have a lot of fun anyway. I'm just terribly impatient for you to come home, I pray it may be soon. Just in case it is sudden darling, always ring NORTHWOOD 2200 Extension 178, and they will always tell you where I am. I love you sweetheart, your Margaret.

Margaret to Joe 6th January 1945

My darling sweetheart, you must imagine by now that I have completely forgotten all about you, having written so erratically for two weeks. You have been in my thoughts the whole time though, more than ever before, if that were possible, because I never know now when I shall see you, and how much I want you here is far more than my pen can describe. Its funny darling, you'll probably call this "dripping", but I'm sure you will understand, I feel more every day as though we belong together, and those lovely dreams you tell me about, are just like mine.

In your sea mail letter you asked if you could be the only one ever to be really close to me. Darling, even if you didn't want it, it would be like that, the thought of anybody else ever being as near to me as you have been, and will be, is shudder-making, and when I think of us being married, it just somehow seems right. I know I shouldn't say this darling but one of the things I dream about, often, is a little boy, exactly like you, it would be wonderful to have a small edition of J.T.P. – those are wizard initials, Joe!

I had a sudden thought today, a stupid one, but you must hear it, I just happened to be thinking of us, when, idly into my mind came a picture of you with somebody else, and not me, it caused me a moment of sheer misery, unreasoning panic. Too silly of me dear one, and forgive me if I am indulging in adolescent imaginings, but if I ever wake up in the morning, knowing that I haven't you, then I am lost and life is quite truly not worth living. It's hard to imagine now how I filled my thoughts before we met, life must have been very empty I think, or perhaps I was not wise enough to know it, and existed in untroubled ignorance of what real and lovely happiness is.

I feel, deep down inside me, that we shall be very happy Joe, because you love me as I you, and we are idealists, the worthwhile things in life have been shown to us, and we have taken them, knowing their value, and they will show us in their turn, more beauty of mind and spirit than we can guess can exist.

I love you with all my heart and soul and know quite truly that although everyday tiresome things can, and do, force them selves to the fore of our daily lives, that deep satisfying glow will steadily persist, so that in the end, it will be the only lasting thing. I need you badly sweetheart, and when you come home everything will be so much easier, because of you. Yours always, all my love, Margaret

Margaret to Joe 8th January 1945

Darling, it must be very difficult for you to imagine anything being cold, at the moment, but here it is so cold that even the beauty of the country which, with successive frosts and now a thin layer of snow, is really lovely, cannot comfort me. I'm working in Ops with greatcoat and mittens on, and still shiver.

Don't worry about V2's darling, we are some miles out of London and although we do hear the bumps in the distance so far none have reached us. My people are not so lucky. As you know they are in East London and are incredibly plucky. Already during the war they have been blasted 5 times. The house we lived in at Dagenham was rendered useless by a bomb during the blitz, I was still at home then, a sweet 18 year old , and when we came back from a concert one Sunday afternoon with the whole family, except Frankie, it was only to discover we had no place to eat or sleep for that night, all very sad. Mummy has been away with the kids several times but hates to be away from Daddy, so she always comes back to London where he has to work, and now the two boys are back too, Peter at the local secondary school and Stanley at the school across the road. They have both changed their schools far too many times during the war, it's difficult for Mummy to decide what to do, she doesn't mention going away again, I have the feeling she is a little fatalistic about it and would rather stay and take a chance, just so as to be at home, with what little home she has left. Somehow I feel she is right, they are all so happy together, it has been dreadful to move away and to be parted so much, and so many times, too.

Joe my dear, I have been wanting to ask you, do your parents know about me? And will they mind? About the leave I mean. It seems terribly mean to steal you for two whole weeks out of three. After all, my parents see me every week but yours haven't seen you for what will be about 18 months. You must tell me if you think they will mind, I should hate to hurt them in spite of the fact that I want every second of your leave to be mine. I love you, dear one, yours always, Margaret

Margaret to Joe 8th January 1945

Margaret to Joe 8th January 1945

Darling Joe, every word anybody ever said about the beauty of the country in snow is true, every word I mean. This afternoon I went up the hill and through the golf course to get to the hairdresser at the NAAFI hostel, and the snow covered my shoes completely, just as I reached the door of the hostel the sun was coming out with a deep red glow covering the whole of the horizon.

Just beyond the house is a valley with the hill rising beyond it gradually, with a gentle sort of reluctance, and there was a little black dog rushing madly about trying to swallow all the snow in sight, I'm certain it must have been the first snow he had ever seen, and quite the happiest day in his young life. Darling, I must know when your birthday is, please, do you know you are 3 years older than I? I think that is rather perfect, and Joe, can we have a dog?

Margaret, my young aunt, you know the one who married recently, was telling me the other night about her honeymoon. Her husband's sister has a small house in Surrey and she turned it over to them lock stock and barrel for as long as they wanted it, and then went to live with her mother to keep out of the way. Don't you think it was marvellous of her? Margaret hadn't seen Ted for nearly 3 years and she said it was really the most delightful and wisest thing they could have done, to get right away from everybody they knew and find out all about each other, because although they have known each other for years they had both changed a lot during that separation and it was so much easier to be alone. She was a little frightened about cooking, but Ted was so clever about it, she still isn't sure whether she has hidden talent or whether he has quite unusual powers of self control, or maybe a more than averagely good digestion.

I received a compliment from my baby brother, Stanley, yesterday, which really gave me an unwarranted amount of pleasure. He just said, what was my boyfriend's name, I told him Joe, and he said well I reckon he likes you, when I asked him why he replied Oh well I think you're rather (pronounced rarver) nice. Considering that, quite apart from being possibly the most loveable youngster one could meet, he pretends to be the toughest thing in creation, you can understand that I had the utmost difficulty in restraining myself and not hugging him, which would have annoyed him intensely. He's 11 years old tomorrow and reckons he's not far off being the most grown up member of the family. He still loves to be allowed to sleep with me, although my imagination has rather let me down lately for bedtime stories, it's a pity he's growing up, I loathe the idea of not having him whispering all his little secrets to me in bed any more. Write lots darling, I love you, Margaret

Joe to Margaret 9th January 1945

My darling, you must be disappointed with my letters these days, I cannot seem to get what I want into them. Often I begin to write with definite things in my mind to tell you, but on reading them over find that I have missed the important points or have muddled them up. This is often due to the disturbances around, as there is usually no place to write but in the Mess, so please forgive me, little girl.

This climate certainly spoils the memory and slows everyone down. I noticed it particularly when first arriving out here, it would be necessary to tell people everything twice before they could grasp it. For myself I often have not a clue on my doings or whereabouts, say, ten days previous. And I find myself thinking of you as someone who I am always yearning for and who I cannot live without. To remember what made me fall in love with you – those many things that I will try and tell you about some day – it is necessary for me to ponder on days when I knew you in Oban. Because it was only for a short while dear, and a long, long time ago, almost 17 months in fact. The 17 months have made me surer with every month that "we two" is inevitable.

Your letters have been wizard. We have learnt so much about one another through our letter writing, mine have always lacked something I'm afraid.

Reading your past letters I imagine that latterly you have not written as light-heartedly as in your previous ones. I often sit down to write to you in lighter vein but find myself thinking of serious things and you get quite a different letter to the one I intended, but do not let my moods affect you darling. You must always be your own sweet self, we will have lots of fun together all day and every day. Do not forget, it will not be long before I am home now and, damn it, when we do meet up, we both turn a page of the old life's history, and gosh what a page it will be, lets make a book of it! All my love darling, Joe

Margaret to Joe, undated, assumed to be mid January

First fragment of the letter torn....but it seems it really is to be a white winter, yet another and heavier fall greeted us this morning, still very lovely, but oh so cold, and wet underfoot. Literally the only thing to take one's mind off the cold is to work, or sleep. I suppose a long walk would be the answer, but the thought of the first freezing mile, before the old circulation gets going, is enough to decide me quite definitely against it.

Coming on watch this morning was a most hazardous business, my bicycle tyres are old and very smooth and the surface of the road was, as you can imagine, with a frost following immediately upon a snowfall, treacherous. I slid from one side of the road to the other, only just keeping my balance, and proved to be a positive menace to pedestrians and the few motorists on the road. It would have been far safer to walk – but time – and the fact that I'd stayed too long in bed forced me to use a quicker method of getting to Ops, and of course, it proved to be far longer by the time I'd pedalled sideways and sometimes backwards, most of the way.

I can't help thinking, or hoping, darling, that you might be on your way, because I've had no mail for some weeks now, it's a nasty feeling, this having no mail from you, your letters are the only ones I ever really want from the postman, I find it most difficult to concentrate upon anything, it's silly of me isn't it? But you are so far away, and the relief of a letter is more delightful than I can possibly describe.

It's really rather foolish to worry about letters not coming, because so many things can happen to them en route, it's rather amusing really and truly, when you realise that my life is governed, in happiness or misery, by a funny little man with glasses and a most sad face, staggering up the hill with a sack and a bicycle, hating everybody who ever writes to anybody, because he has to carry them on his back. There are days when I love that little man, but there are other, many more days, when I could quite easily strangle him, convinced that he so deliberately holding your beloved letters from me.

Did I tell you that Joan Collins, the ex-Nairobi Cypher Queen is going to show me a picture of the whole squadron? I hope to see it today, if she hasn't gone to London. Please don't miss writing darling, if you possibly can help it, it's the only thing I value in the whole week. All my love sweetheart, Margaret

(until this promotion Margaret's WAAF rank was senior to Joe's RAF rank).
You ask about Christmas – I can describe it all to you in three words – I was working – and also on New Years Eve, so I reckon I can spare you the details. I can still awake a fair amount of enthusiasm for parties, but not at H.Q.C.C. There was one recently, the night after New Years Eve, which was quite fun. Nancy asked me to entertain an Army friend of hers whom she had arranged to bring and then couldn't get down from Langham, he was quite amusing so really it wasn't too bad.

Frankie has been sent to a ship, I can't say much about it except that I think if you are home at the beginning of this year, you will meet him as I had hoped.

Darling sweet, please don't worry about V.2's, really and truly its quite all right here, so don't give it a second thought. I'm glad you got my cable, but surprised it took so long, it was sent a fortnight before Christmas, just to make sure, and the Post Office said it should only be three days.

Darling, I have a confession to make, the photograph I have been waiting for so long, has arrived, and Joe, honestly it isn't worth sending because it just doesn't look like me at all. The only thing I can do now is to get another one done at another place, where I think they take 3 weeks, and then send it on to you. If you should come home before it arrives then I can give you one personally with my own fair hands.

Joe carried this photo in his wallet for the rest of his life

I do hope you are getting my mail now dear, I know how horrid it is when there is none. All my love dearest, yours always, Margaret

Joe to Margaret 13th January 1945

My darling, I am still stuck in the same hole in Madagascar, my letters of last week were addressed incorrectly and I shall probably be court marshalled, even that would be a welcome change.

Yesterday I nearly wrote you a complete letter on the decadent priesthood, particularly overseas padres. He arrived, the squadron padre I mean, direct by air from the squadron, knowing full well that we were here, almost 20 of us, but did he bring our mail, did he hell! He is only down here on a jolly, material things that matter do not interest him, and spiritual things "it is so difficult over here you know" and he fusses around like an old woman. And he had to sit next to me making noises over his food like a pig and stuffing himself to the brim. If he only knew how I was feeling, actually I believe he did, and he thinks he is flying back with me – HA HA! I am boss of my aeroplane, if my feelings <u>do</u> improve and I take him, he will sit in the bilges, and I hope he is sick! Meanwhile my bitterness is slowly subsiding.

Sorry about this sweetheart but forgetting, or not remembering, mail is the greatest sin that can be committed overseas. It is the more unforgivable because of my worries that I wrote to you about last week. Damn funny how I have been tormented this last week by a subconscious, ominous feeling in my mind that all is not well with you. Even if it turns out that I have been a worrying fool, please write and tell me if there is anything worrying you darling, about this time?

I have been reading through all the letters you ever wrote me, they are wonderful letters, quite a lot of them now too. Hope to goodness we do not have another period of letter writing like this one, it is such a poor substitute for being together but better than nothing I guess. Rather strange having to get to know about one another by letter, because we did you know. Thank goodness we were able to learn the things that matter between us in Scotland.

There are so many things I want to know about that are probably written in your letters that are on the way. The six letters I whipped off in reply to the sea mail letters you attached a certain amount of importance to, must have arrived, I do hope they all made sense. And I wonder if my parcel arrived and whether Maltby looked you up. I am told that F/Lt John Penhard left for UK about a week ago and should arrive at the beginning of February, he is a good chap. He promised he would write to you when he arrives, hope you will not mind, he is an Aussie. Cheerio for now dear, Love, Joe

Margaret to Joe 14ᵗʰ January 1945

Darling Joe, I must write today, even though there is very little to tell you really. I don't think I told you that I went the other day to see "Blithe Spirit" at the Duchess theatre - with Penelope Dudley-Ward playing the spirit of the man's first wife. It's a lovely thing, all about a playwright who marries for the second time in middle age, his first wife having been very young and attractive, died of pneumonia, his second wife attractive, sophisticated, but a very different and older type. They had a mad spiritualist to dinner one night and she conjures up the spirit of Elvira, the first wife, who can be seen and heard only by her husband. The resulting confusion and misunderstanding is lovely to see, the second wife thinks he has gone mad and won't believe there is a third presence in the room, and when he is being rude to Elvira, Ruth, the second wife, swears he is insulting her, every time Ruth says something Elvira makes a nasty crack and Charles answers Elvira and Ruth thinks he is answering her, and so it goes on throughout the whole play. If it is still playing when you come home darling, we must see it, I'm sure you would love it.

We are on three watches still, Mabel has left now, for the P.D.C. she had a number of people up to the Mess last night for drinks, I was going on duty so only saw her for about a minute, for which I was really rather thankful, because for one dreadful moment, when I was saying goodbye to her, I was sure she was going to burst into tears. It must be quite a wrench for her really, she's been here 3 years and knows just about everybody there is to know. I don't believe she has many friends outside the service anyway, so in a way it's almost like leaving home to her.

I'm going to see my family on Tuesday, they'll be pleased to know that Frankie isn't going abroad yet.

Joe, you often mention a man called Bill, is he one of your crew? I think you must think quite a lot of him, he often crops up in your letters to me (*this would be Bill Graham, Joe's Australian navigator. He and Joe were the only officers in their crew and would have spent a lot of time together*)

Darling, I have been trying to find a piece of leopard skin to match my lovely bag, I want to make a collar for a coat, most of the ones here are imitation and they look horrid. If you go into civilisation again do you think you could find a small piece to match? It doesn't matter if you can't. All my love dearest, yours always, Margaret

Margaret to Joe 15th January 1945

Darling, the most amusing thing happened this morning, one of the Y Branch types tore a great rent in the knee of his trousers, and borrowed a needle and cotton to mend it, he showed me the result, which to put it mildly, was ghastly. I told him that if he gave me the trousers I'd make it look a bit more respectable. He straightaway shot off to the cloakroom, sent a clerk into the Ops room with the trousers, and sat there shivering for about ten minutes while I struggled with the tear.

Of course, while I was sitting there doing the wretched thing, all <u>sorts</u> of people had to come in and ask for things, and looked aghast at the Duty Plotter enthroned in the middle of the Ops Room, sewing a pair of trousers. Poor little man, he still looks rather as though he'd been put through a hedge rather rapidly, but at least he isn't showing his bony knee through the tear.

It's most sordid here at the moment, the snow has gone into a grey mass of slush, and underneath there's a freeze, which is anything but pleasant, or safe. I've seen so many people sit down quite suddenly, with a surprised look on their faces, I've just given up laughing.

There's a party in the Mess scheduled for the 19th, I don't think I shall go, that is, unless my mood improves, I feel just a little anti-social at the moment, there's no reason, except the small and possibly weak one, that I find it too much effort to be pleasant to people I don't care two pins for. It's all right darling, its only a spasm, its just because its so long since we had any time off at all, that I'm beginning to feel slightly mutinous, it'll pass.

Pauline has had her board for India, but doesn't know yet whether she has passed, I do hope she has, in a way, because new places and new work will help her forget her nasty experience, which still seems to be on her mind sometimes, when she is feeling a bit low.

The thing I wait for now darling, even more than your letters, which are terribly important, is the cable saying that you are coming, it can't be too soon for me. Do write lots of letters dear, I do look forward to them so much. All my love darling, Margaret

Joe to Margaret 16th January 1945

My darling, at lunchtime today I was surprised to see all of our Mess boys looking glum, with hands bandaged up to the wrists. Apparently Lysol had been issued by the NAAFI for the first time and floors had been scrubbed with it. About half an hour afterwards the boys had complained of sore hands and were duly sent down to sick quarters. But the joke was this, the boy who works outside, also used the Lysol on his "seats" and a Frenchman had cause to use one while still wet. Now this stuff has a delayed action, and shortly after this everyday occurrence a very worried Frenchman presented himself too, at sick quarters, I imagine the orderly is now out of bandages! – eating food standing up presents its difficulties, or lying on the stomach, a little like camping out.

Joe at the Squadron base, hard at work.

The sergeants mess at Diego Suarez, which doesn't look much different to the officer's mess above.

There have been some Dutch Officers (M.N.) ashore. What grand people they were, the best one could hope to meet anywhere. Any RAF officers near their ship would be quickly whipped into a cabin and presented with a cold bottle of Tennants (British) beer. And not just one beer but many, with Bols Dutch Gin Liquer. But they are not good fellows because of their generosity, everything about them is first class, their manners, speech and outlook on things generally. They all speak English, French, German and Dutch fluently, lucky people. We shall have to improve our, or at least my, French when we go for our holiday abroad darling, we might be able to go, who knows? We could if we used the youth hostels providing they start again after the war. There are hundreds of things we should be able to do anyway.

Did I tell you that some Belgian friends of mine (whom I met in 1942) got in touch with me, through a staff sergeant? They would like nothing better than for us to go and stay with them. They invited me dozens of times when I was living with them – I told them I would look them up after the invasion, so why not? (*this would have been Roger and Stephanie LeBlois who became lifetime friends*) But you might prefer Paris, I have some friends there too, I wonder if they are still alive? (*Rene and Raymonde Coache, also to become lifetime friends*).

Later Good news darling, tomorrow we return! I shall soon know now if your letters are still coming, cannot write more now until I know. All my love sweetheart, Joe

Margaret to Joe 18*th* January 1945

Darling, I do hope everything is all right, the mail has not been very fruitful now for a couple of weeks, I'm not worrying stupidly darling, but your letters have been coming regularly now for several months and its queer not to have any at all. When I have your letters I feel that I can do anything, without effort, but when they don't come, I feel quite lifeless, everything is too much trouble, and the only moment during the day which means anything at all is when the postman comes.

Sorry dear, please don't think I am grumbling, indeed I think I am very lucky in many ways, one of our plotters has a fiancé who has been overseas for four years, can you imagine how dreadful that must be? Poor thing, she worries most of the time now in case he finds her changed for the worse. I wonder what you will think of me when we meet? Tomorrow, or Monday, I am going to have a final fitting for my blue velvet dress, it looked quite good in its raw state, all pinned together, I do hope it looks proportionately good in its highly civilised finished state too.

Joe, I wonder if Audrey would care to come up to have dinner with me one night? Should I ask her d'you think? You will remember perhaps that she wrote and suggested that we meet in Town, when she was on leave, but unfortunately her suggestion arrived just a wee bit too late, I had to go on duty, and there was no way of letting her know that I couldn't be there, I was rather disappointed, because I really had looked forward to meeting her.

Incidentally, I wonder if you have noticed how very crumpled my letters to you are? It's because I always put an odd one in my bag, in case I get a moment to write during the day, sometimes I'm afraid they stay there for several days before they get written, or at least just recently it has been like that, because nowadays, when we are not actually working, we have to catch up on sleep, twice now I have fallen asleep for a moment in the bath, gosh the water's been jolly chilly when I've woken up. Still, all that's nearly over, we have a new girl under training, so when she is "finished" we'll have a bit of relief. Nevertheless my sweet dear, when you come home I shall have two weeks leave or bust! I love you very much, yours always, Margaret

Joe to Margaret 19th January 1945

My darling, I am still at the place I wrote from at the beginning of the month. After being airborne for an hour or so on the 17th I had to return. Disappointed? What do you think, it is now more than three weeks since I received your last letter. My hopes are optimistic....*letter torn and part missing*.....I do not know, it seems that your letters have been regulating my week, darling.

The food here is excellent. Lots of eggs, every kind of fruit and chickens at 11/6d each, are only a few of the luxuries which, coupled with no exercise are helping to distend my stomach. My sister, Margaret, who you may remember is married to an army type from Derby, is living at home now in delightful anticipation of a baby, and if I am home soon I feel I can offer her some competition.

Luck is becoming my unhappy state but you have my assurances that I will take steps to rectify it dear, although the thought of taking any steps at all right now in this heat is agonising. But I promise I will walk a mile tonight darling, just for your sake and, if its OK with you, will stop half way to partake of the local rum and citron, which will be for my sake I suppose. Afraid I am writing like a drip this afternoon which is so well in keeping with my perspiring self, that I will stop for a while.

21 Jan –Having read over my letter I am in two minds about sending it, but it so happens that the stamps are already stuck on and stamps are scarce. We arrived back today thank goodness and I am anxiously waiting for the person who looks after the mail to arrive.

There is nothing definite about our tour expiring but the chances within the next few weeks seem quite good. But there are so many rumours going through the Mess that it is not wise to take too much notice of them.

The Padre has now redeemed himself. He has been chosen for a football match and when somebody suggested he was an ex-international he replied "Well, not exactly an international, but I did play for the Stafford Clergy against the Leicester Police in 1925" Bye for now, darling, Love, Joe.

Margaret to Joe 20th January 1945

Darling Joe, I had a letter yesterday describing your merry-making at Christmas, the thought of you standing dripping beer and then turning round and pushing the bloke off the wall is really very funny, but darling, must you really go around breaking peoples necks? Or anyway nearly breaking them. If ever I do or say something which annoys you, will you push me off a wall? Or maybe just give me a gentle tap on the dome with a large hammer? In a way I'm glad you like fights, I like them too, we'll have some wonderful scraps when you come home, the only rule I make is that you don't pull my hair, that's a thing which definitely has an unfortunate psychological effect on me.

The mess party turned out to be great fun after all, everybody was very merry and bright for a change, and nobody really thought about anybody else's rank, which of course is most unusual here.

I think I told you a story about rabbits, or kippers, and when it was re-peated to me this morning, it sounded most vague and terribly complicated, apparently I'd got far with it and then forgotten the end of the story, so of course the whole thing sounded a trifle weird. Quite frankly I don't really think I ever knew a story about rabbits or kippers, so why I ever started it I can't imagine.

I met Norman Cooper, one of the lads who was with the Norge (?) squad-ron, just before you came up to Oban, I don't think you ever met him dear, did you? He's a little Canadian, about five feet nothing high, a round pink beaming face, and a wizard wit, most amusing, we had a long chat about the old Oban days. I afraid I absorbed far too much drink though, I felt quite wizard last night but had to make a terrific effort to get up in time for duty this morning. I'm going to have to catch up on some sleep though, because we really did stay up to an incredible hour this morning, seeing who could tell the tallest story.

Write hundreds of letters darling, please?, and if you come home soon I might even let you push me off a wall. All my love darling, yours always, Margaret

Margaret to Joe 22nd January 1945

Darling, I met somebody just back from Nairobi today, a WAAF Cypher Officer called Joan Collins, do you remember her? She has been telling me all about the mess, and what a nice squadron yours is, she told me too what a nasty climate it is, I know that of course from you, but it seemed to bring it home to me with some force coming from Joan, who can tell me verbally, it must be absolutely frightful. It's marvellous meeting somebody who actually met you out there, she thinks you might quite possibly be home very soon, I do hope she's right.

Another thing I discovered is that Rupert Taylor is now the Chief Nav. Officer here, I have seen him about in the Mess for the last few months but never knew until now that he is your ex-chief.

Darling, do you really drink the dreadful local wine that Joan speaks of? She said it's really rather like raw methylated spirits, wouldn't that make one frightfully ill? I don't like the thought of your being ill, Joe, I want you to stay well and fit.

Dear one, I know you don't like dripping letters, but I must tell you again how much I want you home, and how damn useless life will be until you come home to me. I thought that after a while I should become resigned to just filling in time whilst waiting for you, but I'm afraid that becoming resigned is harder than I imagined. It's so silly when you have as little to do to have to stay away for so long. It was a little unsettling talking to Joan Collins really, I did envy her so much, and longed to be able to do as she had done, just fly over and see you. If I could only see you for one moment, I really wouldn't mind coming back and waiting again. There has been no news of you now dearest for over two weeks, I wonder if you are out on attachment again? When I consider how completely I depend upon your letters over here, I realise how much worse it must be for you to be without home news. Have you been getting my letters regularly darling? I do hope so, it would be dreadful to cause you any unnecessary worry. God bless sweetheart, I love you always with all my heart, yours always, Margaret

Margaret to Joe 22nd January 1945

Darling sweetheart, I've been thinking a great deal today of the first time we shall meet, when the day arrives, I shall be very frightened I think, frightened in case I'm not as you think of me. A rather queer thing happened this evening, I was reading a book, a very technical one on Navigation when suddenly, unexpectedly, a picture of you flashed into my mind, you were so close that it was a shock when I realised it was only a thought, and that you really weren't there at all, it upset my good intentions to read D.R.Nav completely, I just had to put it down. Darling, it may not be long now, it's a lovely thought that soon I'll get a 'phone call or a telegram, I wonder how I really will know of your homecoming? And then the unbelievable will be true, I shan't believe it until I see you really and truly there. If I can't see you at the very first humanly possible moment I shall simply die. All my colds have finally disappeared and I feel full of the joys of Spring once more, I do hope I haven't a beastly cold when I see you darling, I hope too that it won't be freezing when you come home, you will feel it terribly after East Africa.

Have you had any more work to do recently? It must be quite unbearable to sit about with nothing useful to do, I wish you were here with so much time to spare, it would be marvellous, I could be with you in all my off duty time, imagine seeing you practically every day, although my work would suffer very badly.

Darling, is there anything you want me to get for you, before you come home?

I'm on night duty now and intend to get in a couple of hours sleep, because I'm going to see Mummy tomorrow and if I arrive looking tired she'll jump on me. Tomorrow is Monday, the first post of the week, a letter from you, usually, I wish it were morning now. I love you terribly much, Your Margaret

Margaret to Joe 24th January 1945

Darling, There's a great pile of work waiting for me but I can't settle down to it, I'm due to hand over my watch in a couple of hours which will mean a mad rush starting about one hour from now. I tried to find out some gen the other day, about your homecoming, but the sugar-daddy (your term darling) wasn't playing, I don't think he knew as a matter of fact, he's one of those types who like to have people imagining they have all the inside dope on everything.

Joe, when you come home will you spend the first week at home? That would be best I think, because then I should have time to arrange my leave.

Pat, one of our plotters, there are four of us altogether, is waiting for her Bernard to come and I have a feeling that both you and he might arrive at the same time. If that does happen, our leave, Pat's and mine, will certainly take a bit of organising, because we both want two weeks and if they come during the same time, it'll mean leaving the other two girls on two watches, which can't be done. Bernard apparently is due about the middle of February, I do hope you come either before or after he does, because I just couldn't bear it if you were here and I couldn't be with you.

Have you heard more frequently from Audrey recently, Joe? I have several times thought of writing to her again but really it isn't fair, it would be better to wait until you come home I think, don't you?

It was sweet of you to ask your chum to get me some stockings darling, as a matter of fact the stocking question here is most trying, the only stockings which are not difficult to get are not worth wearing, and look quite ghastly. I bought two pairs of service grey, rather nice silk ones, the other day, and have succeeded in laddering every single stocking, I'm afraid my language rather shocked my roommate when I discovered the last ladder, but I reckon it was excusable, there's nothing worse than trying to get decent ones, and when one ladders those, well life just is the absolute end.

However, if when I meet you sweet, I am stocking less, you will be able to sympathise with my cold and blue legs, for assuredly it looks as though that's what'll happen. What a mournful letter! Sorry darling, I love you, Margaret

Joe to Margaret 26th January 1945

Darling, I have just read a short story in the Penguin New Writing (number 19 Oct-Dec) called 36 hours. It tells of the feelings and worries of a man who is about to become a father, the title gives a small indication of the contents.

After I had read it I felt quite scared, gosh it is all very terrible! You see, Toto, my darling, it is so easy to allow my imagination to wander (in fact it is now beyond my control) and the very thought of you.... I should feel such a brute, and yet there is no way out if we are to accomplish our dreams? But if all the money I had would help, you know I would wish no better use for it and I think money does make a difference in such matters? Damn it, I suppose I am a sentimental fool thinking about things like that, I feel for you such a lot these days. Do people in love write to one another like that? We two are so very... (*illegible section*)... we meet, and did not realise what the score was until we have parted, in fact until we are thousands of miles apart. And from this end I wonder if the unity that did not materialise before will happen when we meet again, and although I am sure it will, I have no proof. So instead of writing such things as ...(*illegible section*)... would you prefer to be the peacetime wife of an Air force officer, a civil pilot or an ordinary civilian? – the RAF might mean being abroad for two years, the civil pilot for several years with long leaves and the other being at home always? If we can choose shall we live in the city, town or country? Where shall we spend our honeymoon? Let us promise one another never to go to sleep at night without telling the other if there is something on our minds, would you like to spend a holiday living quite rough, sleeping in a tent, stopping where we want, going where we want and being quite unusual, do you mind if I do not talk very much before breakfast and may I read the headlines of the paper? – Instead of writing lots of silly and serious things such as these, I must write to quite another person, who I am vain enough to believe shares my hopes, yet until we are sure it must be. When that time comes we shall soon begin to delve much deeper into our own personal selves. Even after about six months of strenuous letter writing I feel I know you so much better dear, in fact I love you in a slightly different way, a deeper more solid way, I guess it is because you have let me know you better. Will write again tomorrow answering your letters and telling you my chances of an early departure. Do you think I love you darling? Try stopping me! You did once! Second thoughts? Joe.

Joe to Margaret 27th January 1945

My darling, this letter will be more scrappy than usual because I am going to answer the little queries you have asked in your letters this year.

It gives me a pleasant feeling to know that your folk know that there is someone after their daughter. I hate meeting people who I am forced to meet, I cannot behave naturally, but I already feel quite differently about the Dillons. Please let us not do any visiting until we have spent a few days together? And you must come down to Kent too, my Mum knows about you, but only that you are a special friend, she can only guess <u>how</u> special. I have not expressed myself too well above when I used the word "friend", I mean people I am introduced to who are perfect strangers in every way.

It is highly probable that when I arrive back I shall spend a few days in London at the Air Ministry before I get my official leave, which will give us time to make arrangements. If things go wrong and I have to do my full time it will be 12 weeks from now before you get any leave, a hell of a time for you to wait, darling, for your leave. Indications are quite good however but there cannot be any certainty, sorry to be so difficult.

So your young brother thinks you are rather nice. What wisdom for 11 years! Perhaps after the war they will be (both brothers) able to come down to Kent for a few days, or would they find it too dull? If Frankie is sent East do give him my address and brief him to write to me, if he goes around the Cape it is 10 to 1 his ship would call at Mombassa and I am often there. It would be grand if we could have a couple of evenings out together.

I hate to tell you Toto but two of your miniature photos have disappeared and I have only one sadly bent one left. They were lost because I have no wallet now and there are no buttons on my shirt pockets. Do not bother to send a big one but if you should see a person waving a camera around, stand in front and demand your picture be taken and slip a print inside an A.M.L.C – very important you know, imagine us both walking round and round Trafalgar Square (not too sure about the vowels) Nelson's Monument – without recognising one another!

Will you write and tell me what size piece or pieces of Leopard skin you require and I will get it. And can you make anything with the Indian material I sent? You will have to get the bottom drawer cracking one of these days young lady you know! Did you like the elephant heads? Please use the buttons for anything you want, they are probably useful things for years to come, all women seem to keep innumerable sets of buttons. By the way sweetheart my birthday (my 27th) is on April 30th, when is yours? I love you, Joe

On June 6th 1944 the Allies had launched Operation Overlord, or "D" day, the invasion of German occupied Europe through Normandy. This was the largest amphibious assault in history and was very successful in pushing the Germans back. In mid December 1944 the Germans made a massive counter attack against Allied lines. It was initially successful creating a bulge in the lines. However Allied air superiority and lack of fuel for the Germans meant it could not be sustained and on Jan 28th 1945 the Battle of the Bulge took place and the German army was in retreat back to Germany and the European war was nearly at an end.

Margaret to Joe 29th January 1945

My darling sweetheart, my whole life is changed today, after a silence of several weeks a whole batch of your beloved letters has arrived, all at once, oh gosh it's wonderful, I could sing and just go quite crazy, but I don't think the Controller would appreciate it at all. You see, my dearest darling, I have been thinking exactly the same as you, that something dreadful had happened, and, well, I can't describe how absolutely ghastly life has been with that thought right in the front of my mind the whole time. As for the thought of there being somebody else, that's quite mad you old silly, I haven't a double personality, or anything quite so sinister, and I'm far too crazy about you to even think about anybody else.

I stood the suspense as long as I possibly could and then telephoned Audrey to see if she had heard from you, I'm afraid I gave her rather a shock, she wasn't available the first time I telephoned and I didn't think of leaving a message, but phoned later that evening, she imagined it was bad news from home which made somebody phone so persistently. However she cheered up enormously, she does sound sweet darling, she and her Jack are going on leave in February or March and we intend to meet in London, I so wish you could be home by then Joe, it would be marvellous if we could all meet together.

Darling, I wish it were humanly possible to help you in some way, it must be ghastly to be stuck in some of the dreadful places you have to go to, if only I could come and see you sometimes, it would be wonderful. I expect the weather has held up all the mail, no doubt you have some of mine by now, please don't ever worry about me dear, Mummy and Daddy know how much you mean to me and if anything ever happened they would let you know right away, I promise.

Every time I see them now they ask how you are and are most anxious to see the man who has settled their erratic daughters hash so completely.

Daddy was very disapproving when I sent you the little miniature photographs, he said they were most unflattering and you would want something much more like me to keep in your pocket book, but he seems to have a number of illusions about my beauty (?)

Audrey said she would feel very shy about meeting me, my goodness, if she only knew how petrified I am of meeting her, but she sounded so lovely and sweet on the telephone, I'm not half as frightened as I was before. Your idea of a Sunday at home, when we are together, sounds lovely and I cannot improve upon it darling. I shall probably want to hold your hand the whole time and kiss you at quite the wrong moments, but perhaps if people know just how loopy about you I am, they will forgive.

You said that my letters had become less light-hearted darling, please don't mind that will you? It's just that I long for your homecoming so much that everything else seems so much waste of time, and then we have been working hard too, I just never seem to find the time or energy for frivolous things, I know that sounds awfully weak, but waiting for you becomes just a little trying to one as impatient as I, and every time I look at the map, you seem even farther away than before. But as you say, it won't be long now sweetheart, I pray for you all the time, keep safe dear one, and happy, and don't worry about me, I love you with all my heart and soul, and want only you, you will be convinced of that when you do come, I shall make a point of convincing you. Write many letters darling, and wire me when you are to start for home, I love you, yours for ever, Margaret

Joe to Margaret 31ˢᵗ January 1945

Darling, on arriving back at the squadron a day or so ago I was welcomed with the news of Scotch Whiskey in the mess, 20 bottles of it! But this good news was dwarfed by news of much greater importance, darling, a relief crew is arriving on Thursday, two days hence! The C.O. tells me that I must not bank on it being my relief but….!! Even from here getting home might take six or seven weeks. Please continue writing little girl, I will send an E.M.F. signal when I am posted, then please write to Officers Mess, Eastleigh, East Africa Command. I am sure to be stuck there for a while, mark your letters TO AWAIT COLLECTION or something like that. Hope I am not being too optimistic, gosh when I do get home I shall be too happy even to talk to you, but after that, what a time we are going to have together. You just won't know what has happened to you! You think you will be cold? Not with me around Toto!

Not sure what's happening here

Enough of these tantalising thoughts I wonder if you heard about the hurricane that hit Mauritius at the beginning of January, it was given out on the radio. I flew priority supplies and personnel to the island a few days after it had passed. It was quite a severe cyclone, winds at 95 mph, but fortunately only 15 people killed, lots of injured of course. Most of the native huts were knocked down and a lot of European property severely damaged.

The native men do little or nothing to make good the damage but the women are hard at it carrying bamboo and grass to make more houses, these natives certainly have the gen, believe you me kid, I have picked up a few tips from them! The roads were passable when I arrived, the giant banyan tress having had passageways cut through the branches wide enough for a lorry to pass.

These trees are similar to those shown in the Swiss Family Robinson, with roots growing from the bows. Our mess had been practically demolished but by some stroke of good fortune the bar was intact, I now believe in divine intervention! Sacrilegious? Sorry.

When you write after getting this darling, just tell me once again that you like me and that when we meet everything will be all right, please, because I love you so very much and cannot appreciate life without you, it would be so empty. Yours ever, Joe

17. February 1945

265 Squadron diary 1ˢᵗ February 1945 up 2200 (1ˢᵗ) down 12.10 (2ⁿᵈ) Meteoro-logical research flight in new CAT, to/from Diego Suarez

Joe to Margaret 3ʳᵈ February 1945

Darling, when you write will you please tell me if I can bring you any-thing that you cannot get at home. How about cosmetics? I can now send you material for making the undies you wrote about a while back – will be able to choose my own colour too – ahem. This will arrive under a duty free label in about eight weeks time. Gosh, I am really getting excited now, not at the thought of going home so much, as seeing you darling. Do please tell me if there is anything I can get you, it will give me a big thrill to get it for you, it is easy to send stuff now, and I might as well begin to look after you now, as later.

Yesterday I sent a parcel home, contents mostly for the family, but there were odd things for you dear. I will not risk sending the three pairs of stockings I have for you (from Durban). They are rayon, size 8 ½, and seem to be quite good, hope you like them.

Our C.O. has been posted to Oban of all places! His name is Louw, a wiz-ard fellow, he left today. I will not try to explain my position re my return to UK because everything just now is so mixed. Your letters are coming OK.

So, you want to fight with me do you, you obviously do not know how strong I am! It will be wizard fun though. You know Toto it will take us a few days to get to know one another, I feel I can write things to you now, that I would be too scared to say to you, say the first day we meet, we must get tight on that first day, it will help loosen us up, or would you prefer not?

I do hope you manage to see Audrey perhaps for dinner, she wants to meet you. She is getting quite a serious thinking kid now, her man's influ-ence I guess. It won't be long now kid, all my love, Joe

265 Squadron diary 5ᵗʰ February 1945 W/Co Louw returns to UK

Joe to Margaret 5ᵗʰ February 1945

My darling Margaret, I am feeling a trifle bad about a few things, let me tell you why. To begin with you have held back your leave for me, and I am unable to give any definite date of my return. And I know that you are badly in need of that leave. At this end we are now many new crews over estab-lishment, and the postings to UK do not come through. Although it is probably a matter of finger trouble at H.Q. I can do nothing about it, except patiently wait. To cap everything and to make me feel an utter cad, we are being sent on leave out of the way. This leave does not interfere with embarkation leave in any way of course, and we will be immediately recalled if and when postings come through. Something might happen before we leave in a few days time.

To counter all this however I am told that the trip home from <u>here</u> now takes only 8 days or less! There are numbers of empty transports going home. From all this darling you must realise that I am feeling guilty, but am at a loss to know what to do about it. To ask you to hang on to your extra leave puts me on the spot, if I am to stay overseas another 3 months from now to complete the 18. The set up makes such a thing ridiculous but ....So there you are dear, I must leave it to you to decide, I cannot help you, it would be so easy for me to be selfish.

I shall be able to get you some leopard skin if I get up to Nairobi, and write to you every day, the mail leaving daily from Nairobi. Yesterday a sea mail letter from you arrived written on Dec 5th. It was a lovely letter darling, I do hope you will not be disappointed with me, or perhaps in years to come look back at your earlier ambitions and be one small amount sad that you did not follow them. There seems no reason at all why you should, but no one can see into the future to the extent of being sure of what it holds. But we two can be sure of many things darling, things that we both know are important. Bye for now sweet, love, Joe

265 Squadron diary 7th February 1945 A/S up 0315 Diego Suarez down 0925 Seychelles

Joe to Margaret 7th February 1945

Darling, Once again, under the net – sorry. I am finding it most difficult not to celebrate every night now that the posting is through but if I am to leave the command "square" I cannot. The old cheque book could be brought into use, but that is ours and would hardly be fair, the allowances book will have to be made to last out. The 5/- a day overseas allowance (approx) is very useful, I will miss it.

You know old girl, this bloke of your is getting a hell of a pot on him! No, it is not mythical, it is the genuine article. I do so hope it goes when I get back to UK, should have a tiny one I guess, getting on for 27 you know, not a kid now, you know.

This bl___ Mombasa weather is really at its worst now, my whole body is bathed in perspiration (yes uncovered) and the time is nearly midnight. My movements have been booked and will arrive at Eastleigh on the 16th March, which should mean Northwood by the end of the month, or shortly afterwards. Do absolutely nothing dear until I ring you in UK. I may be able to fly from Cairo (24 hours) or 10 days by ship, the Gods decide.

African scene, location unknown

Strange things happen these days. Cigarettes suddenly become rationed and letter cards most difficult to obtain, and I go round to all manner of people swapping them, fortunately I have quite a supply of cigs, and often smoke a pipe anyway, not that smoking matters.

Am being kept awake by monkeys in the trees, they are quite wild (the monkeys) and seem to have lots of fun. The drunken singing from distant huts becomes so familiar overseas that one takes little notice of it, many lily white boys who "would not touch it " when they "came out" will go back confirmed drunks.

Keep writing darling, you know how much you letters mean to me. Always yours, Joe

Joe to Margaret 8th February 1945

Margaret sweetheart, I am writing this in the air which explains the shaky handwriting and the untidy A.M.L. Instead of going home on leave as was arranged I have been sent to Seychelles, but will be away soon. The adjutant has promised me faithfully that he will signal for my return if a posting comes through, and in the meanwhile time continues to slip past, no one can stop that. Today I bought several hanks of embroidery cottons, about eight colours made by __ I have forgotten, but it is good stuff. Tell me if it is of any use to you dear, because if it is I will save it for you, please don't think there is a veiled suggestion behind it (as when your best friend buys you stationery, or Lifebuoy for Christmas) you did mention in one of your letters that you made things, so I bought them.

As I have been writing, small islands have passed the view from my window, some of them are only about 50 yards long, each with its clump of coconut trees. And even those 50 yards long have a couple of native huts and are inhabited, although they might be 10 miles from the nearest adjacent island. They are mostly of volcanic origin and somehow rise almost sheer out of the water up to 500-1000 feet. Others are coral islands, the type you read about rising only 6 feet above water level and surrounded by a coral reef complete with lagoon. The water is blue and clear and these islands grow nothing but coconuts. Life is very serene and easy, but people only live for effect and themselves and the climate makes it impossible to concentrate on anything. For myself I know that I will miss the sun when I get home but I know I shall gain a lot more.

Apologies for the number of "I"'s in this letter darling, it is because I have none of your letters to answer and I have got that hopeless mood today. Have just remembered, the cause of this despondency is due to the Gin I soaked last night. Bye for now dear, keep smiling, I will be with you soon, Love, Joe

Joe to Margaret 9th February 1945

Margaret sweetheart, am giving you my new address although I am still at Mombasa, please excuse the mess at the top, guess it is the whisky.

Tonight I walked to a high-class hotel and sat on the veranda and watched the dancing. The band was shocking but pleasant in so far as one wanted to jig to it. And, as always, I thought of you dear, wondered whether you were tall, fat or thin, but you once fitted under my arm didn't you and had a wizard little waist then. Some of the girls at the dance (WRENS) looked graceful in their evening gowns while others looked clumsy, I have only ever seen you in service dress, wonder how you look in civvies, have no fear darling I would love you in anything, you know that. Nevertheless it is rather pleasant wondering how my girl will look when I see her, I know I shall be very proud of her, how could I be otherwise?

Saturday the 10th – the light went out on me last night so am finishing this letter in more legible form. There is a slight hitch here at Mombasa, matter of transportation and priorities, and in consequence we did not leave yesterday, but few days will be lost. It is strange how quickly one gets tired of waiting about, when that all-important posting is sitting in the adjutant's office back at the squadron.

Will have to destroy some of your letters dear (*on reading this the editor felt like screaming "don't you dare"!*) as I have so many now and they make quite a bundle. Space will be most valuable travelling part or the whole way by air. If it is possible to save them I will because I value them, will be rather nice to read them in years to come.

It may be difficult to get that skin home darling, since a special license is needed for all skins and that license cannot be got for just the plain skin, not made up into anything I mean. Maltby was able to get those odds and ends out by putting them into bond, since he is Canadian. Will do my best as you know. This material you need is difficult because imported material cannot be exported, hope to be able to let you have some clothing coupons when I get home, they might help. All my love, Joe

Margaret to Joe 10th February 1945

Darling, in your last letter you apologise for writing dull letters to me, don't worry too much about that dear, we can't always be bright and cheerful, we should be quite unbearable if we were like that always. You must be very tired of waiting about with no definite news of coming home at all, but still darling, it can't be very long now, can it? and it's really worth waiting for.

I have two photographs for you now, one in uniform and one in evening dress, although you can only see the straps of the dress, it's a head to shoulders effort. I haven't seen them yet darling, but the man who took them should be bringing them today, so I'm keeping my fingers crossed and hoping they are nice enough to give you. I should hear from Audrey sometime this ... *letter partially torn, fragment missing* ... Joe, dear, if you think you may be coming home at any time now, it will be better if I keep the photographs for you till you come, won't it?

I have been thinking quite a lot about leave in London. You know dear, London just now is frightfully costly, far too expensive for the average person, and I think really and truly that it would cost a small fortune to spend a week on leave there, perhaps we could stay for a few days? Then too – I do want you to see something of my people whilst we are there, do you mind darling? The district where we live is really most uncivilised and there is very little likelihood of finding ... *letter partially torn, fragment missing* ... When Frankie comes home on leave the rearranging is most amusing, we have to have a conference to decide where we are all to sleep.

The last time this particular place was bomb blasted, Mummy went away with the two boys and I used to go during the week to see how Dad was getting on, there was only one serviceable bed left to occupy, and one night

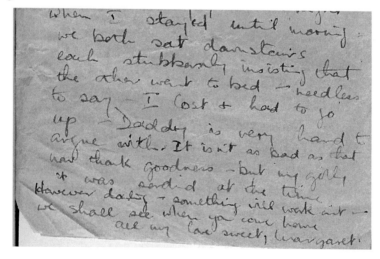

When I stayed until morning – we both sat downstairs each stubbornly insisting that the other went to bed – needless to say – I lost & had to go up – Daddy is very hard to argue with. It isn't as bad as that now thank goodness – but my girl it was sordid at the time. However darling – something will work out – we shall see when you come home – all my love sweet, Margaret.

Joe to Margaret 11ᵗʰ February 1945

Margaret sweetheart, to arrive back on the squadron and to find four of your letters awaiting me demands a letter back on the spot. It is amazing how your mail puts me into a good mood on the spot, in fact I find myself beaming at everyone, buying far too many people drinks and generally behaving like someone who has received a letter from the most adorable girl in the world. And when I try to answer it, I find that I am full of something I am quite unable to express because of a hopelessness that can only be relieved by seeing you again, do you ever feel like that dear, you can put your thoughts and feelings so much better into words than I shall ever be able to.

Yes, I remember the cipher queen, but very vaguely, she was at Seychelles for a while I think. Seychelles is the only base frequented by us that the WAAF show up, just a pair of them on a 9 months tour, they are lucky, Seychelles is beautiful, I have described it before. Quite a surprise to hear that Rupert Taylor is Chief Nav. Officer, is he still a Group Captain? I have flown him around quite a lot, flew him to Durban about nine months ago, he knows me well.

Strange coincidence, Bill, my Aussie navigator, went to school in Sydney at Hunters Hill and Taylor's wife comes from there! Even that will not influence him into sending a recall signal to UK. I suppose he probably would if he could because we always got along well together. He would probably be interested to know that our late C.O. W/C Louw got an OBE in the New Years Honours list, and is now on his way back to UK.

Mum has been ill in bed with flu and bronchitis, I am worrying about her. Margaret, my sister, now at home, writes to say that she narrowly missed pneumonia. Poor Mum, she needs a hell of a lot to send her to bed, and then she is always seriously ill. Please be careful yourself dear, you seem to be having a terrible winter this year. Six more weeks and the worst of it will be over for you I hope. Will probably be on the mainland tomorrow so you will be getting my letters 12 days or so from posting. All my love darling, J

265 Squadron diary 12ᵗʰ February 1945 A/S Diego Suarez to Seychelles

Margaret to Joe 12ᵗʰ February 1945

Dearest Joe, today is my birthday, the 24ᵗʰ year, I can't believe time is going so quickly, when I met you I'd only just had my 22ⁿᵈ birthday, do you realise it's nearly two years since we met, Joe? You will find me changed rather, Joe, but not enough I hope to make me completely unrecognisable, but just to reassure you, let me say that even if I'd never met you, I've looked at your picture so often I'm sure I should know it was you a mile away.

Joe holding the Squadron cat

You sound very excited in your last letters, I pray that we are not disappointed, although if only we knew exactly <u>when</u> you were going to leave for home, it wouldn't be so bad, this waiting.

As far as your career in peace-time goes darling, I want you to do whatever appeals to you most, if you really want to go on flying, then obviously to join a civil flying organisation, or to stay in the RAF, would be the thing. Quite naturally I should want you with me every day, but dear, I couldn't be happy if you were not, so just go ahead and do whatever you want, and don't worry too much about the money side, we shall need some of course, especially if we both want bawling brats about the place, but as long as we don't starve, and you are quite content with whatever work you decide to do, then I shall be happy too. Darling, I should like to live in the country, just far away enough to avoid being bothered by crowds, but a lot depends upon what happens to you, doesn't it? However we can discuss all these things when you come home, unless you want to do something about the civil flying or RAF straight away, in which case go ahead, dear, whatever you decide will be my decision too.

Audrey is most excited about her wedding arrangements, she wrote telling me that she is to be married either at the beginning of April, or on the 30th, your birthday, I do hope you are home for it darling, she will be most disappointed if you are not.

You ask me to tell you that I like you, the funny part about it is that not only do I feel quite stupidly crazy about the thought of being with you (the thought of you causes the most disturbing and quite unmaidenly emotions!) but also, I "like" you, do you understand what I mean darling? I think that if we continue to love, it will be a lasting and deep affection which will grow out of that first exciting feeling, because I think you "like" me too, don't you, dear sweet Joe? I shall be a little shy of you at first, just until I feel that you are really there, and not in my dreams, but not for very long. Yes, dear, we shall be together for a few days before we see anybody else, I shall want you to myself terribly. I love you darling sweet, Margaret

Margaret to Joe 13th February 1945

Darling, it's almost half way through February now, in just a few days I shall be meeting Audrey, and in not too many days after you will be here. You might be on your way when this letter reaches base, how absolutely marvellous to think about! We've both grown up rather darling, haven't we? We were only 25 and 22 when you went away, but now, well, for my part I seem to have grown 10 years older, instead of nearly two, how about you, do you feel 27?

I'm hoping frantically that you will be home for your birthday, we shall have to celebrate both yours and mine together. Oh gosh! Joe, we have such a lot of time to make up for, lets just celebrate and celebrate at first, until we are both tired of it, shall we? Darling, when they post you after your leave I hope its to a place where I can see you on my stand-offs, but the dreadful thing is that your kind of stations are all so very inaccessible from here, unless I can fly to a spot nearby which is sometimes possible. Any other places would mean a beastly stooge job, which would make you miserable darling, I should hate to see you doing some dull job unhappily. But still, as long as you are here, that will be wonderful, just imagine being able to ring you up instead of having to wait 2 weeks for each letter from you. I shall be fearfully jealous, and if you are not there when I ring, I will suspect some other woman of trying to ensnare you, just as Daphne did, but she didn't succeed, did she? By the way, I believe she, together with yet another unborn babe is on her way to Canada, so we have no more intrigues to expect from that direction.

Yes darling, I think you have the right idea about clearing things from our mind before we sleep at night, without doubt. As for having babies, why darling, thousands of people do it, it's no bother really, or at least, it doesn't appear to be, the only thing which disappoints me rather, is that one can't just gallop along and say Okay I'll have one of those, and take it home, It seems such a hell of a time to wait for anything, doesn't it?

But those who know, seem convinced that it's quite worth waiting for, so I reckon we might as well try it and see what opinion we form. Agreed? I love you darling, Margaret

PS There seem to be a lot of "darlings" in this letter, but I can't help it, that's the way I think about you.

Joe to Margaret 14th February 1945

My dear Margaret, I am now at Mombasa and will be leaving for Nairobi in two days time. This morning I have been reading through lots of old Daily Mirrors and was astounded at the number of important home topics about which I know nothing, it will take me quite some time to catch up with things again. The Mirror was not necessarily my choice, but it is the only paper (other than a version of the Times) to be sent overseas and most of us here like to keep a watchful eye on home. It will be wizard to be able to read a daily paper printed a few hours earlier, with a cup of tea and a cigarette, but to breathe cool air is one of the chief things I look forward to, and do you know what I look forward to most? Somehow I think you know, you will soon anyway.

Yesterday I bought myself a pen, there will be no need for me to borrow pens again, until I lose this one, and you will get more letters Toto, that is if you are good and write lots to me, because I shall soon be home to keep you in order, you know the kind of thing, "sorry dear, no more cigarettes for you today, you have had your 50"!

I have written home asking Mum to enquire at my local garage re the use of a car. There is little petrol to be had but if we could get enough for 300 miles or so, we could get around and have a hell of a leave together. Then you might say that it would make a hole in the savings? For my part I think the occasion warrants complete forgetfulness so that years later we sit at each end of a long table cutting bread and cheese for the "eighteen" we shall be able to say to the others "had we been more careful with our money when we were young we could be having H.P. sauce with our bread and cheese!" But a woman's brain is better than a man's about these things so I do really leave things to you sweetheart.

I am drawing a little chart, each square of which represents one day and the last square is May 7th. Each day a square is blanked off, it makes me feel good, although the chart shows a pessimistic view for May 7th is the end of my full eighteen months overseas and it is ridiculous to think that I shall be kept overseas so long.

Now that I am on leave I shall be able to write often my darling, so chin up, always remember that I love you, Joe.

Margaret to Joe 16th February 1945

My darling, I'm so relieved to know that you are getting my letters all right now, don't feel badly about not being able to give me definite plans for coming home, it isn't your fault, it's simply the Air Ministry behaving in it's usual mystifying way, and for heavens sake enjoy your leave, don't reproach yourself for a moment with the fact that I'm saving mine for so long, I shan't lose it, its simply deferring it until later, that's all, and I don't see the point in wasting a whole week of leave now, when I can spend it with you, just by waiting a little. Darling, I'm getting excited too, or rather just plain scared, scared that you'll find me different to all those things you've been imagining for the last few months, if you are prepared to modify your ideas about a half, then you might find something like your imagined Margaret, but Joe, just at first I'm going to be so thrilled to see you that I'm just not going to be able to think of your reaction to me.

Today is Friday, on Sunday I'm going to meet Audrey in Town, it's funny that I am at last to meet her, we somehow seem to have missed it before.

It's Saturday now, I didn't get the chance to finish writing yesterday but read your two latest letters about a dozen times, in bed, before I turned out the light. It is sweet of you to say you will get things for me dear, but there are so many things I want, or rather need, that I almost dare not start thinking about them. You see, for more than four years now I have bought hardly any mufti at all, it has never been really necessary, and frankly, until now, when you are at last to see me in mufti, I have never really thought much about it. However, if you can get some underwear material I shall be more than grateful, because otherwise I shall be reduced to wearing service issue in a short time, and that's a thought which affords me no amusement at all.

As far as the leopard skin is concerned darling, a small piece will be enough, just enough to cover the collar and lapels of an ordinary tailored coat so that it will match the lovely bag you sent me. The elephant's heads are wizard, I'm saving them very carefully for you. The Indian sari is so lovely I haven't dared touch it yet, but someday it will make something very pretty. I'm longing for you to come home and can't help feeling that it might be sooner than we both think. I love you very much darling, yours always, Margaret

Joe to Margaret 18th February 1945

My darling Margaret, once again about 6000 feet up, almost on the equator and quite cool, feel more like human being again. And the 6000 feet up is Nairobi not the cockpit of a Catalina. Yes, it is really good to live in a proper room again, with parquet flooring, windows, doors, lights and not a single lizard in sight, even flies are scarce

This hotel, like others in Nairobi, is better than a wartime London hotel, better food, lots of room boys and bar boys, they steal of course, so what! Dinner consists of 12 courses if one could possibly get through them, and no restrictions. In addition the drink situation is really good this time. Bill (my navigator) and I have bought <u>part</u> of our liquor ration from the N.A.A.F.I. and have stocked up the wardrobe. Our stock (with what we have bought) is now 1 bottle of scotch, 2 of whiskey (Canadian Club) 3 of Brandy,

2 of Gin and a vast amount of beer. I am getting out tomorrow into the country, Bill drinks every hour of the day and night and is perpetually tight, it is too much for me (in many ways), gets a trifle boring after a while anyway. *This will have been an officers holiday camp which is why there is no reference to the rest of the crew - Ed.*

Later have just met two S/LDR Canadian liaison officers who know the Canadians on this squadron. They told me that two crews with RCAF captains have been posted and are probably now in Cairo. It is disappointing because one of them is not due to leave until after us, things are moving anyway.

I wonder if you remember this hat that I used to wear in Oban, rather a grimy effort. It got into rather a bad state, no kidding, badge coming apart, no band inside and so on. A couple of days ago I dropped it into an Indian hatter for repairs. The result is magnificent, a new peak of a different blue, Army Medical Corps buttons blacked over each side and the badge sewn together again, hope you like it, I will have my little one at the ready, just in case you refuse to walk with me. Love, Joe.

Margaret to Joe 18th February 1945

Darling, I expect you are on leave by now, indeed it must be almost time to return, I pray there is some news waiting for you when you get back. I have been talking to Audrey on the telephone this evening, making arrangements to meet, she must have thousands of things to do, poor kid, it seems rather selfish to take up some of her time on leave, but she doesn't seem to mind at all. I think her Jack must be rather nice, not to mind tearing around to meet me when they must have so much planning to do, he's coming with Audrey you see, when she comes to see me. We are going to have lunch together and then I believe she wants to do some shopping. We are both going to wear mufti, which will make everything a lot easier, perhaps she won't remember then that I am of the blighted WAAF Officer brand, although I somehow think stupid things like that don't matter much to Audrey.

Gosh Joe, now that it's nearly time to see you, I can't contain my patience for this last little time, I find myself excited one minute and impatient the next, and every time someone mentions anyone coming home, I can't help thinking why in heavens name it isn't you, darling. When it is you, it won't be a bit like anybody else's homecoming, it'll be ten times more wonderful, what shall I say to you, how shall I be able to tell you how it makes me inarticulate when I think of loving you and being with you, not just in letters, but really and truly. Just a drink or two on our first day together <u>will</u> help us both darling, you are quite right, but we won't get too tight will we? Because if we do, you'll have a tearful woman on your hands, or at least I should imagine you would, people say that anybody who is overwhelmingly happy bursts into tears, and I shall be delirious, so you can judge the enormity of the possible flow.

Joe my sweet, when we meet, don't wait too long before you tell me all the beautiful things you write, I love reading them, but to hear them will be heavenly. You have my phone no. haven't you, but on second thoughts dear, it might be better if you send me a wire saying or simply giving me somewhere to ring you, or don't you think that's a good idea? Anyway darling, wire and as far telephoning is concerned, just do as you think best, only come to me at the earliest possible moment, please? I love you dearest Joe, yours always, Margaret

Joe to Margaret 20th February 1945

Margaret my darling, today, as always, I have been thinking lots about you. Funny how you seem to appear at all times of the day, into all kinds of situations and I sometimes wonder how our conceptions of one another vary, they are based to quite a large extent on letters and also on memories, but we will soon be able to know ourselves once again. I believe as the days become fewer I become more frightened, it seems terrible to suggest, but I really think that to save lots of time (getting to know one another again I mean) we will have to look at one another from high stools along a bar. Write and tell me off darling if you consider this sacrilege. Hope you will not expect me to be brown and handsome; just to make certain am sending a picture of a dispirited F/Lt taken a few days ago (actually I am not bandy legged) at Nairobi. Still here in this big metropolis, but have a reservation on the train out of town tomorrow, thank goodness.

And now the apology! About two months ago I remember searching through your letters Toto darling, for the date of your birthday, and not finding it, asking you for it. The very next thing I know is a letter posted only 8 days ago on the day of your birthday! You must have told me the day my sweetheart but my memory is hopeless, please forgive me, I do so hope you had a jolly celebration, we will have the next together. Yes it will soon be two years since we met, what a waste of time it seems, we are both quite large children now, if that is any compensation, know the ropes a bit, yes?

What understanding letters you write darling, you are a grand kid, thank goodness it will not be long before we can be sure of one another and begin to sort out our little world from the craziness all around, always your own, Joe

Margaret to Joe 21st February 1945

Darling Joe, your adorable letters are arriving now with a fair regularity, so the other occupants of the hostel find me almost possible to live with. There's one effect upon me which they have, and which had better be explained to you. When you write you often ask numbers of questions and I'm really never sure if I have answered them in my reply. The reason is that when a letter from you arrives the uppermost feeling it produces is a ridiculous delight at being, so to speak, as much with you as it is possible to be just now, and I just sit down and write, not replies to all those things you want to know but just silly little thoughts that cross my mind, because the things I really want to say will have to be said when you are home and I am holding you close to me, and not really believing you are there.

Darling, don't be unhappy, we have waited a long time now, but although it seems years, it can't be so very much longer before we can be together and do all the things which we should have done two years ago, and which we could have done, had it not been for my stupidity in not seeing farther than the end o f my nose. We have a lot to talk about darling, haven't we? I do make things dear, mainly because it's economic, and also because it gives me pleasure to make something pretty and to know it's all of my own creation. I want our children to be pretty, dear, what do you bet on the chances? With your colour hair and your nose, in fact very much like you altogether, do you mind if I think that your children will be pretty?

I didn't meet Audrey last Sunday after all, we decided it was better to meet on a day when we could spend more time together, she was travelling from Ilford with Jack to your home on Sunday and could only have spent an hour or two in London, so we are having lunch together tomorrow, I do hope she likes me, Joe, wouldn't it be simply dreadful if she didn't?

I believe I did describe the amount of leopard skin I should like didn't I? Thank you for all the lovely things you are getting for me, and for the sweet thoughts behind them all, you are a darling Joe, I know you don't like letters that drip, but I really must say that I love you very dearly, with every letter, I know it more surely, perhaps especially when you are not so cheerful, because then I know how terribly I want to make you happy, I pray you will be, darling, when you are with me, I want it so much, and if you were ever disappointed in me, in any way, it would break my heart. I know it won't be long now, but it can't possibly be too soon for me.

Yes, Rupert Taylor is still G/Capt., I'm afraid that even if he moved heaven and earth he could do nothing to bring you home, he is a specialist here, Navigation only, and you know what these big shot blokes think of people poking their noses into other blokes jobs, but it doesn't matter dear, we can wait a little bit longer. All my love darling, Margaret

Margaret to Joe 24th February 1945

My dearest, it's difficult to write to you now, when the only thought in my mind is of your coming home, every moment I wonder how long it will be, sometimes I feel excited, and expectant, quite convinced it will be any moment, and other times it seems impossible, that it will be years and years before I see you. It won't be long darling Joe, will it?

Do you remember the first time I went to the Alex with you? I asked your name, and you grimaced when you replied that it was Joe, I love your name, perhaps because it belongs to you, I don't know, but whenever I hear it spoken it gives me a lovely feeling inside, that's mainly how I feel about you darling, excited and happy, but underneath, all the time, safe and sure, I wonder if you feel as secure with me, I hope you do, because there is no pretence about my love for you. In some ways my dear, it's an amazing thing that we are still in love with each other, we started off in the most difficult of circumstances, and we both made very determined efforts to put each other out of our lives, and look where it got us, into a state of irrepressible longing for each other again. When I think back I realise how much I must have hurt you in Oban, for no good reason, except unbelievable stupidity, it makes me sad looking back, but the future, darling, holds nothing but the certainty of happiness, perhaps a little sorrow too, but shared always with you, which seems to me a miracle, I really believe it is.

Pat's Bernard has arrived after 4 ½ years away, I couldn't help feeling happy for her, because I know how I shall feel when I hear your beloved voice again, indeed I marvel at her self control, she did none of the wild things which I am sure I shall do when I know you are home. Oh darling, if you telephone me and I am out, I shall die a thousand deaths, I never spend more than a part of my day off at home now, for fear that your wire may come and I should not be there to receive it immediately. Imagine, when I receive it, it won't be more than a week afterwards before you actually phone or wire me that you are here, oh gosh darling, just look, even my handwriting suffers when I think of it. It will be all right when we meet, I know it, you said you would be so happy you would be unable to say anything at all, I shall be like that too, quite speechless, what a couple of dumb people we shall be, I wish it were tomorrow we were meeting darling. All my love, yours always, Margaret

Joe to Margaret 24th February 1945

My darling, I am sitting on a veranda, it is midday, the equator is only a few miles, yet it is delightfully cool – reason, this spot is about 7000 feet up. And as I write I watch tiny little bubbles rise from the bottom of a glass of cool beer to the top – all's well with the world! Lucky me. When I am able to pull my eyes away I can see a number of beautiful birds chirping away merrily and showing off their vivid red, blue and green feathers. There is a tame fawn (that is not it's correct name) jumping about the lawn, and through the trees I can see the lake and in the background dark high mountains. Mount Kenya is not many miles away, it has snow on its summit the whole year round but it is usually covered in clouds.

This must sound quite pleasant and it is, but everyone is very occupied with one another and there is little to do, since I came alone (*most of Joe's crew apart from Bill Graham were NCO's and would have had their leave elsewhere, this sounds like an officers playground*) I managed to pull myself away from Bill at Nairobi to this little spot, a small hotel miles from anywhere called Naivasha. The golf and tennis I had hoped for did not materialise, the golf course is miles away and the tennis court worn out. It would be wonderful if you were here darling, we could have a whale of a time just walking, talking, boating, drinking, in fact just having lots of fun.

But I have been wanting you with me for such a long time now it seems a little pointless to tell you how much I want you here.

I do hope your colds are now gone and that it is warmer for you. It must be rather nice sitting by a warm fire with a good book, nice music, nice company –going to bed is always the worst I always think, unless you are lucky enough to have central heating, once inside and warm, wizard. Silly of me to think about things like that, but I have been 15 months without them.

It seems that I have not written for several days but was out of air letters and had to borrow some of this type. May have to wait until I reach Nairobi before posting them. All my love, darling, Joe.

Joe to Margaret 25th February 1945

Margaret sweetheart, this leave of mine is getting me down. Tonight a well-meaning old Scotsman of 55 (he told me he was 55 quite 100 times), quite tight, insisted on drinking with me and later eating with me. I could not shake him off and after 2 hours of him am feeling way down. If I had any sense at all I would pack my bags and leave tomorrow but I don't expect I will, it is too much trouble I suppose.

An RAF type did drop in early in this evening and we had a couple of beers together, but we did not stay for long – the "Pongo's" (army officers) generally speaking are just not worth even trying to talk to.

Darling, do you snort? Tonight an elderly woman sitting on the next table to us (she is a nice person) made snorting noises through her nose whenever she laughed, a bit trying for the husband I thought if she has always done that, imagine the pair of them at the Grosvenor – he, the husband, either deciding on a jokeless evening to prevent the inevitable snort, or endeavouring to cover up with his handkerchief – a long vehement blow – any laugh of his wife's which went the wrong way. Funny thing, but if the laugh was prolonged, the poor woman would snort with every chortle, each snort a little smaller than the last. I have been trying to work the whole thing out and have decided that the reason for her laughing through her nose was that her top set of dentures were loose. Rather than allow them to drop when her mouth opened to laugh, she preferred a nice feminine snort, I might be wrong.

Darling, please look after yourself, the thought of there being no You to come home to is too terrible to think of. Love, Joe.

Joe to Margaret 26th February 1945

Darling, yesterday I walked to the other hotel in Naivasha to find a large number of the squadron N.C.O.'s staying there. Some of the fellows had left Madagascar after we left and they tell me that our crew is posted! Take it for what it is worth dear, but I expect it is true. I feel a bit of a fool telling you about every possibility and hope of my return, only to tell you in my next few letters that nothing is happening or that I am going on leave. My leave ends on the 4th of March, but it may be several days before I can get back to the squadron, continuous rain might hold the aircraft up for two or three days. It made me feel good to get the news of being <u>possibly</u> posted, and I celebrated it by an energetic day, golf on a terrible links and several games of tennis. To my surprise I found quite a good tennis form, do you play Toto, I don't think I have asked you before? The day finished with a terrific party and no food, from which I was awaken this morning by a baby which cried solidly for two hours, have not had too much experience of that kind of thing, yet!!

I often wonder how Gladys, my eldest sister, coped with her four, now aged between two years and seven. They are lovely children and I know she thinks it was well worthwhile now. Neville, her husband, has recently left for India, the kids will be a great comfort to her while he is away. Glad was still looking very young and gay when I left home and tells me in a letter that she has got her figure back. It is truly amazing how it comes about. When I get home your namesake, my other sister, will also resemble a beer barrel, her husband is in India and will probably be away for three years. We two are really quite lucky you know darling there are many men (single) who have been out East for four years and many have at least two years to do. Many will stay in Kenya, it is quite a pleasant country and there is work to be had, and lots more will stay in S.Africa, the climate and conditions are so good. That is all for now, my darling, that telegram will not be long now, all my love dear, Joe

Joe to Margaret 27th February 1945

Margaret my darling, this man of yours is writing to you at 21.00, and in bed! The bar is still open but am too fed up to even drink, because there is just not a soul to talk to – at least that I want to talk to. Strangely enough now that I am here thinking and writing to you, I am quite happy, it will be my luck for my pen to run dry, the number of this room is 13!

I wonder if you have met Audrey yet, I do hope you have, I am sure you will like her. She must be up to her neck in arrangements, schemes and things, it must be hellish exciting preparing to be married. A couple of nights ago I began to imagine myself in the role of best man and even went so far as thinking out a speech, he does have to give one does he not? It will be quite a small wedding I expect, perhaps we will both be there, what fun. We might even be leaving for our glorious fortnight when Audrey and Jack leave for their honeymoon, who knows? Not quite the same thing but very nearly, it will be quite a new experience for me to be with someone the whole time for a fortnight! But gosh how I look forward to it, there are several couples here and often I visualise we two and what <u>we</u> could do together. If that ever materialises it would be rather wizard to tour around the countryside staying at any place that interested us for just as long as we chose. A couple of days by the sea, some in town, some in the country, putting up at any little country pub that catches our eye, going highbrow at the Royal every so often and lowbrow at Mrs Brown's the following day. Tell me how this idea strikes you Toto darling, you know I am easy about everything, the only important thing is that we <u>must</u> become reality to one another, and as long as we can be together, that is all that really matters.

I have now four unposted letters for you, and will not be able to post them for two days. When I get back to Nairobi I will post two on one day and two the next, just to surprise you – pity you have got my letters in dribs and drabs, have amazed myself at the number of letters I do write to you darling, I must love you an awful lot, but you must get tired of me telling how much I love you, always your Joe

Joe to Margaret 28th February 1945 Naivasha

Darling, it seems that you have a small boy on your hands. Today I went off to the other hotel for tennis and lunch and there being no transport back had to walk, and the rain came, tropical stuff, 3 inches to the hour, naturally I got very wet and dirty and after a hot bath and a noggin of whisky felt OK again. But the whole point of it is that I immediately want to tell you about it, which means writing, and there really was nothing to it!

So you understand what I mean, little girl, when I say that you have a small boy on your hands, because it is always happening, little things, nothing at all, and I want to tell you about it. It is fortunate for you dear that I rarely do. Things like – the other evening while I was drinking I watched a ragged native walk up to two other natives who were waiting for him. As he came up he doffed his hat and stretched out his hand to shake each in turn who also removed their hats. With each shake pearl-white teeth showed from each native as he smiled a welcome. Absolutely nothing I suppose, but the little scene coming from those people was so simple and gentlemanly it struck something in me, and I immediately wished you had seen it. I could not write trash like that to anyone but you darling, they would not understand, do I expect too much of you dear?

Last night I lay awake for hours trying to work out the best plan for us to adopt for this leave, it is all rather complex. It is probable that I shall be given leave from the Air Ministry in which case I shall need a railway warrant for Devon or wherever we are going, rather than the short distance warrant to my home, but a car may be forthcoming. No doubt things will straighten themselves out, I shall see you in London before going home and we can discuss the situation, that is, if we can really talk sensibly to one another during the comparatively short time we shall have together.

Tomorrow I leave for Nairobi where your mail awaits me!!! All my love darling, write often, always yours, Joe

18.   Coming Home

Margaret to Joe 4th March 1945

My darling, twice I have tried, in writing, during the last week, to tell you all that is in my mind, it has been clear to me but when my pen is ready to start, the power of expression dries up and leaves me unhappy and frustrated and I know that until it comes to me, of it's own accord, it is useless to attempt, you would receive nothing but an empty jargon of words which mean nothing, and fail to convey to you all that is slowly building inside me.

Somebody accused me of being deliberately tragic, I didn't really understand what they meant at the time, but now, as time passes and I grow to a greater knowledge of myself, I think perhaps they used the wrong word, intense perhaps might be a better word, a trait credited to a young unformed character, intense because it is unsure of itself and everything, because life has quite suddenly ceased to conform to a hitherto untroubled pattern, but why only to a person such as this, why not to someone who has seen a little of life, has learned to know it's failings, and yet can still feel and wonder, can still be made sad or happy by it.

It has really gone, for the moment, the wish to tell you so many things is there, with such force as to be almost unbearable, but it won't be written, it will someday darling, all of it, perhaps it will be easier to tell you when you are with me, and I can see understanding in your eyes, I know that you will feel all that I am feeling, because we shall be close, just as close as we always are in my dreams.

There have been no letters now for over a week, not long, measured in time, but, strong and lovely as my delight in you has become, it still needs reassuring, it will be reassured tomorrow, and again tomorrow, was there ever a person so beloved and yet so hated as a postman?

My mind is still clouded from a fruitless discussion last night with Anne, a co-plotter – a talk which started with purpose in mind, but which was distracted time and time again, each of us feeling what the other failed to make clear, and yet powerless to control the trend of thought, so never succeeding in reaching any conclusion. As I went home I felt only a sense of wasted time, and distaste for the sound of my own voice.

No doubt your leave is over now dearest, write a lot please. I love you more than I can describe here. Yours always, Margaret

Margaret to Joe 6th March 1945

Darling, our attachments have started at last, and I'm quite terrified because it looks as though we shall have to go whenever and wherever we are told, if it is possible I shall try to persuade the people concerned to allow me to go last of all, which means that I shall have another nine weeks before going, but if it is not possible, then I shall go in 3 weeks from now, so as to get it over, and pray that you won't be sent home while I am away. The attachment lasts for three weeks, Pat, our senior plotter has said that if you do arrive whilst I am away, it should be possible to recall me to go on leave without any trouble, so it will probably only mean a delay of a day or so, but I should hate not to be able to see you at the very first possible moment.

Do you mind if this letter is extremely dull, darling? I'm feeling cold and a little tired, but knowing how you look forward to letters prompts me to finish this now, in case I have no opportunity in the morning, tomorrow being a working day. Our Senior Controller, who, if you remember, took my photograph a little while back, took some more this afternoon, as he wasn't really satisfied with the others when they were finished. This effort to give you a decent photograph seems to be terribly difficult, dear, doesn't it? I really am sorry, it would have been better if I had had one taken from my last picture, but I didn't think you would like it, it looked so unlike me.

Just at the moment writing is not an easy task, one of the lights has fused, and there's a collection of women gathered around the ... (*fragment missing*) ... all the fuses to discover which one has gone, so every couple of minutes this light goes out, sometimes in the middle of a word, it certainly doesn't make for continuity of thought.

Sometime next week I hope to discover some places where we might spend our leave, darling, do, if you can, let me know soon which part of the country you would like, I might be able to find a place which would come to a tentative arrangement. I believe Audrey and Jack are going to Cornwall for their honeymoon, do you like Cornwall darling? It has a complete fascination for me, but you mentioned the Norfolk Broads once didn't you? Would you rather we went there? It doesn't really matter to me where we go, as long as it is quiet, and we can be completely ourselves. Your recent letters have not been happy sweetheart, don't be sad, it can't be long before you are home. All my love always, Margaret

Margaret to Joe 13th March 1945

Darling Joe, these letters, the last ones you will receive before we meet, will be unbearably dull for you, for several reasons. First and most wonderfully important is that I may see you almost any day now, and I can think of nothing but that, if I keep telling you how much I am looking forward to it, and how excited I get whenever thinking about it, you'll simply be bored, so what to do? There's no solution darling, except just hurry and come home, then the problem will be solved.

Did I tell you that I had a flip in a bean the other day? It was marvellous, and made me quite exhilarated, and sort of outside myself. It's funny darling, but when we were way up, above the clouds, you were there, in my mind, the whole time, and I could see us both very clearly, and in a way, from a detached view. I liked what I saw too. The letter you wrote to me in reply to the one I sent you in December, came back to me, you said perhaps I might be sad, after a while, because I had not followed my earlier ambitions. It wouldn't be fair to you if I said that they no longer mean anything to me, they are still there certainly and I do think of them sometimes, but would you be convinced, sweetheart, if I told you that I think you are worth any number of ambitions? After my still fairly recent behaviour, in Oban, perhaps I shall have to try really hard to convince you of my true feelings, but I have an idea, darling, that when you have been with me for a little while, you will believe what I say, you have my promise that I will tell you the absolute truth. My letters seem to have made you happy, I hope with all my heart that when you hear from my lips what you have seen written down that you will be even happier, and assured of my very deep love for you. We shall be a little strange just at first, dear, but not for long, I'm sure. All my love, dearest, yours always, Margaret

Joe's mother to Margaret 14th March 1945

Dear Miss Dillon, This is just a short note to say that I do hope that you will be able to come to Audrey's wedding, as we shall be so pleased to meet you.

No doubt you have heard the wonderful news that Joe is on his way home, although he may be held up for a week or two in Africa, we are hoping that he will be home by the 7th April, then it will be a great day for us all. With best wishes hoping we shall see you, yours sincerely, Delia Pack

PS As Egerton is such an out of the way place and the wedding is so early, we should be pleased for you to spend a night or so here, if it will help you

Joe to Margaret 14th March 1945 Eastleigh, East Africa

My dear Margaret, last night Bill and I went along to this flat of a friend of ours who recently got married out here. He married a WAAF officer, he is now a S/Ldr. It was a most enjoyable dinner party, our hosts seemed to get along quite well together, although the female side is already beginning to nag a little, but she is two years older than he. Life is easy for people in E.Africa. African "boys" do all the housework, cook the food and serve at table, they are paid about 10/- a week. How would you like that dear? The newlyweds are both Aussie and are going back to UK in the near future, we might be able to fix up a night in town with them? Incidentally Alf (the S/Ldr) informs me that my posting is right through to UK which dispels any possibility of a hold up anywhere.

Have been talking to a chappie who was in Oban three weeks ago, he gave me some red hot gen on things in general. He did say that the beer was terrible, is he right or does he not know where to go? He was a Canadian anyway. He told me that practically all "gash" (?) aircrew of C.C. are on indefinite leave, nice thought that.

Several of us have been watching the antics of two small monkeys in front of the mess. They were racing from one tree to another, in the mess, through the gardens and pretending to ignore us although they were really showing off. Everything was all right until someone hissed at them, when they stood at bay with bared teeth making a curious noise. This brought the mother of these monkeys helter skelter down a tree and straight at us. It must have been a funny sight when four officers turned and ran into the mess with three monkeys close on their heels! We took refuge in the dining hall with a closed door between us and the enraged monkeys and felt quite foolish, such is life in Africa.

Hope you get my letters from here all right darling, there is no post box and I have to push them under the door if the postman is not in. Bye for now Toto sweetheart, never forget for even a moment that I love you, very badly, Joe

Joe to Margaret 19th March 1945 Eastleigh

My darling, let me try and tell you about things that have happened during the past three days or so. After waiting so long at Mombasa to get back to Madagascar I was more than relieved to find myself doing a last shoot-up of the camp at about 16.30 on the 15th. That night a farewell party and off to the club in town where a load of females from a ship provided partners for a dance. We did not dance of course but stuck to the ale and around 23.00 a very fat jolly nurse allowed me to decorate her with flowers, yes – in the bar, dear, she was good fun.

The following day, the 16th, hell of a head of course, but feeling "posted" for the first time, waving a paper, my clearance chit, dashing about the camp and finding it quite impossible to take a ridiculously silly grin off my face, and realising how many wizard people I was leaving behind, and feeling momentarily unhappy but not for long. Managed to get through by about 16.00 and only had to fake two signatures. Had a long interview with the newish C.O. and had so many compliments paid me I really began to think I had done something for the squadron. And during the interview darling, he told me that he had given me a good write up to the Air Ministry and had recommended me for 6 months on a staff job! I will probably curse him one day but right now – well, what do you think Toto?

Having torn myself from lots of junk, got your letters put in an "official documents" censored package, and distributed worn out clothes to the boys, Bill and I found ourselves with overweight baggage at the nearby 'drome by 18.00. It was the quickest ever clearing but the weekly plane back to the mainland was leaving at 0600 on the 17th, incidentally we had to get the movements officer drunk at the previous night's dance before he would put us on.

At about 20.30 that night (the 17th) our ex C.O. rang us to say that he had laid on transport arrangements for a party in our honour at the squadron. And you cannot guess who had asked the C.O. that we might come over? – it was the airmen – we felt hellish proud. Their mess closed down at 23.30 that night with us the worse for wear – damn it, one cannot drink ¼ pint of sherry brandy without feeling that way! From there we were escorted back to our own mess where airmen, some N.C.O.'s and Officers continued the party. By 0300 on the 17th only four of us remained and the C.O. remained with us drinking and chatting (sensibly) until 0500 when transport arrived! He was a wizard fellow, most perturbed about my future (God knows why) gave me the names of friends of his at C.C. Northwood to look up...will continue on other A.M.L...

around the other passengers talking unintelligible Australian. We piled in at about 10 after the hour, but I was fast asleep before we were off the ground. The D.C. landed twice before reaching Nairobi and after my first 3 hour sleep felt b------ for the rest of the trip. But we reached our destination at last (at 16.30) where a letter from our ex flight commander awaited my arrival – and what was it about? – to attend a squadron anniversary party that night at 18.30! Whizzo! We made it, about 30 mostly ex-squadron types were there, erks, N.C.O.'s and four officers – lots of drink, food, songs, wizard company, much confidential talk with the airmen – and a lasting memory – Laughs of the evening? – a pongo being thrown out, a ragged old man being introduced all around as the new flight commander (yes, he had many drinks) the black waiter walking around with Bill's Aussie hat on, and many more. We slept at the S/Ldr's place, Bill on the floor (he lost the toss) and the next day, Sunday the 18th, tennis, resting and some drinks that night.

And all that has made a wizard send off, will not bother you with any more. We were not able to get gen on our departure for Cairo that day (Sunday) but today I learned that we shall probably be going the whole way to UK by air. Unfortunately there is little hope of our leaving Nairobi for the next 9 days, but do not anticipate a long wait at Cairo and <u>might</u> make Audrey's wedding on 7th April.

Hope I have not bored you too much with all this little girl, but am damned excited and wanted to tell you about everything. There were lots of lovely letters awaiting me at the squadron when I arrived, will answer them tomorrow. In the meanwhile darling Toto, could you write to RAF Officers Mess, 22, P.D.C. Middle East Command, Would get a big kick to find a letter from you when I arrive. All my love, dear, Joe

From 23.3.45 all of Margaret's letters to Joe are redirected to Victor Villa in Egerton, his parents address. It is clear that the Air Ministry knew Joe was to be posted home even though, from their correspondence, he did not. Many of these later letters Joe probably did not receive until after they were married.

Margaret to Joe 23rd March 1945

Darling Joe, it's now only seven days to the end of the month, I'm quite sure you must be on your way, so you'll probably not get this letter until you are home.

Your story about the monkeys was lovely, to think of four great men running like blazes away from three little monkeys is too funny, although I imagine they can be very dangerous if really aroused. Twice recently I've had to cross out the date on my letters, it's because time now means nothing, and will mean nothing until the phone rings and you say you are home.

You know I love receiving your letters darling but now it is even a little disappointing to see them come, because each one means that you may still be on that other continent. Don't worry about bringing things home dear, just bring yourself, that will be all I need. If your Aussie friends are to be in Town when we are darling, it would be great fun to spend an evening with them, but don't lets see too much of people, Joe, not just at first, I do so want to get to know you again, and there are so many things I want to know about you and to tell you too.

After some days in the clean air, away from underground and tedious work, I feel almost normal and it only remains to see you to complete my cure, so get crackin' darling, the sooner cured the better.

Anne, one of the plotters, and I, went to the Turkish baths some days ago, it was most amusing, it'll be better to tell you all about it when I see you, because if this letter should be censored, the censor might think I had a very sordid sense of humour.

Any minute now sweet, is the time, isn't it, don't make it too long, each minute is like a lifetime.

In case I've never mentioned it before, I love you very much, much more than I thought possible, for me I mean, always yours, Margaret.

Margaret to Joe 24th March 1945

Another day gone darling, a whole 24 hrs nearer, I'm getting quite frightened now, in case I've grown different, or you imagine me wrongly, or a thousand things which might happen, stupid isn't it?

Your mother has written to me asking me to go to Audrey's wedding and to stay a couple of nights, it's sweet of her to take so much trouble because she doesn't know anything at all about me yet. Oh gosh, that's another thing, suppose she doesn't like me, that would be truly terrible, I couldn't bear her not to you know, because you love her very much darling, don't you? I have said that I'll go, but I hope you are home by then, I shall be more courageous if you are with me.

It's very unsettling this waiting, but it must be much worse for you, it must be wonderful to know that you are actually coming home, after so long away, and your family are looking forward to it terribly.

Looking forward doesn't describe even a fraction of what I feel darling, you know don't you, how much it means to me? The thought of seeing you again fills me so full of happiness, and fright too, that I'm unable to think clearly let alone write. I wonder where you are now, at least in Cairo I hope.

The mood changes every minute, now I'm certain the telephone will ring any moment, and now it seems that it'll be weeks, I'm afraid to go out, and can't stop in, can't read, can't be bothered with people, yet all the time wanting to talk to somebody, so that I can get back to normal again.

You are wise darling, when you say, we'll make our plans while you are at Air Ministry, if we can talk sense, it will be an awful effort for me to talk sense, you will have to do all the talking and try to make me listen.

It's still not really believable this news, and I shall not be able to believe it until I see you – gosh! Just listen to that "when I see you", just like that, its only a matter of days now, bring on the dancing girls and let the band rip, I'm just about ready to burst. All my love darling, always yours, Margaret

26 March 1945 *Joe arrives at 22 Personnel Transit Centre, Almaza, Egypt,*

Joe to Margaret 28th March 1945

My darling sweetheart, Cairo at last, but a bit of a disappointment for us old girl, I am afraid. The almost immediate air passage to UK that I expected will probably not be forthcoming, sorry. As you have read, the POW's liberated by the Russian Armies are being returned home at the earliest possible, their route obviously being via the Med. And all air transport available is being used with the resultant bottleneck here. I believe most of them are now "through" however, and I am hoping furiously, but if a sea passage is necessary our big day may have to be postponed to the end of next month. Hell of a disappointment of course, but to comfort you without being too optimistic, something might happen to get me home sooner.

To cap everything we are living in tents in the desert and at night the ground nearly freezes! – no kidding. My face is horribly chafed with the cold winds and I cannot keep warm even thro' the daytime. It is impossible to be miserable however, because this is the last stop to you dear, and it is good not to have what one wants too easily, wish to God your leave was not being held up though, I know you need it, my life seems to be one big laze day in day out, very empty.

By the way sweetheart, we landed at an out of the way 'drome on arrival and my carefully prepared plans re the Egyptian customs were in vain, I had destroyed a film among other things, I was almost disappointed! (about the customs I mean) There is lots of stuff to be had in Cairo but the cost – phew!

It is rather pleasant to sit in delightful expectation of going home, seeing my folk and above all, working things out with you, dear, seeing England, Mum Dad and the rest, is something that I shall probably do on and off for years to come, but such a lot depends on our D Day, our future in fact, pity about Audrey's wedding, little hope of being able to make it, why not try and go down for it darling, Mum will love you I know, and you will love her, I know that too, because I know you both. Love J.

Biff to Joe date unclear March/April 1945 Senders address Biff, Airborne Nag Smarden

My dear Joe, at last I can tear myself away from the shaking dept and answer your welcome letter and to let you know the old firm is still going strong and anxiously waiting for you to fly home and try your luck, I suppose it will be the same and poor Biff will have to pay.

I might mention I have squared my debts up since you left and the shadow of the workhouse is farther away. Smarden is about the same and I don't think there is any special news from that front, only Joe Gunner has gone away so when you come home you can do as you like. Laurie was home a little while back and I chivvied him about the twins and asked him what you thought about it, and he said something about you had got a few sets about, but you were lucky because you did not keep them. I don't know what he meant (just a minute a couple of clients are coming in)

There we are again. Just managed to win a shake. First for a week. I am glad to say Mum and Doris are keeping well and the little boy doing fine. I have trained him to have a light ale each day in memory of his (Uncle Joe) I was ever so pleased to hear I might see you soon. Oh boy I shall be tempted to push the boat out. And now my dear old pal all the very best and hurry up and get home Yours as B4 Biff.

PS try and guess the title after your name and address *(it shows 3 dice with the numbers 165, this may have been a mistaken reference to Joe's squadron number which was 265. Biff was the landlord of the Flying Horse in Smarden, a pub Joe used a lot before the war, being just far enough away from home in Egerton, and would use after the war as well)*

Biff at the Flying Horse.

Margaret to Joe 28*th* March 1945

Darling, yes I know this letter should have been written days ago, but all week I've had a feeling you would be here, and only now, at the end of it, have been convinced that you weren't coming, but now I look forward to next week.

This afternoon before going on night duty, I went to bed as usual, the orderly informed me at about seven-thirty that somebody had 'phoned at six, and upon being informed that I was sleeping, asked if they could ring me on duty. The effect of this news was drastic, I felt like slaying poor Arnold for not waking me, because quite naturally I thought it must be you darling. However I went on duty at nine, and no further call was, or has been forthcoming up to now, so it couldn't have been you. It will remain a mystery because I just haven't a clue as to who it might have been.

It's a great surprise to hear that Hugh Sheldon was your C.O. – I knew him slightly here, he was quite a personality in the Mess. I know Southall slightly too, it was he who flew me up to Wrexham the last time I visited Pauline, seems to be rather a nice type. My idea of heaven is for you to be posted here sweetheart, the only thing which really worries me is exactly what you mentioned in your letter, being away from a squadron, and some of the Command jobs are frightfully dull, but could you bear it, just for a little while dear? It would be wizard if we could have some time together here at C.C.

It's a relief to hear that Audrey apparently doesn't disapprove of me anyway, mostly because, apart from wanting your people to like me, I liked Audrey on sight.

The thought of talking over our leave in a London pub maybe next week, is too wonderful darling, be quick coming home, time is dragging terribly, all my love sweet, yours always, Margaret

On March 29th the last bomb fell on Britain, the war would be soon over...

Joe to Margaret 30th March 1945

Darling, you probably found my last letter a trifle scrappy, but it did at least give you the "gen". Rumour has it that those unfortunates still awaiting transportation to UK in three weeks time will at last be rewarded and the trip is 10 days. I tell you this for what it is worth and think we can look upon that date as being the most pessimistic.

Having just read two of your letters written on the 11th and 12th of this month, I feel so very sorry for you sweetheart, you were taking two days off, remember, and perhaps at this very moment you are expecting a call from me to say that I am home and when I can see you, and where, and can you get leave the day after tomorrow, and can you put in a couple of reservations at the Ambassadors or any place you like – and – but damn it I am still here, so must stop raving, that time is not very far away. Am feeling more like a human being in this cooler climate and freezing nights, feel I can cope with you now, keep you in order, spank you when necessary, and love you better too. Yes, it's grand to feel on top line again, mentally and physically. But for all that there is something which I cannot describe that makes me feel wildly excited, it is because my whole life is about to change and it will be quite the biggest change that will ever happen. Not like as a boy going to school for the first time, his first job, or his first solo flight but – oh hell why have I started trying to tell you about something that I could not even describe, much less write about!

You have not mentioned your brothers of late in your letters, the elder one Frankie. Was he eventually posted for overseas service or is he still at home? And I trust all your folk are on the top line and not like the daughter of the house, overworked. They may get a bit of a shock quite soon now, are we fast workers? But then it might not shock them, I am sure my own Mother has read through the lines, hope you go down to see them at Audrey's wedding, they are very easy people to get along with, because you are "not a bit snooty" (as Audrey puts it).

You may feel a bit "down" after receiving this but cheer up darling, we are only 2000 miles apart now instead of 5000. All my love, Joe

Joe to Margaret 31st March 1945

My dear Margaret, since I posted a letter to you yesterday, it seems reasonable to assume that you will get this one and yesterdays letter together.

And if you do as I do, you will read the oldest letter first, yesterday's. Because if you have you are now thinking something along the lines of – it seems a hell of a time to wait or "will this man of mine ever get home". And having made you thoroughly miserable with this thought of 3 or 4 weeks waiting I think I can now make you happy again, which all adds up to this. After posting your letter I walked back to my tent to find a note awaiting me – report to movements immediately! – imagine my sprint to the movements office. On arriving the impossible happened, one man had been off-loaded from a ship which is homeward-bound, in a very short time, and I am to take his place – but why me, there are hundreds waiting to go home and many have been waiting much longer than I have? We must have someone guarding our interests darling.

If I can guess accurately at time of departure, speed and so on, you should get that phone call between the 14th and 18th of April, could be earlier or later. How does that fit in with things sweetheart, will it clash with the return of your fellow plotters' boyfriend or has he already shown up?

Your letters have not been getting through to me since leaving E.Africa, so if there should be any queries or news of importance I shall remain ignorant until my return. This may be my last letter to you darling, only about 7 days from the time you get this and I shall be holding you tight. Hell, aren't we lucky! All my love little girl, Joe

Separately Joe wrote We left Diego Suarez on March 15th 1945, via Dar-Es-Salaam and Mombasa to Nairobi in a Dakota, then Juba, Khartoum, Wadi-Halfa, Cairo and the UK (*by sea*).

Posted 26 March to 22 Personnel Transit Centre, Almaza, Egypt, 206(Maintenance) Group (on his way home to UK)

2nd April 1945 1 Personnel Despatch Centre, West Kirby, Liverpool 28 (Training) Group (Finally back in the UK)

Family folklore has it that Margaret, working as a plotter at Coastal Command, followed the progress of Joe's ship on it's way from Cairo to Liverpool. This is entirely possible but she would not have known it was the ship he was on because he would not have been permitted to tell her the name of it.

19. Back in Blighty

Joe returned on 2nd April 1945 to No. 1 Personnel Despatch Centre, West Kirby, Liverpool.

Joe and Margaret finally met in the 3rd or 4th week of April in a pub in Euston station. In his 50th anniversary address (see next chapter) he said " we met for the second time (Oban being the first in 1942) in a pub at Euston station, it was the happiest day of my life, just 5 weeks later we married at Poole, I had to push it a bit in case Margaret changed her mind". Since they were married on 2nd June this meeting at Euston must have been towards the end of April. Presumably Joe had to remain at Liverpool for several weeks after arrival for administrative reasons. There are no letters because now they would be able to talk on the telephone. This will also mean that Joe missed Audrey's wedding on the 7th April. The reason for a pub at Euston must be that Euston is the station for trains arriving from Liverpool.

The plans for leave and holidays appear to have come to nothing since on the 3rd May 1945, just a week or two after their first meeting at Euston, Joe was seconded to BOAC, and transferred to Filton near Bristol, and then to Poole in Dorset, to fly Sunderlands which he had last flown in 119 Squadron 2 years earlier.

Joe to Margaret, Undated, Flt/Lt B.O.A.C. Harbour Club Poole, Dorset

My darling, am still trying to find myself, in England, new surroundings, new people, new plans, and always uppermost in my mind and thoughts, <u>you</u> dear. It is still a little too much, I want to find my groove, be able to think about one thing at a time, but all in good time I suppose. Tomorrow I pray for a letter from you with news of lots of time off at Whitsun, so that we can spend a few more hours together, we have so much more to learn about one another. I can almost count the hours we have spent together since my return, but what can one do about it (*this letter is between their first meeting at Euston and before the one below when he becomes a First Officer, so late April/early May – Ed*)

My comments in my last letter about getting married in three weeks were probably unnecessary, I will tell you what happened when I see you. Damned funny how it seems so necessary to marry at the earliest possible moment, after having waited so long, and knowing comparatively so little of one another. But the fact remains that it does seem important, although marrying will make such a small <u>material</u> change in our lives just now, since the War Office do not appear to anticipate releasing married women from the forces at the present (*Margaret was released from the WAAF on 7th August when presumably they were able set up a home*) If you feel as I do darling, I have a suggestion to make. Rather than wait a month or so to make arrangements to be married in a church, those arrangements and leave which cannot be forecasted ahead will be extremely difficult to fix, under the circumstances, what do you think of going to a registrar just as soon as we can have a few days together, and "marrying" a second time in a church, when you are "demobbed" and our plans more definite? Think about it and tell me what you decide, and if you don't like the suggestion, we will forget about it. Gosh, I can hardly believe we are engaged (*they must have decided to become engaged at Euston*) to be married to you is just about all I ask of life. I know we can be perfectly happy.

Have visited a couple of clubs with the lads of course, they were both quite nice, we must belong to one of them, if you like either place. Last night I went to a show, put over by the Anglo-Russian ballet, it was marvellous, pity you could not have been with me. It is impossible to stay in at night in my present digs, if you could see them you would understand. Have just received a fat letter from you, sorry about the ring, perhaps you will have it by now (*presumably the engagement ring*). Will phone just as soon as I arrive in London, probably Friday morning. Will close now as I am supposed to be attending to the lecture. All my love, darling, Joe

Joe to Margaret 13th May 1945 First Officer (not to be abbreviated) J.T.Pack, B.O.A.C Harbour Club, Poole, Dorset

My darling sweetheart, it seems damned strange writing to you again on ordinary paper and within a couple of hundred yards of a 'phone box! How I wish you were here! Your letter did not reach me until today, Sunday, or I should had to have dashed off to see you, but I could not go on spec as I did not know your folk's address. As it is I have to spend from about 3pm on Friday to 0930 on Monday moping around Bournemouth drinking punk beer. The extra time off this weekend is due to having been inoculated on Friday afternoon, some job this! And by working a crafty fiddle, I am expecting to be in London for a Yellow Fever jab on Friday morning (18th) and will not be required for duty again until Tuesday 0930! The time I am not spending with you darling, I will use at home working on the caravan, would prefer to spend it all with you of course. If I do not hear from you soon, will ring you and get the gen. With any luck at all you will be practically unemployed when you return on Monday, hope so for your sake sweetheart.

I have lots of news for you dear, mainly that I may be on "the line" within a couple of weeks or so, that I am expecting to have cheaper and better digs soon, that we may have to make the most of a few days leave in about three weeks time (if that is not too early for you Toto sweetheart) and also that I am happier than I have ever been before, now that our love has become such a wonderful reality. And all that I will not attempt to write about now, because I will be seeing you soon and it is too much for one letter Perhaps you will have the little hoofy (?) when I do come, I do hope so. Enquiries I have made and information in the daily papers seems to indicate that married women are not automatically demobbed, only those with a family – too bad, but maybe we can file it.

Please don't be too disappointed with our "bods" in Kent dear, they mean little to me, you will meet people that we both like when you eventually come down to Poole.

Am looking forward to seeing Jim and your Mum again this weekend? It is a good thing you had a couple of days with them they need your company too. Had you come back with me to Bournemouth you would scarcely have survived the journey. It was necessary to walk from Cannon Street to Waterloo and to board the train I had to fight for a portion of corridor large enough to stand in, but it was worthwhile because I <u>think</u> (?) you enjoyed your second stay at Egerton. Must dash to catch the last post, all my love, darling, Joe

PS Quite soon I will be sending my letters with: Your loving husband or Your old man. Do you like the idea?

Joe to Margaret 23rd May 1945 BOAC Harbour Club

My darling, after talking to you tonight I feel I must continue, if only this way. You would be amazed if you realised how talking to you cheered me up. The whole day one of my front teeth has been aching fiercely, the b------ thing is aching now, but I refuse to be cowed by it.

Sorry about having to transfer the last three minutes to you dear, perhaps you will not be charged with it. My friend assured me that a call to London was ¼ and I armed myself with 3/- but found the cost was 3/- a "nip" ... *Page 2 missing* ... will hardly see anything of one another again, why not get us a double room so that we can talk until one of us falls off to sleep? I can be awfully good you know.

Dear Toto sweetheart we are going to have lots of fun when we finally get together, you do not realise how much I love you, yet. My only hope is that you will never become even a little bored with me, because then you would not love me. When I remember how poor a conversationalist I am, I feel genuinely unhappy and inferior to other people better gifted. And I think of your conversational... *Rest of letter lost*

10 days after this letter just 5 weeks after their meeting at Euston station they were married on 2nd June 1945 at Poole Registry Office, presumably the nearest for Joe's new posting with BOAC. The witnesses were Gladys Manchip (Joe's sister) and F.D. (Frankie) Dillon (Margaret's brother). Joe was resident at Flat 4 "Pelham", Branksome Park, Bournemouth and Margaret at Frithwood House, Watford Road, Northwood, Middlesex. They would have to wait until leaving the services before being able to set up house together. It is not known who else was at the wedding, Joe's parents were not since they sent a card "Wishing you both Oceans of Luck, Mum and Dad x"

On 7th May 1945 the Germans surrendered and the 8th May was VE day, they would have been very exciting times for newlyweds.

Margaret and Joe marry on 2nd June 1945

In a letter to friends written in 2004 Joe wrote the following:

We were married in Poole and then drove down to Egerton to see my parents the following day. My Standard 1929 car had been left at Oliver's garage to be checked out. We collected the car and started our honeymoon the following day, which had to start at the Flying Horse, which we knew well.... Shortly after leaving, turning a corner, one of the front wheels came off and I saw it bowling ahead before the car dropped down. We were still quite near to the Flying Horse and had no alternative but to walk in (it was early evening) to tell Biff, the landlord, about our predicament. Without being asked several of the chaps in the bar quickly left and found the offending wheel, lifted the car and replaced the wheel, found 3 of the wheel nuts had worn loose, tightened them and we set off again with 3 nuts holding the front wheel on!

This appears to be outside the Flying horse with one of the helpers.

The Flying horse in more recent times.

It was not a long honeymoon since Joe is recalled by BOAC.

Joe to Margaret 14th June 1945 c/o 73a Wimbourne Rd Bournemouth

My darling Wife, take off time has been delayed to 20.00 hours tonight so I am able to whip off a quick note to you. Was so glad to hear that you can get more leave on my return, it will make up for the disappointment of our broken honeymoon. As you know this trip is to take 10 days but it might take 11 or 12 days and I may have to stay in Poole a day or so before going on leave again. It occurred to me that I can ring thro' to you on my return and you may be able to get your leave and come down to Bournemouth. We could then continue our tour back to Kent, what do you think of the idea?

I am longing to see you again dear, our short experience of married life was far _too_ short It was very wonderful while it lasted. I shall be thinking about you all the time darling, ten days is not such a long time.

Hope you manage to visit Egerton while I am away, they will love seeing you. Have not time for more darling, all my love, Joe

Margaret was discharged from the WAAF on 7th August 1945, presumably from this time on they were able to live together.

Joe to Margaret 21st August 1945 Karachi

My darling sweetheart, it seems strange writing to you again, dear, thank goodness it is only a temporary means of talking to you. I met Colin here, and since he expects to be home on the 27th thought I would run you off a few lines so that you will receive them a few days before my return – am due home on the 2nd of September by the way not the third.

Am longing to hear what you are doing with yourself darling, whether you tried for the job or went down to Kent or otherwise. I am already counting the days to seeing you again, it still seems a hell of a long time to wait. But I know I am the luckiest man in the world to have you to come home to. There is just a grain of hope that there will be a letter from you awaiting me when I get to Cairo on the 24th but there is hardly time, I live in hope. It is possible too that today news will arrive from Mr ------ that will make a big difference in our two lives, everything is very uncertain for us, but who cares? I think about you every day and all day darling, and long for the time when we shall always be together.

Having your photographs with me has helped to make this trip quite a pleasant one to date. I have kept you in "Random Harvest" which has enabled me to have a quick smile at you every hour or so of the day, yes, you are quite my most beautiful wife, dear, life would be worth nothing without you.

Today I visited the town and chanced to visit a shop which was quickly selling out of some rolls of material from England. The colours were quite pleasant and I thought of your need of blouses, so I bought two pieces each of 1-¼ yards, the colours being blue and fawn. The price was a shaker –

17/6 per yard but it seemed good stuff. On getting back to the hotel a member of the crew assures me that he bought similar material in England for 2/8d a yard, so right at this moment my mood is black! Am hoping he is wrong however, otherwise you will be most disappointed, and so will I. Am expecting to do little shopping this time, the Jap war ending has made things a little unstable. (*Hiroshima was bombed on August 6th and Nagasaki on August 8th. This was effectively the end of the Japanese war although the formal surrender was not until September 2nd*) Sheets and blankets may still be obtainable however and the usual tea and fat.

Am just off to the local cinema so will close now, only 12 more days and I shall see you again, gosh I wonder if you know how much your old man loves you? Joe

Joe was discharged from the RAF (on secondment to BOAC) on 21st June 1946, having flown with BOAC for more than a year after coming home, flying to Cairo, the Persian gulf, Karachi, Calcutta and Rangoon. Two months after his discharge they were to welcome their first son.

After the war Joe and Margaret had a successful business career in West London. Despite their correspondence about having a rugby team for a family they settled for a brace of boys and they produced four grandchildren, all of whom are shown below.

They eventually retired to a village called Smarden in Kent. Smarden is about 5 miles from Egerton where Joe was born and where this story started. They bought an oast house about half a mile from the Flying Horse which has

featured in this story (did the name of the pub give him the idea of joining the RAF?) and is obviously the place where Joe learnt to drink before the war, safely out of sight of his parents, and once he had obtained a motorcycle.

Margaret and Joe at the Oast house in Smarden

Very recently the editor met George McKendrick who was also in 265 Squadron and knew Joe. When asked what sort of person he was George replied he was "a regular guy, he joined in everything, he wasn't one of those who were always writing letters".

20.   Letters and writing after the war

Letter from M. et Mme Roger Leblois, Hoeylaert, Belgium 31st October 1946

Dear "little" Joseph, we just receive your letter of the 28th and we are happy to hear from you and to know you are alive and well. Also that you are married and that you have a little baby. I should love to know Mrs Pack and your little son and I'm sure I'll like them very much. We should be very glad to have a photograph of you three. If you want to receive our photo, let us know and I'll send it.

I hope to see you again and to make the acquaintance of your wife. That day will be a very grand day indeed.

After you left our home and Brussels, we often thought of you and nearly every day we were speaking of you, wanting to know what happened and anxiously waiting some news.

Now, my dear boy, let me ask you not to thank us for what we have done for you in 1942. I'm afraid you won't understand what a pleasure it was for us to give help to one of our friends while the boche were everywhere in our country. It was simply marvellous. Don't forget your promise to send a long letter giving us lots of news. I'm anxious to receive it.

I'm intended to go to England next year, if possible. I promised to the sergeant Tippen who was staying here for about 18 months to visit him and his family. We know his wife because she was an A.T.S sergeant and stayed at La Hulpe, a place very near Groenendael. When they were engaged, they came to spend the evening with us. Now they are married and got a little boy too. My husband is godfather and I am godmother. If I get a visa in June or July 1947 I surely will go to England and won't forget to go and see you in London. But don't forget, dear Joe, that you promised us in 1942 to come back here after the war, if possible. Well we hope it will be possible and that you'll come with Mrs Pack and your little son to spend a few days at our home. After the liberation we were hoping to see you back in Belgium with the aircraft and we have been expecting your visit every day as we didn't know you were then in East Africa.

We still have the photo taken in 1942 with your name and address on the back. My husband had been hiding it the same day the Germans were killing the doorkeeper of the Ministry (you know that gentleman who came with you to our house). He put it in a bottle and buried it. The first work he did as soon as the Germans left Groenendael, was to disinter the bottle and take your photo out of it. It was in good condition and we were really very glad to see it again and also a little proud to show it to the first English soldier we met here.

If this letter is not well written, will you please excuse me, because I have nobody anymore to help me. Will you also excuse me for using the typewriter but I have had a nervous breakdown and to write a long letter by hand is still difficult for me.It is getting late now and I shall have to finish my letter. I hope to hear from you very soon again and close with all my very best regards and good luck. From yours sincerely, Roger and Stephanie Leblois

Roger Leblois ran a horse racing stables and is kitted out for the part

The Unsent letter (Margaret did a creative writing course in her later years) to Roger and Stephanie Leblois

We spent many happy times together at your home in Belgium and at ours here in England. Always so excited and happy to meet again. I shall never forget the first time I met you both. I had heard a great deal about you but we had to wait for the war to end before I could actually see you.

It seemed always difficult to express in words my own love and gratitude, for the danger in which you placed yourselves whilst hiding Joe in your home, after he was shot down. I can only hope that you understood and realised how I felt. I know you always thought of Joe as your son and we think of you as precious friends, beyond compare.

Of course you knew much later on that Joe's parents had received a telegram saying he was "Missing believed killed". Their world must have collapsed but, due to the care given to him by you and all the other Resistance people over several months up to that point, incredibly, he appeared at the door of his home the very day after the telegram had arrived. His mother opened the door and he was standing there.

At the time Joe and I did not know each other. Had I been the one to open the door the shock would have been unendurable, as it must have been for Joe's mother.

You have gone from us now, but our memories are bright and clear. We speak of you often with all our family and you will be everlastingly a part of our lives.

Raymonde (Coache) written by Margaret, also not sent

Every now and then, if one is lucky, into one's life comes a special person.

I have been privileged, through the wartime contacts of my husband, to meet a number of people, English, French and Belgian, all of whom have risked their lives for others. Like any other group of human beings, each different in character and personality with wide difference in age.

Looking back into the past, I remember most, if not all, of our friends. There are some, however, who are never forgotten, and Raymonde is one such friend, and saviour.

She was tall and handsome, dark haired and with piercing brown eyes. It would have been difficult to tell her a lie. She was married to Rene, a small, rotund Frenchman, with a permanent twinkle in his eyes. They were devoted to each other. During the war they lived, as they had done for many years, in a flat in Paris, in fear and hatred of the Nazi regime, but not too afraid to help stranded airmen and soldiers sent to them by the Resistance, to be hidden in their flat until such time as they could safely be passed on to other helpers, hopefully, one day, to be in England again.

While staying in the flat my husband, a pilot who had been shot down, and two Scottish lads, also in hiding, were taken by Raymonde to the Metro. Before leaving she gave them each a ribbon of blue, white and red silk, cut into the shape of a "V" for Victory.

Raymonde wore her national scarf. This was all in blatant defiance of the German decree to take part in no national display. It was Bastille Day in 1942. However, Raymonde and her small group paraded past as many German soldiers as they could find, but they appeared to be unnoticed.

Later in the war, Rene was discovered helping the Resistance with communication, which was his skill, and he had to escape to England.

There was a price on his head, but he got away safely and finally joined in dangerous work with British Intelligence. Raymonde had to stay behind. There was no hope of getting her out, by now she was well known and was being watched by the Gestapo.

She was subsequently sent to a concentration camp; in fact she was moved from one camp to another until she had finally been in 8 different ones, because of her stubborn activities in helping other prisoners, in all sorts of ways. Eventually she was told that if she continued to write letters for prisoners, she would have her hand cut off.

I am sorry I cannot do justice to Raymonde. As I write I am full of memories with her and her compatriots, and I still find it difficult that human beings can go through so much and survive.

Also I feel overwhelmed with sadness. RAYMONDE – BELOVED LADY.

Letter to Joe from Gracie Fields "Leaving USA for Hong Kong Dec 4th 1964", written on Americana of New York notepaper

Dear Mr Pack,

Thank you for your kind letter, its too bad that my husband was an Italian and seemed to have been the cause of the last terrible war.

Now I'm married to a Russian (born, now Italian) so, I guess if there's any more dreadful trouble I'll get it again.

I've done my job through two great wars and pray there'll never be anymore. But if it should happen, I'll be doing my best to help make people happy, as I've always done. I'm still British. God Bless you, sincerely yours, Gracie Fields PS These wicked stories are untrue

It is not known what letter from Joe this replies to.

Letter to Joe from Andrée De Jongh, Brussels, 24/1/1967

Dear Joe,

First I must ask you to excuse my mistakes, to write in English is much more difficult for me than to speak.

Thank you so very much for your nice welcome at your house on Sunday 8th January. I was so happy to see all the members of your family, and so deeply touched by your kindness. Will you please say my gratitude to them all, and especially to your wife, who prepared such a wonderful dinner! – I am afraid she had a lot of work with that, and just on Sunday time, when she should have rest!

Thank you also for all you did for us during the four days in London.

Those days were wonderful, and we really hadn't imagined such a reception. That was too generous indeed and I am afraid it was terribly expensive for the R.A.F.E.S. not only in money, but also in work and time. Really, dear Joe, we were happy during those days, because we found, faithful and intact, the friendships formed during the war. It was impressive to meet "our children" again after twenty years (or more sometimes) and to see that they had nothing forgotten. We were the very happy "mothers" (and grandmothers!)

My dear Joe, I wish you and your family all the best, and thank you again for so much kindness. Very sincerely yours, Your <u>old</u> mother, Didy

Joe and Margaret to Andrée De Jongh 11/4/1967

Dear Dédée, thank you for your delightful letter, which we received a few weeks ago. We were honoured to have you at our home for those few hours during your very busy stay in London.

I believe my mother has already written to you. Although she is now very old I am sure you will appreciate how she felt towards you when I was able to tell her just a little about your great heroism in helping both her son and many others back to England. Margaret and I will know how she must have felt because Jeffrey, our elder son, is now about 21.

Now, after all these years, that I have learned what happened to so many of you wonderful people, so often only months after I escaped from Europe, I can only feel guilty that we were the cause of such terrible things happening to you. I can only think now that I am a lesser being, or perhaps we were all too young then to realise what might happen to us. You will know that you have the everlasting gratitude of, not only we whom you helped, but the wives and families of us all and thousands of British people who know what you did and the sacrifices you made. I only hope that you think we have not let you down.

Do please tell your mother (who, I believe, is still with us) that another of your "sons" is in contact with you again and will always be eternally grateful to her brave daughter.

I was surprised that you had only been to England twice since the end of the war, although you told us of the years you have spent in Africa. We would be delighted if you could spend a few days with us here. As you know, we have lots of space and you could do whatever you wished, without having "official" visits anywhere. Margaret could have a few days off from the office to take you around and she could take you over to see your brother-in-law if you wished. Do please think about it seriously, we are very easy people to get along with and London, and England, is quite an interesting place.

We are wondering if you will be going to Ethiopia, there was a film about the country on television the other week. It is very different from the other parts of Africa that I visited. I would think that the climate is less hot in most of the country, a little like Kenya perhaps.

Do please keep in touch with us, let us know what you are doing. I know you have lots of letters to write to your many friends but you must give me the opportunity of making up for lost time.

Please let us know how you feel about a visit to London. Yours very sincerely, Joe and Margaret Pack

Letter from Raymonde Coache to Joe dated 22nd February 1967

Dear Joseph, Your letter is arrived with delay as we live 71 rue de Nanterre, and not 51, but what a pleasure we have had recognising you on the photograph from so large time, you are no more the very young boy that we have hidden in 1942.

We hope that your sons look like you after your departure.

My husband has rejoined the Free French in England with some good fellows of the RAF at the end of 1942.

As for me, I was arrested in June 1943 and condemned to death by the Germans.

I have known 13 prisons and two camps (Ravensbruck and Malthausen) from where I was liberated by the Croix Rouge Internationale on the 29th of April 1945. I was rather in a bad condition.

During that time my husband gone back in France for missions and was arrested in Belgium, where he was imprisoned during six months, and was liberated miraculously.

That is what happened after your leaving from Asnieres.

We keep an excellent remember of you and your companions that we have hidden at home.

We keep in contact with three of them, one lives in Leeds, the other in London, and the last one is Canadian.

We have a girl aged 20 years. If we go to London we shall be very glad to see you again and to make acquaintance with your family.

Sincerely yours and thank you for your so kind letter, Raymonde Coache.

The Coaches visiting Joe and Margaret in London

Letter from Albert Bidelot, Inspector of Bridges and Gutters, sent in 1980

Thank you for your good wishes at Xmas. I, in return, send you mine for 1981. I will now describe in detail how I came to find you back in 1942. Being an Inspector of bridges and gutters as well as "Geometre expert"(*a surveyor, in that part of Holland waterway maintenance was very important - Ed*) I was, that day, out to measure the area in which I found you, because the canal was to be made larger. I had 3 helpers with me that day, and one of them was next to me when I discovered you and mistook you for a German soldier, that is why I first spoke to you in German. You addressed me in English and offered me the money the RAF had given you in case of such a situation and I refused it. I gave you a little of what I had on me to eat and told you to wait for me while I went off to find some civilian clothes for you. I sent my boys home and cycled 8 km home where I rang one of my neighbours (a doctor) and asked him for some civilian clothes.

The doctor offered me some cigarettes which I refused. I then asked him if he would accompany me back to Neeroeteren (his wife was Canadian) as he spoke fluent English. He said it was too dangerous, but he would put me in touch with someone who could help. That same day at around 6pm there was a knock at my door. It was a clerk from Elens de Stokkam (solicitors) the brother of Gertrude Moors, one of the country's greatest heroines. He brought me a suitcase with a suit, shirt, tie, shoes etc. He said he would wait for me to return. I set off on my bike and when I reached the place where I had left you – no Joe Pack. I called for you, but received no reply. I had tears in my eyes. I thought the Germans must have found you, or that you had given up waiting.

I went to one of my "helpers" who lived in Neeroeteren and was told that G Groserman of Ophoven (12 km from Neeroeteren) had returned to the forest accompanied by Hilven of Ophoven, and that the latter had taken you on his bike, having given you an old pair of trousers, took you home with him, accompanied by the "helper" Grosermans. I was furious that the Grosermans had done this to me (he was an unemployed teacher). I knew Hilven, who was part of the secret army of which I was a member, but Grosermens was a good for nothing, he might have betrayed us all.

I returned home, where I found the clerk from Elens waiting for me. He assured me that you would be in good hands and that the next day you would be taken to stay at Gertrude Moors, who was part of the escaping society Comète. I tried to see you the following day, but was not allowed to. I had to prove myself over a period of several months. I later found out that from the Mill at Dilsen, you passed through the hands of the leader of the Comète – Paul Schoenmaker de Neerharem (*and then)* you were passed on to Mathieu Tras, and after that I lost track of you.

I now give you a few details about Comète of which I remained a member until April 1944. In June 1943, the first members of the Comète were arrested by the Gestapo. Moliers and Vandinerde Maaseik died in an extermination camp – Gertrude Moors died in a gas chamber at Auschwitz. In

November 1943 Paul Shoenmaekers of Neerharem and his son were decapitated at Fort Halle (Germany), their statues stand today at Rekem near Neeraren. I replaced Paul Shoenmaekers at the head of Comète *(in Holland)*. The lawyer Elens and his clerk Moors were arrested, the lawyer was imprisoned in Breendunk until September 1944 and died a few months later. In August 1944 some of my very close friends were stopped at Hasselt, they had helped 53 pilots, 10 of which I had found myself and taken to them. My wife and I are from Liege so we are Walloons, we speak French primarily, as well as 5 other languages. I must tell you a further story about Jean Grosermon(*One of Bidelot's colleagues who discovered Joe*). A few months after the day when I found you I sacked him and employed another helper, I entrusted him with my secret messages to Comète . He would have to go by train to deliver these messages. He was very sadly stopped by the Gestapo and later died in a concentration camp. He was married with 2 children. I gave him the posthumous title of "under officer" which made a big difference to his widows pension. To think he would be alive today if I hadn't sent Grosemon away.

If there is anything else you'd like to know don't hesitate to ask. It was the Florent Biemaux family – Walloons like me, heroes. Mrs Biemaux came out of Auchwitz in June 1945 and died shortly afterwards, along with her son (aged 20) who died in an extermination camp. Mrs Florent Biemaux, my great friends escaped from the "Ghost" train which was to take them to Germany. She was the sole survivor of this tragedy. The map shows the 6 places you stopped at after Asch and before Lanaken where our friend Mathieu Erab lives. I have 2 daughters – Maryse and Mathilde born in 1934 and 1935. My granddaughter is an English teacher.

Albert Bidelot

Letter from Joe to Mathieu Tras-Nijs, dated 9th November 1980

Dear Mr Tras-Nijs, It is now several weeks since I met you, for the second time at Lommel, not very many kilometres from our first meeting in June 1942. But today is our Remembrance Sunday (Nov 9th), and I particularly remember those who gave their lives during the Great Wars of our times, and especially those of my Belgian friends to whom I owe so much.

It was wonderful to meet you and Albert *(Bidelot)* during our stay at Lommel, my thanks are particularly due to Dr J. Bussels who must have arranged the meeting. I certainly did not expect to meet you and Albert ever again.

I still remember clearly sitting on the pillion of your bicycle and being taken away from the German border and away from almost certain capture and life in a P.O.W camp. You, in your turn, faced a much worse fate had we been caught. I wonder if you realised the danger? At the time you seemed to take the whole matter as something of a joke – but I noticed at Lommel that you seemed a very happy person.

You provided me with a jacket and a pair of corduroy trousers in place of my uniform for our cycle ride. I have always thought that you took me up into Holland to a farmhouse; do you know if those people who took me in are still alive? And would you know their name and address? Also the young man (Ex. Belgian Air Force I believe) and his girlfriend who brought me a bicycle and cycled with me the following day to a windmill somewhere in Holland(?) to be interrogated by an English speaking doctor. Would you know about them?

Yes, they are now dimming memories of about 38 years ago *(and Joe's recollection of events is not always correct – the windmill was in Belgium, at Dilsen)*, but are no less real and my appreciation and thanks go to the very brave people who risked so much for me and other evading airmen; we of the R.A.F descended on you unasked but not unwelcome.

I was one of the lucky ones who eventually arrived back in England about 3 months after you and Albert found me and was able to carry on the war against Germany for our mutual freedoms.

After this long lapse of time and then meeting you again, it seems I know nothing about you. Did you survive the war without serious harm? Do you have a wife and family? I have a wife, Margaret, whom you met at Lommel and two married sons with families. I shall be retiring in a couple of years or so, life is catching up with us all.

It was impossible to communicate verbally with you at Lommel and the Secretary of our Society, Mrs Harrison, has kindly offered to translate this letter into Flemish.

Our Association is called the Royal Air Force Escaping Society which was formed after the last Great War, to enable us to keep in contact with our helpers abroad like yourself – do you know about it?

I am also writing to Albert, in French, but it is taking rather a long time to get my letters written and translated. Are you in contact with Albert?

Once again, my very best wishes to you for the future, it has been a long time, but better late than never!

Mathieu Tras-Nijs arriving at London Airport with all his medals, the triangle on his beret is the insignia of the Armée Secrèt. He was 29 when he helped Joe.

Extracts from a letter from Leslie Baveystock to Elizabeth Harrisson, secretary of the RAF Escaping society

Dear Elizabeth, I have had a most interesting letter form my historian friend Jacques de Vos. For a book of "Escaping" through Limburg has just been published by a Mr Bussels, and Jacques de Vos supplied much material concerning the escape of our crew who have all been mentioned in the book. Unfortunately it is written in Flemish but Jacques supplied me with a translation of the pages concerning us. The Nijskens family are of course included as also is a photo of their farmhouse in Bree. Also mentioned in the book is the story of another escaper and his name is Joseph Pack. It is quite apparent that Joseph covered almost the same track as we did going from Limburg to Dilsen then on to Liege where he was contacted in the same church of St Denis and I believe stayed in the same house. Apparently this Joseph Pack was at the recent ceremony at the unveiling of your plaque (*in St Clement Danes church*) and I was wondering whether you have his address in England for I would very much like to contact him.

For back in 1974 I retraced my journey back from where our plane crashed to Brussels but I never knew the address where we stayed in Liege or the names of any of the people who lived in the house where all five of our crew sheltered for several days. And I think perhaps that Joseph Pack may be able to supply me with a few facts that would make my story complete. For neither Gisele or Dédée knew the names of the people who sent us to them from Liege. There is no doubt that both of their fathers would have known but alas they are both dead. Anyway it would be interesting to make contact with Joseph for I think he too stayed with Gisele and her family.

Letter dated Sept 10th 1981, name and address of sender torn off

Letter dated Sept 10th 1981, name and address of sender torn off

Dear Mr Pack, no doubt you were surprised when you picked up this letter and saw that it came from N.Z. And no doubt you wondered who could be writing to you from the opposite side of the world. But, though we have never met, and although until a week or two ago I did not even know of your existence, nevertheless we have much in common. In fact, we obviously trod the same ground and stayed at the same places, probably slept in the same beds, and all within a few days of each other. But, of course, that was over 39 years ago.

So now I must explain. Firstly although I have lived with my family in NZ since 1949, I am an Englishman. I was born in Finchley, London (1914). Married in 1938 and lived quietly in Friern Barnet. Joined the RAF in 1940, trained in Staverton and then Canada, and then went through an O.T.U at Cottesmore on Hampden Bombers in the winter of 41/42.

Posted to 50 Squadron, operating out of Skellingthorpe, where they had Manchesters (deep groan) and found myself doing Ops as a second dickey in spite of the fact that I had never touched the controls of a Manchester, and knew F.A. about them. I flew with a crew I did not know on the night of May 30/31 on the first 1000 Bomber raid on Cologne (*Joe was also on this raid*). Result – shot up badly over target, set on fire and lost an engine. Struggled back as far as Limburg in eastern Belgium where the crew were ordered to bale out. It was too low for the skipper to escape and he was killed in the crash (*having held the aircraft steady to allow his crew to escape*). Too long a story to mention here but he got a posthumous V.C. (*all the crew survived except Manser*) Incidentally it was only my fifth Ops trip.

The plane crashed near the village of Molenbezal (*actually Molenbeersel*) only a few hundred yards from where I landed, and soon after I met up with one of our crew. We were hidden by some wonderful farming people named Nijskens, who put us in touch with the Underground and on the night of June 1st we left the farmhouse and proceeded to the Mill at Disen (*actually Dilsen*) where we arrived in the early hours of June 2nd 1942. Left by a sort of tram/train and went to Liege where we met up with all of the crew (5) except the dead skipper and the navigator who had been caught by the Germans. One of the men who took us from our "pick up point" in Liege was a chief of Police, and the pick up point was as we came out of the Church of St Denis. We stayed for three days then went to Bruxelles where I and a crew member named Bob Horsley were picked up by Gisele Evrard and we stayed with her family for five days. The other three crew were picked up by a young man named Henri Van Steenbeck and they stayed with the Steenbeck family for 12 days. The flats we stayed in were on the ground floor of two apartments in the Palace of Justice Apartments.

And if I am correct, I believe that is just what you did only a few days later.

And how do I know. Well some years ago a Belgian historian named Jacques de Vos who lives in Ghent made contact with me... *rest of letter lost*

Thanks to Oliver Clutton-Brock – the writer of the letter was "the celebrated Sergeant (later Flt/Lt DSO, DFC &Bar, DFM) Leslie Baveystock. The skipper of the Manchester who perished and got a posthumous VC was Pilot Officer Leslie Manser. This is described in a book by Leslie Baveystock called Wavetops at my Wingtips, published in 2001 two years after his death. Preparations for the book may well have been the reason for the letter to Joe.

Extracts from a letter from Leslie Baveystock to Elizabeth Harrisson, secretary of the RAF Escaping society March 16ʰ 1982

Since I wrote to you last I have exchanged very interesting correspondence with your member Joe Pack. It is apparent that when I evaded in 1942 I followed almost directly behind him. For he crashed only a week or two before I did, and was taken to the Mill at Dilsen, then to Liege where he stayed in the same house, as I did only days later. Then to Brussels where he was sheltered by Gisele and her family, and so on down the line to Gibraltar.

Letter from Joe to John Evans Paterchurch Publications 24ʰ Jan 1991

Dear Mr Evans, Johnny Elms has sent me prints of the beached Sunderland together with a copy of your letter; how the original prints came from Australia I shall never know..

It was my misfortune to be flying with F/O Cooke (a Canadian) on this occasion (29ʰ March 1943) as 2ⁿᵈ Pilot. We had been flying an anti-sub patrol in the Bay of Biscay. Pembroke Dock had closed in weatherwise and we were diverted to Mountbatten *(Plymouth)*.

Here they had close hauled the defence balloons for us and the cloud base was down to 500 feet. There are some high hills near to Mountbatten and, flying in cloud with only a rough idea of where we were, caused a certain amount of panic. When we saw through the clouds, the sea together with a few boats and the odd balloon, we gathered we had arrived and got down to the water ASAP. Unfortunately we landed down wind, we certainly had no intention of going back into the clouds.

Landing down wind (which was quite strong) is a dangerous manoeuvre, the Sunderland with the wind behind would not come to a stop and that is why we hit the opposite shore. We tried to get out of the aircraft thinking it might catch fire and several of the crew climbed onto the wing.

Although the engines had been switched off, the propellers were still windmilling slowly and one of the crew jumped through the props without being hit, onto soft ground below, about 15 feet, he was very lucky.

I don't know if you wanted to know about this little incident, John, but now you have it. Many thanks for the photographs, I shall square up with Johnny in due course. I may meet you one day. Sincerely, Joe Pack

Letter from Joe to Raymond Itterbeck, Tresorier, Amicale Comete, 6th Nov 1994

Dear Monsieur Itterbeck, thank you for the certificate so kindly provided by the Amicale Comète and presented by Dédée on the 23rd October 1994. I am so disappointed not to have been in Brussels on that occasion.

The scroll reminds me of the youth who arrived unannounced at the German border with Holland on June 10th 1942 and started what seemed an impossible journey back through Holland, Belgium, France and Spain to arrive (by devious means) to my parent's home in Kent three months afterwards. Those brave men who made this possible have had my complete and sincere admiration and thanks ever since.

Without, what I believe was the Comète Line in it's beginning, my escape would not have been possible. Your secretary, Andrée, then a young girl, risked her life to take me to safety from Louvain to Paris. Your President (Countess Andrée De Jongh) who introduced me to Paris, always with a smile on her face, made the perilous journey with us from Paris to Biarritz and St Jean de Luz, climbing the Pyrenees on a dark night to arrive eventually to a comparatively safe house at St Sebastian, Spain. Yes a truly impossible experience and to those brave people of the Comète Line who are not now with us, your families can justly be proud of you and to those who can still enjoy the breath of freedom---- I salute you!!

La Prèsidente of the Amicale Comète was Andrée De Jongh and the Secretaire was Andrée Antoine-Dumon (Nadine)

50th Wedding Anniversary 2nd June 1995

For their 50th Wedding Anniversary Joe made a speech. He had made some notes beforehand and an extract from his notes reads:

"After 50 years reasonably safe to assume the marriage will last...we met in Oban, landed to find smashing young lady section officer Margaret Dillon, 12-14 days later she was posted to HQ Coastal Command at Northwood, I flew flying boats in the Indian Ocean...Airmail courtship..we met for the second time in a pub at Euston station, happiest

day of my life, just 5 weeks later we married at Poole, had to push it a bit in case M. changed her mind"

Joe making his speech on 2nd June 1995.

Letter from Joe to Mr J.S. Dear 47 Park Drive, Baldock, Herts. SG7 6EN.

Dear Mr Dear, I was interested to see your letter in the Ringing World of May 12 regarding your proposed SEAC veterans peal. If I am eligible you might like to consider me or possibly as a reserve if you are looking for ex land-based personnel for SEAC, I was RAF. After operational tours both in Bomber Command and Coastal Command I flew a Catalina to Madagascar in 1943 (265 Sqdn) to fly from there to Ceylon, Seychelles and Madagascar in search of Japanese submarines and blockade runners and I believe that during that time we were considered SEAC. I have a Burma gong some-where. If this is of any interest please get in touch, by the way, I rang one peal of triples and one of major at Ealing last year........ The peal was rung on Wed 27th Sept 1995, average age of ringers was 74. The peal completed in 2 hrs 40 minutes for VJ celebrations at Lilley, near Luton.

A reunion of extraordinary people (extracts from another piece written by Margaret on her creative writing course in Dec 2000)

The reunion took place in a breathtakingly beautiful room in an ancient building in Paris. It had been furnished with elegant pink and white table linen and with fresh flowers on every table, together with replica flags of every allied nation. The lighting in the room was soft and welcoming.

The purpose of the gathering was to reunite friends from all over Europe, mostly from France and Belgium, and also from Great Britain. The French and Belgian people were wartime members of the Resistance who risked their lives and those of their families in order to help allied evaders and escapers to return to England. They were hidden in homes until the time was right to set them on their journey through Belgium and France until they reached the Spanish border, where they were handed over to the British authorities in Gibraltar, who then found space for them on the convoys going on their way home.

Throughout their perilous journeys to reach that far they were guided and protected by the Resistance line, many of whom were young girls, quite fearless and totally aware of the ghastly fate awaiting them if they were caught whilst helping allied airmen and soldiers.

The room was empty of people, until the doors opened and slowly they began to appear. Each one looked eagerly to see who was there, and the smiles and laughter started when they saw friends, very special friends.

Soon there was an unexpected flurry and all eyes were turned to the door. There stood a tiny, fragile woman, clearly very old and known to almost every person in the room. By repute one of the bravest and most stubborn human beings it would be possible to meet.

She had lived in Paris for most of her life, although she was English, so very English that she was referred to in that way, the Englishwoman. She had been there for so many years that she knew a great deal about possible help for the escapers, and her place in the chain of rescue had been vital.

Now she was old, but she looked around the room with joy and amazement.

The elderly lady was the Countess de Milleville. She was born Mary Lindell in Surrey in 1895. In the first World War she served as a nurse and then with the French Red Cross for which she was awarded the Russian Order of St Anne by the last Czar of Russia and the French Croix de Guerre with star, amongst other decorations. She helped evaders in the Second World War founding the Marie Claire escape line based at Ruffec in France after having been arrested by the Germans, escaped to England and then returned to France.

Others at the above event, from a list made by Margaret, were Raymonde and Rene Coache (Dover), Donald Darling (Sunday), Andrée De Jongh (Dédée or Postman and herself a Countess), Elvire De Greef (Tante Go), Andrée Dumon (Nadine), Micheline Dumont (Michou) and Airey Neave (Saturday).

The event was almost certainly organised by the R.A.F. Escaping society, now the Escape Lines Memorial society (ELMS). ELMS is devoted to maintaining the memories of both evaders, escapers and their helpers and recreates today some of the escape routes used in the war.

Appendix ~ Dramatis Personae

At the end of Chapter 3 Joe was "*swinging across the skies on my parachute, like a huge pendulum*" and probably wondering who he would meet, or who would meet him, when he reached the ground. Would he be lucky or unlucky? The following are amongst those who helped him or that he came into contact with. It is remarkable how many women are among them (not excluding the remarkable woman Joe eventually married). Indeed a title considered for this book was "In the company of remarkable women". Another title considered was "Bells, Bombers, Belgians and Boats" (and beer and brandy to continue the alliteration). In the end "Love is in the air" seemed best to encapsulate Joe and Margaret's story.

Albert Victor Bidelot

He was 35 in 1942 and an Inspector of bridges and gutters in the Ministry of Transport (certainly an important job in that part of low lying Europe) and he found Joe on 10th June 1942, the day after his parachute jump. His colleagues were Groserman and Hilven. Both Bidelot and Hilven were members of Comet but Groserman was not. Nothing is known of Groserman and Hilven. Albert Bidelot became the head of Comet in November 1943 when Paul Schoemakers was killed. He was also an officer in the Armée Secrète involved in lodging and guiding airmen and Russian POWs, gathering intelligence and making reconnaissance patrols. He survived the war. It is not known if he was decorated for his contributions.

Gertrude Maria Hubertina Moors

After being found by Albert Bidelot, Hilven took Joe to the Mill at Dilsen where Gertrude Moors lived. Gertrude Moors was chef de Rabattage (chief beater) for Comet. She organised the evasion line in the Limburg area of Belgium starting from early 1942. She and her helpers, including Louis Rademecker below, would collect airmen in this area and get them to Liege. This part of the line was called JAM but it is not known what this stood for. She is yet another of the remarkable women who helped Joe. JAM helped 20 airmen to escape, including Joe, during 1942, until in December it was infiltrated by the Germans and two thirds of its members were either shot or deported to Germany. Gertrude Moors died on 5th May 1945 at Ravensbruck concentration camp. She has been called the Queen of Limburg and Albert Bidelot, in his letter to Joe, called her "one of the country's greatest heroines". She was 42 years old.

In the First World War the Germans had executed Edith Cavell causing a great outcry. In the Second war they avoided this by sentencing female resisters to "Nacht und Nebel" (Night and Fog) and sent them to unbelievably harsh and brutal camps, of which Ravensbruck was the worst, in which it was expected they would die "naturally". Towards the end of the war, when it was clear Germany had lost, they did their best to ensure that none of the prisoners who might testify against them survived. To have survived in these conditions, as several below did, is a remarkable testament to their fortitude and faith.

Andrée De Jongh (Dédée)

She was the founder, with her father, of the Comet line, and it's inspiration throughout its existence, even after her arrest on 13th January 1943, her 17th crossing of the Pyrenees, and incarceration in the concentration camps of Ravensbruck and Mauthausen. She was awarded the George medal in 1946 by King George in person, the first such award to anyone other than a Briton (and closely followed by Michou and Tante Go), the Americans awarded her the Medal of Freedom, the French appointed her a Chevalier of the Légion d'honneur and the Belgians appointed her a Chevalier of the Order of Leopold and awarded her the Croix de Guerre with palm. In 1985 she was made a Countess by King Baudoin. She was 27 when Joe met her in 1942. After the war she returned to nursing and spent many years as a sister in leper colonies in the Belgian Congo and Ethiopia. She passed away on October 13th 2007.

Frédéric Emile De Jongh (Dédée's father)

Extract from the citation recommending him for a posthumous George medal "in spite of everyone imploring him to leave the country, he insisted on remaining at his post. He was arrested on June 6th 1943 and shot on March 28th 1944, aged 56. He stands out as one of the most courageous and devoted of patriots". Joe stayed with Frédéric and Andrée De Jongh in Paris for the first 2 weeks of July 1942.

Micheline "Lily" Dumon (Michou)

Extract from the citation recommending her for the George medal. She "handled more than 250 evaders, and her name became a legend amongst countless airmen as the famous Lily. She feared nothing and was ready to sacrifice all, her story is one of the finest tributes to the heroism of the Belgian people". She was 21 when Joe met her in 1942. She escaped via the Comet line to England on 2nd March 1944.

Andrée Dumon (known as Nadine, Michou's sister)

Like her sister she worked with the De Jongh's from the very start. She was arrested in August 1942, shortly after having helped Joe, having been betrayed by Jean Masson. The father of Michou and Nadine, Eugene Dumon, disappeared, aged 50 in Spring 1945. Nadine today is very involved in the Escape Lines Memorial Society which maintains the memory of those events. The pictures below show Nadine just after the war (right) and in more recent years (left). Nadine escorted Joe from Brussels to Paris and is the "girl" he refers to " our girl was in tears, passing us off to the officers as deaf mutes". Nadine and her husband, Gustave Antoine, stayed with Margaret and Joe in June 1981when they were in London for an RAF Escaping society function.

Andrée Dumon shortly after the war and in more recent times.

Maurice Collignon

Chief of police at Louvaine. Caught and shot 4th August 1943 after having helped Joe in June 1942.

Louis Joseph Hubert Rademeckers (photo right)

He was one of the Commissaires of Police at Liege and a very active secret agent for the Allies. He was arrested on 6th December 1942 and shot 14th March 1943 at the Citadel in Liege. As senior policemen both

Collignon and Rademeckers took huge risks to help airmen and, sadly, paid the price. He was 47 when he helped Joe in June 1942.

Roger and Stephanie Leblois (photo right)

They hid Joe at their racing stables outside of Brussels for about two weeks in late June 1942. They became family friends and Joe and Margaret visited them often in Belgium and they visited London on several occasions.

Rene and Raymonde Coache (photo below)

They sheltered Joe in Paris for the first 2 weeks of July 1942. Joe wrote "Madame Raymonde Coache was taken by the Gestapo early in 1943 (another victim of Masson). Her husband René, escaped to England, via Comet on January 1st 1943. Raymonde survived two concentration camps and the Coache's became family friends after the war. Raymonde's exploits were acknowledged by both Governments (British and French) with medals that she refers to as her "souvenirs". Joe did not know the names of the Coaches while he was with them and only made efforts to

find them in 1964 through the RAFES. From the letter in the previous chapter he finally tracked them down in 1967. The Coaches stayed with Margaret and Joe several times in London and they also met at RAFES functions in Paris. They regularly exchanged presents at Christmas. The present from the Coaches was invariably a cheese which must have been ripe when it left Paris and was especially so when it finally arrived in London.

The Coaches also sheltered Ft.L J. Maclean. The reader may remember that in the raid on Essen there were only 2 air crew who survived being shot down and evaded capture. Joe was one and Maclean the other.

Elvire De Greef (Tante Go)

An extract from the citation recommending her George medal says she was: "responsible for making arrangements for lodging about 400 airmen in the Bayonne area and organising their transfer into Spain. Although she saw again and again important members of the line arrested she continued undaunted, a most heroic woman". She was 43 when Joe met her in 1942. Joe and the other evaders travelled by train from Paris to St Jean de Luz with Tante Go, her daughter, Jeanine, Albert "B" Johnson and Dédée . Tante Go would then have arranged the journey across the Pyrenees with Florentino and Dédée . "B" Johnson escaped through the Comet line on 20th March 1943.

Andrée De Jongh is in the centre of this picture, Tante Go is on the left and Michou on the right. The picture was taken when the 3 George medallists visited London at the invitation of the RAF escaping society in January 1967. From Letters after the War (above) Andree De Jongh spent the Sunday evening of January 8th with Margaret and Joe and their family before returning to Brussels. The visit was widely covered in the Press.

Florentino Goikoetxea

Florentino was the guide who took Joe and his party across the Pyrenees on 31st July 1942. Florentino had not been the first guide used by the Comet line and Joe's crossing was the 14th undertaken by Comet so this may have been one of Florention's earliest crossings.

Florentino was a Basque from Hernani in the Pyrenees. He was born in March 1898 and so was in his mid forties when he guided hundreds of airmen over the Pyrenees. He was caught and shot in the leg in July 1944 but managed to escape. Florentino was awarded the "Kings Medal for

Courage in the cause of Justice" by the King himself, he was introduced as a man who had worked in the field of "import/export" i.e. smuggling! He was also awarded the French Legion of Honour. He became a gardener after the war and died in 1980.

Florentino with Joe after the war

Donald Darling

Known to the French as "Cheri" his British codename was "Sunday" and he was M.I.9's man in Spain, based in Gibraltar. His took responsibility for air crews once Comet had delivered them to San Sebastian, arranging transport to Madrid, then Gibraltar and finally back to the UK. Spain was nominally neutral in the war but practically helped the Germans and Darling's task was not easy. Although Joe does not mention him Darling will have made all his transport arrangements. He survived the war.

Airey Neave

His codename was "Saturday" and he took over the running of M.I.9 from James Langley. Before this he had escaped from Colditz, leading to the famous film. He will almost certainly have interviewed Joe for his M.I.9 report shown in earlier chapters. He survived the war and became a member of parliament but was killed by an I.R.A. bomb in March 1979. He was much decorated.

In his book Saturday at M.I.9 he wrote: "People who have worked in resistance movements or POW's and evaders do not care to dwell on their experiences. What is thrilling to the reader was frightening to the man he is reading about.

The men, often very young, had been exposed to the feeling of being hunted, sometimes for several months. They hated this cross questioning and a desire to sublimate their anxiety, added to the rather soulless War Office systems, did not allay their fears. The shock of arrival, after weeks of danger and excitement, at the hideous Great Central hotel increased their reticence."

This clearly did not apply to Joe.

Little did Joe realise, as he dangled on his parachute, that waiting for him would be four future George medallists (one posthumous) amongst countless other honours. The George medal and the George Cross were instituted by Royal warrant in September 1940. The George Cross was intended to be the civilian Victoria Cross. The George medal is junior to the George Cross but is the second highest gallantry medal a civilian can be awarded.

References and Acknowledgements

The main source material for this book has, of course, been the letters and writings of Joe and Margaret. To fill in the gaps and to give as complete an account as possible the editor has drawn on a number of sources.

The Squadron diaries for 35, 119 and 265 squadrons, as well as M.I.9 reports, are located at the National Archives at Kew and the editor is grateful for permission to include extracts from them in this book.

The RAF Escaping society files are held at the Imperial War Museum and Yasmin Nicholls has helped the editor in this story, as has Elizabeth Harrisson who was secretary of RAFES. Joe joined RAFES in 1961 and was an active member for many years.

Web sites that have been consulted are

»   www.associations.rafinfo.org.uk/
»   www.lostbombers.co.uk
»   www.mod.uk
»   www.belgiumww2.info
»   www.conscript.heroes.com
»   www.escapelines.com

Books that have been read and drawn from are

»   *Wings of the Dawning* by Arthur Banks, an exhaustive account of the battle for the Indian ocean in which Joe is quoted.
»   *Wavetops at my Wingtips* by Leslie Baveystock, Baveystock's RAF career had many similarities with Joe's and they corresponded after the war.
»   *Little Cyclone* by Airey Neave, a fascinating account of Andrée De Jongh and the Comet line.
»   *Saturday at M.I.9, a History of Underground escape lines in NW Europe* by Airey Neave
»   *Sunday at Large*, assignments of a secret agent by Donald Darling, M.I.9's man in Gibraltar.
»   *First Light* by Geoffrey Wellum, an extraordinary account of life in Fighter Command
»   *A Quiet Woman's War*, by William Etherington, the story of Elsie Marechal, an Englishwoman who married a Belgian, worked in Comet, and was arrested but survived. The book gives a harrowing account of the atrocities committed in concentration camps. There is no record of her having helped Joe but it is a gripping story.
»   Volume 3 (1942) of Bill Chorley's series of books on RAF Bomber Command losses of the Second World War was the source of the in-

formation about the aircraft losses, casualties and evaders in the Essen raid in which Joe was shot down.

Individuals who have helped considerably with their advice and encouragement as well as specific pieces of research have been Oliver Clutton-Brock, John Evans and John Clinch. Brigitte d'Oultremont, Philippe Connart and Edouard Renière gave me considerable help with Belgian spellings, conventions and unravelling the Palais de Justice. The editor's wife and family have also helped by their interest and encouragement.

Responsibility for the accuracy of the book remains, of course, that of the editor.